Editor
Heather Douglas

Illustrator
Clint McKnight

Cover Artist
Brenda DiAntonis

Managing Editor
Ina Massler Levin, M.A.

Creative Director
Karen J. Goldfluss, M.S. Ed.

Art Production Manager
Kevin Barnes

Art Coordinator
Renée Christine Yates

Imaging
Craig Gunnell

Publisher

Mary D. Smith, M.S. Ed.

SIXTH GRADE SKILLS

Includes Standards & Benchmarks

Ancient Egyptian Mummy

Haiku

In the fall, leaves drop gracefully–they flutter down a sea of color

5 cm

10 cm

$V = \underline{785} \ cm^3$

Author

Teacher Created Resources Staff

Teacher Created Resources, Inc.
6421 Industry Way
Westminster, CA 92683
www.teachercreated.com
ISBN-13: 978-1-4206-3945-2
ISBN-10: 1-4206-3945-5

© 2007 Teacher Created Resources, Inc.
Made in U.S.A.

Teacher Created Resources

Table of Contents

Introduction

The wealth of knowledge a person gains throughout his or her lifetime is impossible to measure, and it will certainly vary from person to person. However, regardless of the scope of knowledge, the foundation for all learning remains a constant. All that we know and think throughout our lifetimes is based upon fundamentals, and these fundamentals are the basic skills upon which all learning develops. *Mastering Sixth Grade Skills* is a book that reinforces a variety of sixth grade basic skills.

- **Writing**
- **Grammar**
- **Reading**
- **Math**
- **Social Studies**
- **Science**

This book was written with the wide range of student skills and ability levels of sixth grade students in mind. Both teachers and parents can benefit from the variety of pages provided in this book. Parents can use the book to provide an introduction to new material or to reinforce material already familiar to their children. Similarly, teachers can select pages that provide additional practice for concepts taught in the classroom. When tied to what is being covered in class, pages from this book make great homework reinforcement. The worksheets provided in this book are ideal for use at home as well as in the classroom.

Research shows us that skill mastery comes with exposure and drill. To be internalized, concepts must be reviewed until they become second nature. Parents may certainly foster the classroom experience by exposing their children to the necessary skills whenever possible, and teachers will find that these pages perfectly complement their classroom needs. An answer key, beginning on page 230, provides teachers, parents, and children with a quick method of checking responses to completed worksheets.

Basic skills are utilized every day in untold ways. Make the practice of them part of your children's or students' routines. Such work done now will benefit them in countless ways throughout their lives.

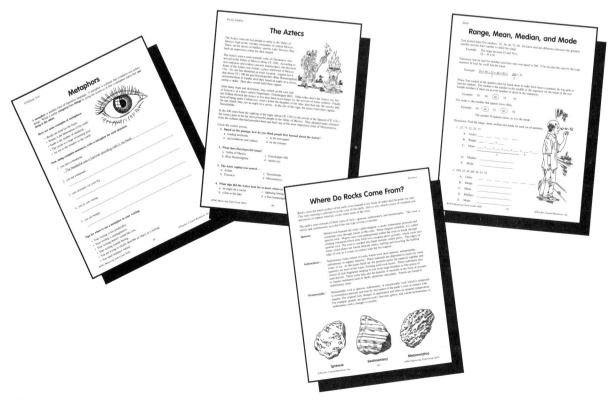

Meeting Standards

Each lesson in *Mastering Sixth Grade Skills* meets one or more of the following standards, which are used with permission from McREL (Copyright 2000, McREL, Mid-continent Research for Education and Learning. Telephone: 303-337-0990. Website: *www.mcrel.org*).

Standard	Page Number
Language Arts:	
Uses grammatical and mechanical conventions in written compositions	
• Uses conventions of capitalization in written compositions (e.g., titles [books, stories, poems, magazines, newspapers, songs, works of art], proper nouns [team names, companies, schools and institutions, departments of government, religions, school subjects], proper adjectives, nationalities, brand names of products)	8,10
• Uses conventions of punctuation in written compositions (e.g., uses colons, quotation marks, and dashes; uses apostrophes in contractions and possessives, commas with introductory phrases and dependant clauses, semi-colons or a comma and conjunction in compound sentences, commas in a series)	9–16
• Uses pronouns in written compositions (e.g., uses relative, demonstrative, personal [i.e., possessive, subject, object] pronouns; uses pronouns that agree with their antecedent)	23
• Uses nouns in written compositions (e.g., forms possessives of nouns; forms irregular plural nouns)	17–18
• Uses verbs in written compositions (e.g., uses linking and auxiliary verbs, verb phrases, and correct forms of regular and irregular verbs)	21–22
• Uses adjectives in written compositions (e.g., pronominal, positive, comparative, superlative)	19
• Uses adverbs in written compositions (e.g., chooses between forms of adverbs such as positive, comparative, superlative degrees)	20
• Uses prepositions and coordinating conjunctions in written compositions (e.g., uses prepositional phrases, combines and embeds ideas using conjunctions)	24–26
• Uses interjections in written compositions	24
Uses the general skills and strategies of the reading process	
• Uses a variety of strategies to extend reading vocabulary (e.g., uses analogies, idioms, similes, metaphors to infer the meaning of literal and figurative phrases; uses definition, restatement, example, comparison and contrast to verify word meanings; identifies shades of meaning; knows denotative and connotative meanings; knows vocabulary related to different content areas and current events; uses rhyming dictionaries, classification books, etymological dictionaries)	27–31, 35–45
Uses reading skills and strategies to understand and interpret a variety of literary texts	
• Understands the use of language in literary works to convey mood, images, and meaning (e.g., dialect; dialogue; symbolism; irony; rhyme; voice; tone; sound; alliteration; assonance; consonance; onomatopoeia; figurative language such as similes, metaphors, personification, hyperbole, allusion; sentence structure; punctuation)	27–29, 32–34
Uses reading skills and strategies to understand and interpret a variety of literary texts	
• Uses reading skills and strategies to understand a variety of literary passages and texts (e.g., fiction, nonfiction, myths, poems, fantasies, biographies, autobiographies, science fiction, drama)	52–53, 56–57, 60–65
• Understands complex elements of plot development (e.g., cause-and-effect relationships; use of subplots, parallel episodes, and climax; development of conflict and resolution)	46–49
Uses reading skills and strategies to understand and interpret a variety of informational texts	
• Uses reading skills and strategies to understand a variety of informational texts (e.g., electronic texts; textbooks; biographical sketches; directions; essays; primary source historical documents, including letters and diaries; print media, including editorials, news stories, periodicals, and magazines; consumer, workplace, and public documents, including catalogs, technical directions, procedures, and bus routes)	50–51, 54–55, 50–59

Meeting Standards (cont.)

Standard	Page Number
Uses the general skills and strategies of the writing process	
• Writes narrative accounts, such as short stories (e.g., engages the reader by establishing a context and otherwise developing reader interest; establishes a situation, plot, persona, point of view, setting, conflict, and resolution; develops complex characters; creates an organizational structure that balances and unifies all narrative aspects of the story; uses a range of strategies and literary devices such as dialogue, tension, suspense, figurative language, and specific narrative action such as movement, gestures, and expressions; reveals a specific theme)	66–70, 73–75
• Writes compositions about autobiographical incidents (e.g., explores the significance and personal importance of the incident; uses details to provide a context for the incident; reveals personal attitude towards the incident; presents details in a logical manner)	66, 69–70
• Writes business letters and letters of request and response (e.g., uses business letter format; states purpose of the letter; relates opinions, problems, requests, or compliments; uses precise vocabulary)	71–72
• Writes expository compositions (e.g., states a thesis or purpose; presents information that reflects knowledge about the topic of the report; organizes and presents information in a logical manner, including an introduction and conclusion; uses own words to develop ideas; uses common expository structures and features, such as compare-contrast or problem-solution)	76–77
Uses the stylistic and rhetorical aspects of writing	
• Uses paragraph form in writing (e.g., arranges sentences in sequential order, uses supporting and follow-up sentences, establishes coherence within and among paragraphs)	73, 76–81
Math:	
Understands and applies basic and advanced properties of the concepts of numbers	
• Understands the relationships among equivalent number representations (e.g., whole numbers, positive and negative integers, fractions, ratios, decimals, percents, scientific notation, exponentials) and the advantages and disadvantages of each type of representation	108–111
• Understands the role of positive and negative integers in the number system	82–84
• Understands the characteristics and uses of exponents and scientific notation	85–86
• Understands the structure of numeration systems that are based on numbers other than 10 (e.g., base 60 for telling time and measuring angles, Roman numerals for dates and clock faces)	153–156
Uses basic and advanced procedures while performing the processes of computation	
• Adds, subtracts, multiplies, and divides integers, and rational numbers	82–84, 87–96
• Understands exponentiation of rational numbers and root-extraction (e.g., squares and square roots, cubes and cube roots)	97–98
• Understands the correct order of operations for performing arithmetic computations	99–101
• Adds and subtracts fractions with unlike denominators; multiples and divides fractions	102-107
Understands and applies basic and advanced concepts of statistics and data analysis	
• Understands basic characteristics of measures of central tendency (i.e., mean, mode, median)	112–117
• Reads and interprets data in charts, tables, and plots (e.g., stem-and-leaf, box-and-whiskers, scatter)	116–123
Understands and applies basic and advanced properties of functions and algebra	
• Solves linear equations using concrete, informal, and formal methods (e.g., using properties, graphing ordered pairs, using slope-intercept form)	124–131
• Understands that a variable can be used in many ways (e.g., as a placeholder for a specific unknown, such as x + 8 = 13; as a representative of a range of values, such as 4t + 7)	151–152
Understands and applies basic and advanced properties of the concepts of measurement	
• Solves problems involving units of measurement and converts answers to a larger or smaller unit within the same system (i.e., standard or metric)	132–135
• Solves problems involving perimeter (circumference) and area of various shapes (e.g., parallelograms, triangles, circles)	136–138
• Understands formulas for finding measures (e.g., area, volume, surface area)	139–146

Meeting Standards (cont.)

Standard	Page Number
Understands and applies basic and advanced concepts of probability • Determines probability using mathematical/theoretical models (e.g., table or tree diagram, area model, list, sample space) • Understands the relationship between the numerical expression of a probability (e.g., fraction, percentage, odds) and the events that produce these numbers	147–149 150
Social Studies: **Understands the major characteristics of civilization and the development of civilizations in Mesopotamia, Egypt, and the Indus Valley** • Understands influences on the development of various civilizations in the 4th and 3rd millennia BCE (e.g., how the natural environment of the Tigris-Euphrates, Nile, and Indus Valleys shaped the early development of civilization; different characteristics of urban development in Mesopotamia, Egypt, and the Indus Valley)	158–171
Understands the political, social, and cultural consequences of population movements and militarization in Eurasia in the second millennium BCE • Understands characteristics of Mycenaean Greek society and culture (e.g., the political and social organization of the Mycenaean Greeks as revealed in archaeological and written records, how geography influenced the development of Mycenaean society, the significance of the story of the siege of Troy)	175, 179
Understands how Aegean civilization emerged and how interrelations developed among peoples of the Eastern Mediterranean and Southwest Asia from 600 to 200 BCE • Understands the social and political characteristics of Greek city-states (e.g., significant similarities and differences between Athenian democracy and Spartan military aristocracy; hierarchical relationships in Greek societies and the civic, economic, and social tasks performed by men and women of different classes; the location and political structure of the major Greek city-states) • Understands elements of Judaism and how it compares to other religions (e.g., the differences between Jewish monotheism and the polytheism of Southwest Asia, the ethical teachings of Judaism illustrated in stories from the Hebrew Scriptures, the major events in the early history of Judaism through the Babylonian Captivity)	174–179 190–192
Understands how major religious and large-scale empires arose in the Mediterranean Basin, China, and India from 500 BCE to 300 CE • Understands the origins and social framework of Roman society (e.g., the geographic location of different ethnic groups on the Italian peninsula in the late 6th century BCE and their influences on early Roman society and culture, how legends of the founding of Rome describe ancient Rome and reflect the beliefs and values of its citizens, what life was like for the common people living in Rome and Pompeii) • Understands events in the rise of Christianity (e.g., the life of Paul the Apostle and his contribution to the spread of Christian beliefs, how Christianity spread widely in the Roman Empire, how the New Testament illustrates early Christian beliefs) • Understands the origins of Buddhism and fundamental Buddhist beliefs (e.g., the life story of Buddha and his essential teachings; how the Buddhist teachings were a response to the Brahmanic system; the contributions of the emperor Ashoka to the expansion of Buddhism in India; how Indian epic stories reflect social values, and how the Jakata tales reveal Buddhist teachings)	180–189 190–192 172–173
Understands the Imperial crises and their aftermath in various regions from 300 to 700 CE • Understands fundamental Hindu beliefs (e.g., how the concept of dharma reflects a social value for the ideal king, husband and wife, brother and friend; the concepts of Brahma, dharma, and karma, the caste system, ritual sacrifice, and reincarnation)	160–161
Understands the rise of centers of civilization in Mesoamerica and Andean South America in the 1st millennium CE • Understands the significant features of Mayan civilization (e.g., locations of Mayan city-states, road systems, and sea routes in Mesoamerica and the influence of the environment on these developments; the role and status of elite women and men in Mayan society as indicated by their portrayal in Mayan monumental architecture; the importance of religion in Mayan society; the structure and purpose of Mayan pyramids; ceremonial games among the Mayans)	193–194

Meeting Standards (cont.)

Standard	Page Number
Understands the expansion of states and civilizations in the Americas between 1000 and 1500	
• Understands how the Aztec Empire arose in the 14th century (e.g., major aspects of Aztec government, society, religion and culture; the construction of Tenochtitlán, the "Foundation of Heaven")	196
• Understands social and political elements of Incan society (e.g., Incan methods for expansion and unification of their empire, daily life for different people in Incan society, the food plants that formed the basis of Incan as compared with Aztec agriculture)	195
Science:	
Understands atmospheric processes and the water cycle	
• Knows the processes involved in the water cycle (e.g., evaporation, condensation, precipitation, surface run-off, percolation) and their effects on climatic patterns	197–199
• Knows ways in which clouds affect weather and climate (e.g., precipitation, reflection of light from the Sun, retention of heat energy emitted from the Earth's surface)	200
• Knows the properties that make water an essential component of the Earth system (e.g., its ability to act as a solvent, its ability to remain a liquid at most Earth temperatures)	201
Understands Earth's composition and structure	
• Knows that the Earth is comprised of layers including a core, mantle, lithosphere, hydrosphere, and atmosphere	202
• Knows processes involved in the rock cycle (e.g., old rocks at the surface gradually weather and form sediments that are buried, then compacted, heated, and often recrystallized into new rock; this new rock is eventually brought to the surface by the forces that drive plate motions, and the rock cycle continues)	203–204, 211
• Knows how successive layers of sedimentary rock and the fossils contained within them can be used to confirm the age, history, and changing life forms of the Earth, and how this evidence is affected by the folding, breaking, and uplifting of layers	205
• Knows that the Earth's crust is divided into plates that move at extremely slow rates in response to movements in the mantle	206–207
• Knows how land forms are created through a combination of constructive and destructive forces (e.g., constructive forces such as crustal deformation, volcanic eruptions, and deposition of sediment; destructive forces such as weathering and erosion)	208–210
Understands the composition and structure of the universe and the Earth's place in it	
• Knows characteristics and movement patterns of asteroids, comets, and meteors	212–217
• Knows how the regular and predictable motions of the Earth and Moon explain phenomena on Earth (e.g., the day, the year, phases of the Moon, eclipses, tides, shadows)	218
• Knows characteristics of the Sun and its position in the universe (e.g., the Sun is a medium-sized star; it is the closest star to Earth; it is the central and largest body in the Solar System; it is located at the edge of a disk-shaped galaxy)	216–217, 219–220
Understands the principles of heredity and related concepts	
• Knows that the characteristics of an organism can be described in terms of a combination of traits; some traits are inherited through the coding of genetic material and others result from environmental factors	221–222
Understands the structure and function of cells and organisms	
• Knows that all organisms are composed of cells, which are the fundamental units of life; most organisms are single cells, but other organisms (including humans) are multicellular	223–225
Understands relationships among organisms and their physical environment	
• Knows ways in which organisms interact and depend on one another through food chains and food webs in an ecosystem (e.g., producer/consumer, predator/prey, parasite/host, relationships that are mutually beneficial or competitive)	226–227
• Knows how matter is recycled within ecosystems (e.g., matter is transferred from one organism to another repeatedly, and between organisms and their physical environment; the total amount of matter remains constant, even though its form and location change)	228–229

Language Arts

Capitalization

Capitalization Rules

- Capitalize names of people, places, nationalities, and religions: George Washington, New York, Italian, Protestant.
- Capitalize dates, historical events, periods, and special events: World War II, Renaissance, Boston Tea Party, Easter, Saturday, May.
- Capitalize titles for people (mayor, doctor, president) only when they are followed by a name (Doctor Stockton, the doctor).
- Capitalize family titles only when used as names: Ask Mom. Ask your mom. I like Uncle Bob. I like my uncle, Bob.
- Do not capitalize school classes unless a specific title is given, or the subject is a language: history, History 1A, English, Spanish, geometry.
- Do not capitalize directions (south, east, etc.) except when they refer to a specific region (the South): I live north of the capital. We moved to the East Coast.
- Do not capitalize seasons of the year: winter, spring, autumn, fall.

Directions: Mark A if the underlined word is correct as it is, and mark B if it is incorrect.

_____ 1. My <u>Aunt</u> is named Terry.

_____ 2. I like <u>Aunt</u> Terry.

_____ 3. Sit by your <u>Cousin,</u> Tommy.

_____ 4. I don't want to sit by <u>Cousin</u> Tommy.

_____ 5. I come from the <u>west</u>.

_____ 6. I live <u>west</u> of the river.

_____ 7. I like <u>spanish</u> class.

_____ 8. I like <u>math</u> class.

_____ 9. My favorite season is <u>Fall</u>.

_____ 10. Is the <u>Mayor</u> in?

_____ 11. Yes, <u>Mayor</u> Ruiz is in.

_____ 12. The <u>President</u> of General Motors is rich.

_____ 13. <u>President</u> Kennedy lived in the White House.

_____ 14. My mother is <u>christian</u>.

_____ 15. I like <u>History</u> 101.

Using End Punctuation

Period: Use a period at the end of a statement.

Exclamation Point: Use an exclamation point to express excitement or emphasis for an important point. Exclamation points should be used sparingly.

Question Mark: Use a question mark at the end of a question.

Directions: Put the correct end mark at the end of each of the following sentences.

1. The sun set on the horizon   Wasn't the sight astonishing

2. When the snowflakes stop falling, we will go to the store

3. Where did you get that beautiful, blue ribbon

4. Hurrah   We can finally go swimming in the ocean since the storm has abated

5. When will the sound of cracking thunder stop frightening me

6. The daffodils are blooming all over the hillside, creating a waving carpet of yellow

7. The gazelles ran smoothly and silently in the distance

8. When will the moon escape from behind the clouds

9. Wow   I am impressed with the colorful vibrancy of fall

10. How often will you be able to come over to my house this summer

11. Although I like the refreshing coolness of snow cones, I usually don't like ice cream

12. Why is the wind picking up speed   Will there be a hurricane

13. The puppy quickly scurried under the bushes, hoping that no one had noticed him

14. I will be glad when this project is over and I feel a sense of accomplishment

Punctuating and Capitalizing Quotes

A direct quotation always begins with a capital letter regardless of where the quotation appears in the sentence. However, punctuating direct quotations varies, depending on their placement.

Speaker Before: When the name of the person doing the speaking comes before the direct quote, the direct quote is preceded by a comma. The quote is punctuated like a regular sentence and enclosed by quotation marks.

> Ann said, *"I hope you find what you are looking for."*
> Mrs. Paul asked, *"Do you know the capital of Peru?"*
> Tamara exclaimed, *"Let me go!"*

Speaker After: When the name of the person doing the speaking comes after the direct quote, the punctuation is varied. If the direct quote is a question or exclamation, then the ending punctuation should be added. If, however, the sentence is a statement or request, then a comma is used in place of a period. In all cases, a period is placed at the end of the entire sentence.

> *"I hope you find what you are looking for,"* said Ann.
> *"Do you know the capital of Peru?"* asked Mrs. Paul.
> *"Let me go!"* exclaimed Tamara.

Directions: Write the following sentences, adding punctuation marks where needed. Capitalize the first word of the direct quote.

1. Michael shouted let's get busy with the paint

2. Those who deny freedom to others deserve it not for themselves stated Abraham Lincoln

3. Has anyone in this group ever climbed Mount Everest asked the mountain guide

4. Mr. Cummings said please watch your step through the pond

5. Donna and Chandra complained we don't want to do the dishes

6. Help cried the frightened girl as she grasped the end of the rope

7. What is the time difference between New York and Los Angeles he asked the flight attendant

Commas

Directions: Use **commas** to separate items in certain conventional, or customary, situations.

Dates	The Towne Book Fair begins on Monday, September 25. Our Constitution was signed on September 17, 1787.
Addresses	The Kentucky Derby is held each spring in Louisville, Kentucky. The address you requested is 453 Bear St., Chicago, IL 69697.
Friendly Letter Salutation and Closing	Dear Grandma Martha, Sincerely yours,

Directions: Read the following letter and envelope. Insert commas where needed.

Tuesday March 16 1999

Dear Aunt Judy

    I want to thank you for the lovely new dress you sent to me for my birthday. I'm sorry you were unable to attend my party on Saturday March 13. We had lots of fun. I plan to come visit you in Lynchburg Virginia this summer. Mother wants you to check your calendar for July. She has booked me on a flight to arrive Wednesday July 27 in the evening. Please write or call to let us know if that date is all right. I can't wait to see you!

Yours truly

Kara

Kara James
7008 Milton Road
Los Angeles CA 90049

Mrs. Judy Kimball
1454 Dresser Road
Lynchburg Virginia 20546

Showing Possession

Using **apostrophes** to show possession is often confusing for students. Yet, there are only a few basic rules.

To form a possessive for a singular noun, add an apostrophe and an s.

the student's records   Mrs. Smith's red car   the dress's collar

Exception: Sometimes a proper name ending in **s** would be too difficult to pronounce with an added apostrophe and an **s**. Therefore, you must use your judgment.

Mr. Jones' backyard   Hercules' victories   Los Angeles' population

To form the possessive for a plural noun, add an apostrophe.

ballplayers' team   citizens' vote   many flowers' stems

Exception: If the plural does not end in an **s**, add both the apostrophe and an **s**.

mice's cheese   women's locker room   children's books

Common mistakes: You do not use an apostrophe to make a noun plural. You do not use an apostrophe with possessive personal pronouns like the following: yours, ours, theirs, its, hers, or his.

Directions: Show possession in the following examples. Check to see if the noun is singular or plural before adding an apostrophe and an **s**. The first one has been done for you.

1. the food belonging to our dog   _____our dog's food_____

2. careers belonging to women   _____

3. comments made by my friend   _____

4. some toys that belong to my baby   _____

5. the horn that is attached to it   _____

6. tickets that belong to the passengers   _____

7. some clothes for the children   _____

8. a store owned by Chris   _____

9. a paintbrush belonging to an artist   _____

10. invitations sent by the hostess   _____

Possessives Practice

Directions: To complete each sentence, form the possessive of the noun parentheses. If the noun is singular, keep it singular. If it is plural, keep it plural.

1. The _____ lounge is upstairs. (teachers)

2. Our _____ motto is "*E Pluribus Unum.*" (country)

3. The _____ department is on the third floor. (children)

4. _____ friends are coming to dinner. (Ross)

5. Where's the _____ room? (men)

6. All the _____ leaders were there. (cities)

7. All the _____ dishes are empty. (dogs)

8. _____ dish is full. (Argus)

9. That's _____ van. (Karla)

10. The _____ practice ends at 3:00. (girls)

Directions: Mark **A** if the underlined word is correct, and mark **B** if it is incorrect.

_____ 1. That's the <u>ladies'</u> room.

_____ 2. I have five <u>cat's</u>.

_____ 3. That <u>babies'</u> mother is Marion.

_____ 4. Our <u>team's</u> mascot is the bulldog.

_____ 5. The <u>mens</u> locker room is closed.

_____ 6. I like old <u>cars</u>.

_____ 7. <u>Chris'</u> mother is bringing lunch.

_____ 8. That <u>ladie's</u> purse is huge.

_____ 9. Your <u>binder's</u> pocket is ripped.

_____ 10. My <u>baby's</u> room is too hot.

Italics and Quotation Marks

To add interest to a passage with many direct quotations, such as a passage containing dialogue between characters, a writer may choose to vary the placement of the speaker's name. The speaker's name can come before the direct quotation, after the direct quotation, or within the direct quotation.

Speaker within: When the name of the speaker comes within (or interrupts) the direct quotation, the second part of the quotation begins with a lowercase letter. Commas are used to separate the quote from the rest of the sentence.

"What are some of the animals," asked Mr. Petok, *"that scientists discovered in the Amazon rain forest?"*

"Finish the dishes and complete your homework," said Mother firmly, turning to look me in the eyes, *"before you even think of watching television."*

Directions: Read each direct quote. Create an appropriate speaker for each quote and place the name or description of the speaker in the location identified. Punctuate the sentence properly. The first one has been done for you.

1. The Egyptian form of heaven was known as the Field of Reeds. (speaker within)

    "The Egyptian form of heaven," said the museum curator, "was known as the Field of Reeds."

2. Don't throw that ball in here! (speaker before)

    _____

3. Have you ever been on a roller coaster? (speaker after)

    _____

4. Emperor Qin had over 4,000 statues of soldiers buried in his tomb. (speaker within)

    _____

5. Plant cell mitosis is a rather simple yet mystifying process. (speaker within)

    _____

6. Do you know if Charlie is coming with us? (speaker before)

    _____

7. Please hide me from the sheriff! (speaker after)

    _____

8. Are you certain that he is the new president? (speaker within)

    _____

Semicolons

A **semicolon** looks and acts like a period and comma combined. It separates complete independent clauses like a period, while also separating items within a sentence like a comma. Use a semicolon instead of a period only when the ideas in the independent clauses are closely related.

I called Jessica. She will arrive in thirty minutes.   (two independent clauses separated by a period)

I called Jessica, and she will arrive in thirty minutes.   (compound sentence using a comma and a conjunction—and, but, or, for, yet)

I called Jessica; she will arrive in thirty minutes.   (two independent clauses joined by a semicolon)

Note: Don't use too many semicolons. When editing your work, decide if it is better to make a compound sentence with a comma and a conjunction, two complete sentences, or a sentence with several commas rather than use a semicolon.

Grammatically Correct: In the deserts of northern Africa, the sun beats down all day practically every day of the year; the plants there, some of which are found nowhere else in the world, are tough, thick, and drought-resistant.

Better: In the deserts of northern Africa, the sun beats down all day, practically every day of the year. The plants there, some of which are found nowhere else in the world, are tough, thick, and drought-resistant.

Directions: Read the following sentences and add semicolons where needed.

1. On our first trip to California, I wanted to visit the San Diego Zoo my little sister wanted to go to Disneyland.

2. Our parents settled the dispute for us they decided we could go to both places.

3. At the zoo we saw a zebra, elephant, and lion the tigers were not in their display area.

4. Three days later we went to Disneyland it has imaginative rides.

5. We can't wait to vacation in California again there are so many sights to see.

Directions: Choose two sentences from above to rewrite as compound sentences joined by conjunctions and commas.

1. _____

   _____

2. _____

   _____

Colons

Colons are used in conventional situations more often than in text. Below are a few cases.

Time	Ratios	Bible Verses	Business Letter Salutations
3:15 P.M.	9:7	John 3:16	Dear Sir:
4:17 A.M.	2:1	Genesis 1:7	To Whom It May Concern:

The most common placement for **colons** in text is before a list of items. If using a **colon** before your list, do not place it directly after a verb or a preposition. A **colon** is most often used with expressions like *as follows* or *the following*.

Correct	On our camping trip we will need to bring sleeping bags, a camping stove, a flashlight, warm clothes, and a week's supply of food.
Incorrect	On our camping trip we will need to bring: sleeping bags, a camping stove, a flashlight, warm clothes, and a week's supply of food.
Correct	On our camping trip we will need to bring the following items: sleeping bags, camping stove, a flashlight, warm clothes, and a week's supply of food.
Correct	This recipe is made from chicken, curry, onions, brown sugar, and sour cream.
Incorrect	This recipe is made from: chicken, curry, onions, brown sugar, and sour cream.
Correct	This recipe includes these ingredients: chicken, curry, onions, brown sugar, and sour cream.

Directions: Read each list of items. Write a sentence with a colon inserted before each list.

1. bait, tackle, net, and hooks

2. ham sandwich, grapes, string cheese, orange juice, and a chocolate chip cookie

3. protractor, compass, calculator, ruler, and pencils

4. basketball, tennis, swimming, and bowling

Nouns

There are two types of **nouns**: common and proper.

- **Common nouns** describe any person, place, or thing.
  Examples: **That young man works at two different jobs after school.**
  The toy store is a fun and exciting place to work.

- **Proper nouns** describe specific people, places, or things and are capitalized.
  Examples: **New York City offers thousands of job opportunities.**
  John Smith can't wait to move there.

Directions: Change the underlined common nouns below into proper nouns and the underlined proper nouns into common nouns. Then rewrite the sentence in the space provided.

1. I've always wanted to see <u>Italy</u>. _____

2. <u>Kathy Petrini</u> owns the <u>restaurant</u> downtown. _____

3. <u>Mr. Minelli</u> drives a red <u>Honda</u>. _____

4. <u>George</u> likes to play <u>badminton</u>. _____

5. <u>Main Street Deli</u> offers free <u>cookies</u> on Fridays._____

6. <u>My brother</u> watches <u>Bugs Bunny</u> on Saturday mornings._____

Here are two sub-types of nouns: compound and collective.

- **Compound nouns** are two or more nouns that function as a single unit.
  Example: **The <u>commander-in-chief</u> fought in World War II.**
- **Collective nouns** name groups of people or things.
  Example: **A *crowd* of people poured into the baseball stadium.**

Directions: Underline the compound or collective nouns in the sentences below.

1. A happy family went to the beach one sunny Saturday.
2. My sister-in-law is knitting me a sweater for Christmas.
3. We rode the trolley car all the way downtown.
4. Jackson led the herd of cattle into the stable.
5. Our class toured the Smithsonian on a field trip.
6. Did you know that the editor-in-chief of the magazine worked in the circus?
7. Rake up that pile of leaves, please.
8. We asked the passers-by if they wanted their cars washed.
9. A flock of Canadian geese flew overhead.
10. The group of carolers sang beautifully.

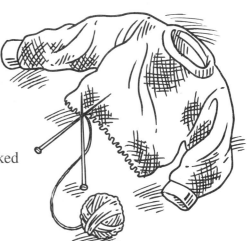

Plural Nouns

Singular nouns refer to one person, place, or thing. Plural nouns refer to more than one person, place, or thing.

1. **Write the plural of the word in parentheses. Hint: Most nouns form the plural by adding *s*. Those that end in *ch*, *sh*, *s*, or *x* add *es*.**

   a. There are over seven _____ in our town. (church)

   b. There are lots of _____ growing in the playground. (tree)

   c. The frightened dog hid between the two _____ . (bush)

   d. Jan put all the _____ on the table. (box)

   e. My brother ate three _____ for lunch. (peach)

   f. The six school _____ were in a line. (bus)

2. **Write the plural of each of the following words. Hint: They are all irregular.**

   a. goose _____   e. tooth   _____

   b. man   _____   f. woman   _____

   c. foot _____   g. child   _____

   d. louse _____   h. mouse   _____

3. **Write the plural of the word in parentheses. Hint: Some nouns that end in *o* add *es* to make the plural. Others simply add *s*.**

   a. We planted _____ in the garden. (potato)

   b. On our holiday, Kyle took lots of _____ . (photo)

   c. South America has many _____ . (volcano)

   d. Hundreds of _____ were bathing in the pool. (hippo)

   e. The brave _____ were all given medals. (hero)

   f. I sliced the three _____ to make a salad. (tomato)

Adjectives

Adjectives are words that describe nouns. They can also describe pronouns because pronouns take the place of nouns. Usually, we find adjectives in front of the nouns or pronouns they are describing.

That's a blue car.

(*Blue* is an adjective describing the noun *car*.)

She's a nice girl.

(*Nice* is an adjective describing the noun *girl*.)

We also find adjectives in sentences like the ones discussed in the verb section, in which a linking verb is linking the subject of the sentence to a word that describes the subject. The describing word is an adjective since a subject must be a noun or pronoun, and adjectives are the only words that describe nouns or pronouns.

Cindy looks pretty.

(*Pretty* is an adjective describing the noun *Cindy*.)

She is smart.

(*Smart* is an adjective describing the pronoun *she*.)

Directions: Underline the adjective(s) in the following sentences. Beside each sentence, write the adjective(s) plus the noun(s) being described.

1. The big truck hit the little car. _____

2. That's a good book. _____

3. My cute kitty is washing her sweet face. _____

4. Ms. Bronowski is nice. _____

5. My dad made a delicious cake. _____

6. That's a silly thing to say. _____

7. I like chocolate ice cream. _____

8. I like the red car better than the blue one. _____

9. This book is old. _____

10. Here's a shiny new penny! _____

Adverbs

Adverbs are words to describe verbs. They also describe adjectives and other adverbs.

> - Usually adverbs are describing verbs: We ate fast. *Fast* is an adverb describing the verb *ate*. He speaks quietly. *Quietly* is an adverb describing the verb *speaks*. Note: Adverbs often end in *-ly*.
> - Adverbs answer these questions: How? When? Why? How did Bob walk? Bob walked *quickly*. When did Bob walk? Bob walked *yesterday*. Where did Bob walk? Bob walked *upstairs*.
> - Some adverbs describe adjectives and other adverbs: He is really nice. *Really* is an adverb describing the adjective *nice*. You read very well. *Very* is an adverb describing the adverb *well*.

Directions: Add adverbs which answer how, where, or when about the verbs in the following sentences. Underline the adverbs you add. Use a different adverb for each sentence.

a. They eat. They eat <u>loudly</u>.

b. She wrote a letter. She <u>quickly</u> wrote a letter.

c. I fell. I fell <u>downstairs</u>.

1. Theresa threw the ball. _____

2. We read the story. _____

3. We flew down the street. _____

4. He ate the pizza. _____

5. Bob hiccupped in class. _____

6. The mummy walked. _____

7. Students talked. _____

8. We watched the news program. _____

9. The teacher listened. _____

10. My friends sat under the tree. _____

Directions: Add adverbs to modify the adjectives or other adverbs already in these sentences. Underline the adverbs you add. Do not use the same adverb more than once.

a. John is nice. John is <u>quite</u> nice.

b. You drive fast. You drive <u>too</u> fast.

c. That's not pretty. That's <u>really</u> not pretty.

1. Your cat is cute. _____

2. That's a wonderful book. _____

3. I bought a blue truck. _____

4. You sing beautifully. _____

5. I talk quietly. _____

Verbs

Verbs are words that show action or state of being.

- To find the action verb in a sentence, you ask this about the subject: "What is he/she/it doing?"

  Jose is riding the bus.

  What is Jose doing? *Riding*.

- The other kinds of verbs are called *state of being* or *linking verbs*. They don't show action; they link the subject of the sentence to a word that describes the subject or a word that renames the subject.

  Jane is pretty.

  What is Jane doing? She's doing nothing. She just *is*. *Is* is the verb. It links the subject, *Jane*, with a word describing her, *pretty*. The most common linking verbs are forms of the word *be*: *is, are, was, am, be, been, being*.

Directions: Underline the verb(s) in each sentence.

1. Ms. Davis talks a lot.
2. She is talkative.
3. I ran into the door.
4. We read *Sounder*.
5. I enjoyed it.
6. I think about *Sounder* all the time.
7. I hope we get other good books this year.
8. I like all kinds of books.
9. I had a root canal yesterday.
10. The dentist was nice.

Directions: Underline the verb in each sentence. If the verb is an action verb, mark **A** after the sentence, and if it is a linking verb, mark **L** at the end of the sentence.

1. Ms. Oudegeest plays with her computer.
2. She also watches TV.
3. She likes *Friends*.
4. Max looks mad.
5. He spit at the dog.
6. Spitting is gross.
7. The dog seems mad now.
8. Karla looked out the window.
9. She saw her dad.
10. Her dad is her best friend.
11. Cathy Lew asked for our attention on the intercom.
12. We heard her very well.
13. She sounded funny, though.
14. Cathy Lew is really nice.
15. Students and teachers like her.

Verb Form Practice

Directions: Underline the correct verb form from the choices given.

1. I should have (knew/known) that I could have (froze/frozen) my toes.

2. As soon as Manuel had (chose/chosen) his subject, he (began/begun) his talk.

3. The coat that I had (wore/worn) only once had been (stole/stolen).

4. The dress that I would have (chose/chosen) was (tore/torn).

5. Has the bell (rang/rung), or would I (have/of) heard it here?

6. The man who had (stole/stolen) the money was (knew/known) by the police.

7. You should (have/of) known that the song was (sang/sung) by Marilyn.

8. Has he always (drove/driven) so carelessly, or has he just (began/begun) to do so?

9. She (began/begun) to see that she had (chose/chosen) the wrong topic.

10. Snow (fell/fallen) after the pond had (froze/frozen).

11. Our doorbell is (wore/worn) out because the children have (rang/rung) it too many times.

12. Two cups have (fell/fallen) off the shelf and have (broke/broken).

13. Barbara (sang/sung) the song that was (chose/chosen) by the committee.

14. I would have (brung/brought) my stereo if it hadn't been (stole/stolen).

15. The telephone (rang/rung) just as I (began/begun) to study.

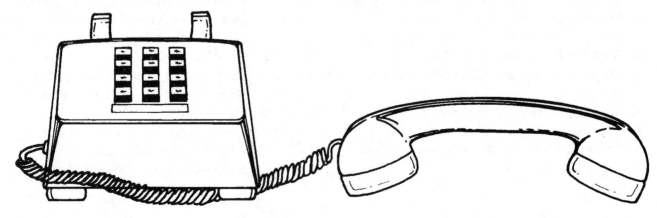

Pronouns

Personal pronouns have two forms: the **subject** and the **object** forms.

Subject I, she, he, they, we   **Object** me, her, him, them, us

As you can see, the pronouns on the left mean exactly the same thing as the pronouns on the right. For example, *I* and *me* mean the same thing. The difference is that the pronouns on the left are used when they are acting as subjects, and the pronouns on the right are used when acting as objects.

Usually we use the correct form automatically. For example, we wouldn't say, "Me like you." We would say, "I like you." *I* is the subject. Sometimes, though, when another person is added to the sentence, we are unsure. For example, which is correct?

1. Go to the store with Bob and I.   **2. Go to the store with Bob and me.**

The second sentence is correct. An easy way to test this is to eliminate the other person in the sentence and say the sentence with the pronoun by itself. Here, we would say, "Go to the store with me." We wouldn't say "Go to the store with I." Therefore, me is the correct form of the pronoun for this sentence, even if we add another person.

Directions: Underline the correct pronoun(s) for each sentence.

1. Bob and (I, me) are going.
2. Stand by the captain and (I, me).
3. (We, Us) girls are going to win.
4. Are Sandy and (she, her) going?
5. You and (he, him) make a cute couple.
6. I'm going to the party with Fred and (they, them).
7. If Lucia and (they, them) go, I'm not going.
8. Give the papers to (she, her) and (we, us) before you leave.
9. You can't play with (we, us) boys.
10. If you go with Ranvir and (I, me), we will have more fun.

Directions: Underline the correct pronouns from the choices given in the following sentences.

1. (We, Us) teachers are going on vacation together.
2. You may go with (we, us) teachers.
3. My sister and (I, me) are going to visit Grandma.
4. She can't go with (he, him) and (she, her).
5. They and (we, us) all did well on the project.
6. My father sent Debbie and (I, me) a card.
7. The teacher wrote detentions for (he, him) and (I, me).
8. A package arrived for (we, us) kids.
9. Don't hold this against Nicki and (I, me).
10. The teacher called on (he, him) and (she, her).
11. We are going to have pizza with the boys and (she, her).
12. (He, Him) and (I, me) are going out to dinner.
13. There was a tie between (she, her) and (he, him).
14. (He, Him) and the clerk got into an argument.
15. (They, Them) and the girls are following us.
16. The students and (I, me) are having a good day.
17. (We, Us) and (they, them) are playing the final match.
18. I wrote a letter to (he, him) and (she, her).
19. I like to ride with John and (she, her).
20. The principal was staring at (they, them) and (we, us).

Prepositions, Conjunctions, and Interjections

Prepositions: A preposition is a word or group of words which show how two ideas are related.

Directions: Write a sentence using the preposition listed.

Example: in front of: <u>They put a sign in front of the store.</u>

1. within: _____

2. under: _____

3. in: _____

4. between: _____

5. on behalf of: _____

Conjunctions: A conjunction is a word that connects individual words or groups of words.

Directions: Write a sentence using the conjunction listed.

Example: He will be ready Saturday **or** Sunday.

6. and _____

7. or _____

8. but_____

9. so _____

Interjection: An interjection is a word or phrase used to express strong emotion or surprise.

Directions: Write a sentence using the interjection listed.

Example: Wow! Are you really that old?

10. Oh no! _____

11. Wow! _____

12. Yikes! _____

13. No way! _____

Prepositions

Prepositions are words that show a relationship between other words.

To see how prepositions work, look at these two words: **fox   log**

Prepositions can show the relationship between the fox and the log:

The fox was *under* the log.   The fox was *on* the log.

The fox was *by* the log.   The fox was *in* the log.

Prepositions always start prepositional phrases. A phrase is a group of words that doesn't make a whole sentence—a group of words that do a job together. These are all prepositional phrases:

under the log, on the log, by the log, in the log

Directions: Under each sentence, copy the prepositional phrase from that sentence. Circle the object of the preposition and underline the preposition.

1. Penguins live at the South Pole.

   _____

2. The students slept during the speech.

   _____

3. The baby was tossed out with the bathwater.

   _____

4. The fish in the pan smelled awful.

   _____

5. The announcer on TV was excited.

   _____

6. I found the keys under the table.

   _____

7. We are going to the movies tomorrow.

   _____

8. The rabbit ran across the road.

   _____

9. Jim put the pizza on the table.

   _____

10. The girls climbed to the top.

    _____

Directions: Rewrite each sentence, adding a prepositional phrase to each.

1. The dog ate his dinner. _____ The dog ate his dinner by the back door.

   _____

2. The boys ran. _____

   _____

3. Josh did his work. _____

   _____

4. Sally read the book. _____

   _____

5. The girls are practicing. _____

   _____

Conjunctions

Conjunctions are words that join or connect other words. It's easy to remember the definition if you emphasize it this way: **con**junctions **con**nect words.

Conjunctions are words like *and*, *but*, and *or*. They connect words or groups of words.

I want a car *or* a truck.

I want to eat dinner *and* go to the movies.

I like Bob, *but* my mom doesn't care for him.

And, *but*, and *or* are the most commonly used conjunctions. There are others, though, including *if*, *so*, *although*, *since*, and *because*.

You may go to the party *if* you clean your room.

I like pizza *although* it is fattening.

Since you are late, we will all be late.

Satinder bought a car *because* she saved her money.

Directions: Underline the conjunctions in the following sentences.

1. Tom likes Linda, but she doesn't like him.
2. I will buy chips or salad.
3. My car won't run, so I have to use my mom's car.
4. I will go if my mother gives me permission.
5. I couldn't leave until my brother got home.
6. I'll call José after I eat.
7. I'm going to do my chores, watch television, and eat a banana.
8. *The Simpsons* isn't on since the basketball game went into overtime.
9. Tom's going with us although he doesn't want to go.

Directions: Fill in the blanks with conjunctions.

1. I would like a slice of cheesecake with cherries _____ strawberries.
2. We can go to the movies _____ go to the park.
3. I like Polly _____ she's nice.
4. I will make dinner _____ I finish my homework.
5. _____ you like chocolate, you will like these cookies.
6. Serena wrote me a letter, _____ I haven't seen it.
7. I like Mexican food, _____ I don't like beans.
8. I will give you my book _____ you keep asking for it.
9. This car has power steering _____ air conditioning.
10. You can go, _____ the girls can't go.
11. The teacher will take down your name _____ give you detention.
12. The best choices would be Anthony, Ricky, _____ Danny.
13. Rusty sent me a card, _____ it was nice.
14. Louise is nice, _____ she is also moody.

Similes

A **simile** is a technique for comparing two things. Similes use the words *like* or *as* to show how the items are alike. Here are some similes.

Her teeth are as white as winter snow.
(Her teeth are white and snow is white.)

The snake was like a garden hose.
(The snake was thin and black and lying in the grass. The garden hose was also thin and black and lying in the grass.)

Explain the comparisons in the following similes:

1. The baby's cheeks are like a rose.

   The baby's cheeks are _____ and a rose is _____ .

2. The full moon is like a cookie.

   The full moon is _____ and a cookie is _____ .

3. The baseball whizzed by like a bullet.

   The baseball is _____ and a bullet is _____ .

4. The coffee is like ink.

   Coffee is _____ and ink is _____ .

Now you try it. Write some similes of your own.

1. The boat is _____
   _____ .

2. The cave is _____
   _____ .

3. Her hair is _____
   _____ .

Read your similes to a friend. See if he or she can explain your comparison.

Metaphors

A **metaphor** is another form of figurative language. A metaphor is a phrase that compares two unlike things. While a simile **compares two things** by using the words *as* or *like*, a metaphor states that **one thing is the other.**

Here are some examples of metaphors:

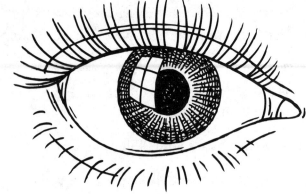

- Books are food for the brain.
- Winter is the hibernation of the earth.
- Earth is the mother of mankind.
- The ocean is a huge swimming pool.
- An eye is the window to the world.

Now, using complete sentences, write a metaphor for each situation:

1. you have a headache

   The headache was a hammer pounding nails in my head.

2. you are exhausted

   _____

3. you seriously cut your leg

   _____

4. you're very strong

   _____

5. you are hungry

   _____

Tips for when to use a metaphor in your writing:

- Your writing is too predictable.
- Your writing is unimaginative.
- Your writing doesn't sound like you.
- Your writing sounds boring.
- You are trying to clearly describe an object or a feeling.
- You need sentence variety.

More Similies and Metaphors

Metaphorical thinking is not difficult, strange, or out of reach. You probably do it all the time, but you just did not know what it was called. A little boy named Justin used a metaphor one day when he came running into the house yelling, "Dad! Dad! It's raining styrofoam!" He was so happy he ran back outside to dance around in the "styrofoam." Of course, it was not "raining styrofoam." It was hail, but it was like styrofoam. However, Justin's description was more playful and descriptive than to simply say it was hail.

Similes and metaphors are literary devices, or tools, to help a writer be more creative.

A **simile** is a way of comparing two things by using the words like, as, or so. Some examples:

- He's as sharp as a tack.

- An ungrateful child is like a serpent's tooth.

- As sand going through an hourglass, so are the days of our lives.

A **metaphor** compares one thing to another without using words like *as* or *like*. For example:

- She's an accident waiting to happen.

- He's a bear in the morning.

  (If you say he looked like a bear in the morning, that would be a simile).

Try writing a simile about life. Begin with, "Life is like . . . "

Here are some examples written by other students:

> *"Life is like a banana. You start out green and get soft and mushy when you're old. Some people want to be one of the bunch while others want to be top banana. You have to be careful not to slip on the peels."*

> *"Life is like a jigsaw puzzle, but you don't have the picture on the front of the box to know what it's supposed to look like. And you're not sure if you have all the pieces."*

Now try completing the following similes (the first one has been completed for you as an example):

An orange is as round and sunny as the sun.

A puppy is as _____ as _____

A star is as _____ as _____

Ice is as _____ as _____

The clouds are as _____ as _____

Snow is as _____ as _____

And here are some metaphors to complete for practice:

The tree is a giant stalk of broccoli.

The rock is _____ .

The rain is _____ .

The moon was _____ .

The wolf was _____ .

The baby is_____ .

Idioms

An **idiom** is an expression which means something different from what is actually written. For example, "to put one's foot in one's mouth" is a familiar idiom. It does not literally mean to place one's foot inside of one's mouth. It really means that you have said something you shouldn't have said.

Here are some examples of idioms:

Idioms	Meanings of Idioms
horse of a different color	that's a completely different situation
spill the beans	tell a secret you shouldn't have
to be downhearted	to be sad
a close shave	a close encounter with trouble
for the birds	useless or silly
crocodile tears	fake tears
going to the dogs	falling apart, losing quality
a fork in the road	two different choices or directions
in one ear and out the other	you aren't paying attention
woke up on the wrong side of the bed	having a bad day
zip my lips	you won't share it, keep it confidentially
bit off more than you can chew	overwhelmed with what you have to do
costs an arm and a leg	very expensive
keep an eye on	to watch very closely
read my lips	believe what I say
count on me	have confidence in me and what I say
raining cats and dogs	raining heavily outside
step on the gas	pick up the pace, go faster
monkey around	goofing off, fooling around
a broken heart	very sad, let down
stopped dead in my tracks	stopped or ended suddenly

Idioms are used to make a point or show the irony of something. A writer uses idioms to keep writing interesting and keep the reader interested. Write a paragraph using one of the previous idioms.

_____

_____

_____

_____

_____

_____

_____

Idiomatic Expressions

An **idiom** is an expression that has a meaning different from the meanings of its separate words. For example, we may say, "Hold your horses," but what we really mean is "Wait, you are being impatient." A. In your own words, explain the idiomatic expressions below.

1. Are you getting cold feet?

   _____

2. She blew her stack!

   _____

3. It is raining cats and dogs.

   _____

4. He is like a bull in a china shop.

   _____

5. I'm just as fit as a fiddle.

   _____

6. He lost his shirt on that deal.

   _____

7. She's as mad as a wet hen.

   _____

8. Keep a stiff upper lip.

   _____

9. It's a one-horse town.

   _____

10. Don't cry over spilt milk.

   _____

B. Underline the idioms in each sentence. Then write a word or phrase for the underlined idiom. Make sure that the word or phrase means the same as the idiom.

1. The referee told the crowd to <u>pipe down</u>.

   <u>The referee told the crowd to be quiet.</u>

2. At basketball practice, we can't get away with anything!

   _____

3. When it comes to fighting, my dad puts his foot down.

   _____

4. I wouldn't turn my nose up at the chance to wrestle him.

   _____

Alliteration

Alliteration is a poetic technique in which the beginning sound is repeated in words for effect. Tongue twisters often use alliteration to create catchy phrases. Notice the effect of alliteration as you try to say the following tongue twisters:

Six silly sailors swam south.

Bobby bought a bunch of brown bananas.

Alliteration Practice

Underline the alliterative consonants in the following sentences.

Example: Snakes slither on the sidewalk.

1. The wind whistled through the willows.

2. Magic markers can make masterpieces.

3. Tommy tried to twist, but tumbled.

4. Greg grabbed the garnish from the graceful bowl.

5. Constance catered to her cat with catnip to keep it from kidnapping canaries.

Use alliteration to finish the lines below.

1. People patiently _____

2. Roger ran _____

3. Six swimmers_____

4. Alan always _____

5. Kelly caught_____

Now, write five alliterative sentences of your own.

1. _____

2. _____

3. _____

4. _____

5. _____

Personification

Personification is a form of figurative language in which an object, an item, or an animal is given the characteristics of a person. It is personified.

Here are some examples of personification:

- The wind picked up the leaves and scattered them throughout the yard.
- The tree stood firm against the strikes of the blade.
- The rug curls up like it wants to hide.
- The door slammed shut to keep the strong wind from coming inside.
- The sun set slowly over the horizon signaling the time had come.
- The papers raced across the vacant lot.
- The chair tumbled over.
- The tree reached its leafy arms skyward.
- Perspiration rolled down her back.
- The floor groaned as the dancers stomped away.
- The wind whispered through the trees.
- The raindrops danced on the window.
- The book sat on the table.
- The paper flew off the desk.

Directions: Add some of your own personification examples to the list:

_____
_____
_____
_____
_____
_____
_____
_____
_____
_____
_____
_____

Helpful Tips on Using Figurative Language

If your writing is clear, easy to read, interesting, and if it flows easily, then leave it alone. The only time to use figurative language such as similes, metaphors, and personification is to improve your writing. Adding colorful words and phrases can make your writing better. Be careful not to add too many, just enough to give your writing some pizzazz.

Hyperbole

A **hyperbole** is an exaggeration or an overstatement used for emphasis. A hyperbole is another form of figurative language used to engage the reader.

Here are examples of hyperbole:

- My dad about died when he saw my grades.
- I about had a hernia when I heard the price of the dress.
- He talked until he was blue in the face.
- She was halfway across the world before she realized she had forgotten her bag.
- I am going to kick that book to Timbuktu.
- The siren was so loud you couldn't hear yourself think.
- Her feet were glued to the ground when she saw the mountain lion.

Directions: Underline the hyperboles in the paragraphs below.

A. It was a rough day at sea. I thought the boat was going to flip right over. The wind came rushing through the sails without a break. The captain almost had a heart attack when he saw the height of the waves. Would we ever see dry land again?

B. The kids were running and screaming around the classroom. You could tell when you walked in there was a substitute that day. It was so loud that you could barely hear yourself think. The substitute was trying to get the attention of the students.

C. This Thanksgiving was wonderful. We had at least fifty people at the feast this year. My mother tried some new recipes and they were all great. I ate so much food I almost burst. I had to take a nap just to be able to walk.

Directions: Write a paragraph below that uses hyperbole.

_____

_____

_____

_____

_____

_____

_____

Directions: Write hyperboles you would like to use in your own writing below.

_____

_____

_____

_____

Language Arts

Vocabulary: Spelling Demons

The following are some of the most commonly misspelled English words.

Word	Syllables	In Context
foreign	for•eign	Do you know how to speak any **foreign** languages?
weird	weird	He had on a very **weird** outfit.
separate	sep•a•rate	Put their gifts in two **separate** bags.
calendar	cal•en•dar	The **calendar** pictured a different dog each month.
a lot	a lot	It took **a lot** of hours to paint the house.
embarrass	em•bar•rass	It will **embarrass** me if I have to get up on stage.
guarantee	guar•an•tee	Did this toaster come with a money-back **guarantee**?
privilege	priv•i•lege	She had the **privilege** of driving her dad's car to school.
rhythm	rhy•thm	The drummer had a natural sense of **rhythm**.
license	li•cense	When you are 16, you can apply for a driver's **license**.
vacuum	vac•uum	Please **vacuum** the living room.
irrelevant	ir•rel•e•vant	Get rid of **irrelevant** information in your essay.
accommodate	ac•com•mo•date	The room can **accommodate** four people.
familiar	fa•mil•iar	Something about that woman is **familiar** to me.
appropriate	ap•pro•pri•ate	Wearing jeans isn't **appropriate** for attending a funeral.

Write the spelling word that begins and ends with same letters as the word given. Some of the spelling words begin and end with the same letters. In that case, an additional line was given.

Example: little _____license_____ (*license* is used again below)

1. four _____

2. airplane _____

_____

3. vandalism _____

4. late _____

5. shuttle _____

6. Internet _____

7. gauge _____

8. chair _____

9. flatten _____

10. express _____

11. petite _____

12. wild _____

13. rum _____

14. What spelling word in this lesson is actually two small words? _____

©Teacher Created Resources, Inc.   35   #3945 Mastering Sixth Grade Skills

Language Arts

Vocabulary: Spelling Demons (cont.)

Roman Numeral Code

Change the Roman numeral code into spelling words from this lesson. Write each letter beneath the Roman numeral that stands for it.

I = a	II = b	III = c	IV = d	V = e	VI = f	VII = g	VIII = h	IX = i
X = j	XI = k	XII = l	XIII = m	XIV = n	XV = o	XVI = p	XVII = q	XVIII = r
XIX = s	XX = t	XXI = u	XXII = v	XXIII = w	XXIV = x	XXV = y	XXVI = z	

Example: XIX XV XII IV IX V XVIII
       s   o   l   d   i   e   r

1. XII IX III V XIV XIX V

2. VII XXI I XVIII I XIV XX V V

3. I XVI XVI XVIII XV XVI XVIII IX I XX V

4. III I XII V XIV IV I XVIII

5. XXII I III XXI XXI XIII

6. XXIII V IX XVIII IV

7. IX XVIII XVIII V XII V XXII I XIV XX

8. XVIII VIII XXV XX VIII XIII

9. V XIII II I XVIII XVIII I XIX XIX

10. I   XII XV XX

11. I III III XV XIII XIII XV IV I XX V

12. XVI XVIII IX XXII IX XII V VII V

13. VI I XIII IX XII IX I XVIII

14. VI XV XVIII V IX VII XIV

15. XIX V XVI I XVIII I XX V

#3945 Mastering Sixth Grade Skills   36   ©Teacher Created Resources, Inc.

Synonyms: Similar Meanings

Synonyms are words that have the same or nearly the same meaning. Synonyms are especially important when you decide you need a more exact or a better word to express your meaning when you are writing or reading. At such times, a thesaurus is a helpful reference.

Because a thesaurus entry usually contains several words that are considered synonyms, you also need to use a dictionary to be sure that the word you choose produces the meaning you want. You cannot be sure that every word in the list will work as a substitute for the one you started with.

For example, you may want to describe in a story a character who is stingy, but you want a word that also suggests that the person hides away money. The thesaurus lists several words that could be used in place of *stingy*: *miserly, tightfisted, penny-pinching, cheap,* and *frugal*. One of these is the word you are looking for: *miserly*. When you look it up in the dictionary, you find that it means exactly what you had in mind: being stingy and especially hiding money.

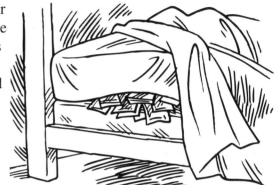

Directions: Use a thesaurus and a dictionary to choose the best synonyms to replace the italicized words in the following sentences. (Remember that one word often leads to another. You may have to go to the next step and look in the dictionary for definitions of one or more unfamiliar words in a definition.)

1. The naturalized citizen, Maria Hernandez, pledged her *allegiance* to her new country.

   a. feasibility   b. helpfulness   c. loyalty

2. Without even a *whimper*, Baby Gerald let a complete stranger give him his bottle.

   a. whoopee   b. cry   c. twitch

3. Even the great Inspector Cleverleaux could not *unravel* the mystery.

   a. tighten   b. calculate   c. untangle

4. The neighbor's barking German shepherd, Daisy, interrupted my *slumber*.

   a. leisure   b. relaxation   c. sleep

5. Because he wanted to *qualify* to go to a top-notch university after he graduated from high school, Terence worked to earn excellent grades in all his classes.

   a. to be eligible   b. to be barred   c. to be innovative

6. Mozart wrote *operas* that are performed throughout the world.

   a. violin solos   b. plays set to music   c. plays about soaps

Synonyms: Similar Meanings *(cont.)*

7. Only an impolite and insensitive person will *mock* others.

    a. photograph   b. ridicule   c. impersonate

8. Molly thought she would *keel over* from exhaustion after running the marathon.

    a. collapse   b. recover   c. become ill

9. My friend Matthew is considered an *ideal* candidate for class president.

    a. indifferent   b. poor   c. perfect

10. The Burmese ruby and the Ceylon sapphire are both *gems* that Mrs. Trumpet likes.

    a. standouts   b. precious stones   c. gymnasium

11. It is *essential* that you eat healthful foods if you are going to remain healthy.

    a. extremely   b. indicated   c. necessary

12. I had to buy a new atlas because the *boundaries* of some countries have changed.

    a. canopies   b. campaigns   c. borders

13. Mr. Chang, our new neighbor, is an *amateur* photographer.

    a. not professional   b. not formal   c. not effective

14. One of the events in speech contests in high school and college is *debate*.

    a. night crawlers   b. formal argument   c. bounty

15. My mother communicated to me an urgent *plea* to clean my room.

    a. pastime   b. query   c. request

16. It is always a bad idea to try to *deceive* your parents about anything.

    a. annoy   b. conceal   c. mislead

17. Sometimes it is difficult to decide what would be *suitable* to wear to an event.

    a. appropriate   b. considerate   c. communicate

Antonyms: Contrasting Meanings

Learning the antonym or the word that means almost the opposite of another word can help you better understand the meaning of that word just as a synonym can. Just as you may find exactly the right synonym in a thesaurus, you may also find an antonym in a thesaurus entry or in a dictionary. There are dictionaries that list both synonyms and antonyms.

Directions: Use a thesaurus and a dictionary to help you choose the sentence that best or most closely expresses the **opposite** meaning of the first sentence in each group. (Remember that one word often leads to another. You may have to go to the next step and look in the dictionary for definitions of one or more unfamiliar words in a definition.)

1. **Pedro Herrera thought the salesman's smile was *artificial*.**
   a. Pedro Herrera thought the smile was confident.
   b. Pedro Herrera thought the smile was sincere.
   c. Pedro Herrera thought the smile was amazing.

2. **The very gracious Lord Hastings *ignored* Louisa's ink-smudged hands when she went through the reception line.**
   a. Lord Hastings noticed Louisa's hands.
   b. Lord Hastings overlooked Louisa's hands.
   c. Lord Hastings admired Louisa's hands.

3. **When visiting the sacred shrine, Murikama behaved very *respectfully*.**
   a. Murikama was reverent at the shrine.
   b. Murikama was alert at the shrine.
   c. Murikama was irreverent at the shrine.

4. **Mayor Lee is a *powerful* member of the city council.**
   a. Mayor Lee is an insignificant member of the city council.
   b. Mayor Lee is a dedicated member of the city council.
   c. Mayor Lee is a distinguished member of the city council.

5. **The Smokey Mountains are especially *gorgeous* in both the spring and fall.**
   a. The Smokey Mountains are magnificent in spring and fall.
   b. The Smokey Mountains are ugly in spring and fall.
   c. The Smokey Mountains are amazing in spring and fall.

6. **Bennie *warily* approached the wounded bear.**
   a. Bennie cautiously approached the bear.
   b. Bennie recklessly approached the bear.
   c. Bennie unexpectedly approached the bear.

Antonyms: Contrasting Meanings *(cont.)*

7. **The candidate *brooded* about the mistake he had made.**

   a. The candidate worried about the mistake.

   b. The candidate took advantage of the mistake.

   c. The candidate was untroubled about the mistake.

8. **Gracie was called a *heroine* after she foiled the robbery.**

   a. Gracie was called a champion after the robbery.

   b. Gracie was called a coward after the robbery.

   c. Gracie was called a cadet after the robbery.

9. **At the flea market, Luke found an *antique* vase for his mother.**

   a. Luke found a very old vase at the flea market.

   b. Luke found a cunning vase at the flea market.

   c. Luke found a new vase at the flea market.

10. **The senator appeared to be a very *dignified* person.**

    a. The senator appeared to be very proper person.

    b. The senator appeared to be a very unseemly person.

    c. The senator appeared to be a very hideous person.

11. **The house the astronomer lives in looks like a *palace* to me.**

    a. The astronomer's house looks like a mansion.

    b. The astronomer's house looks like a hovel.

    c. The astronomer's house looks like a lobby.

12. **Jo Ellen *concealed* the details of her illness from all of her friends.**

    a. Jo Ellen revealed the details of her illness.

    b. Jo Ellen hid the details of her illness.

    c. Jo Ellen criticized the details of her illness.

13. **Romeo decided that he would *forfeit* the race.**

    a. Romeo decided that he would cultivate the race.

    b. Romeo decided that he would give up the race.

    c. Romeo decided that he would participate in the race.

14. **Carl Sandburg wrote a *thorough* biography of Abraham Lincoln.**

    a. Sandburg wrote a sketchy biography of Lincoln.

    b. Sandburg wrote a forlorn biography of Lincoln.

    c. Sandburg wrote a comprehensive biography of Lincoln.

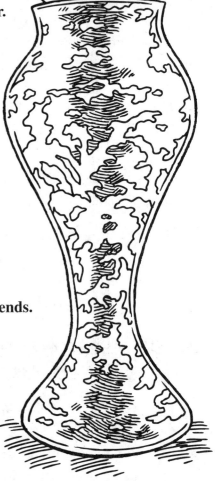

Homonyms

Homonyms are two or more words that have the same spelling or sound but have *different meanings*. These words are problems for many writers, for it is easy to become confused by them.

If certain homonyms are a problem for you, you need to find a way to help you remember what each word means. For example, you can remember that *stationery* is writing paper because of the *er* in both *stationery* and *paper*. Try to think of similar ways to distinguish one homonym from another so that you write both words correctly.

Directions: Select the correct homonyms to fill in the blanks in the sentences below.

1. Mrs. Ridley gave her _____ for all of us to watch the _____ _____ of the colorful hot-air balloons as they rose over Albuquerque. (*ascent/assent*)

2. The sailors on the *Merry Mermaid* were trying to plot a safe _____ (*coarse/course*) through the _____. (*straight/strait*)

3. The furniture refinisher did not want to use the _____ sandpaper. (*coarse/course*)

4. Just as important as remembering to give a _____ to someone else is having the ability to accept one gracefully. (*compliment/complement*)

5. Did you remember to _____ the references you used to write your report? (*cite/site*)

6. The climber kept the rope _____ as he made his way to the peak. (*taught/taut*)

7. If you look over _____, you will see _____ house that they have painted red, white, and blue. (*their/there*)

8. Learning your _____ will _____ (*lessen/lesson*) the chance that you will earn a poor grade.

9. Your _____ is required while I open my _____. (*presence/presents*)

10. Lucinda _____ the test, and that got her _____ the one thing that she had been dreading the most. (*passed/past*)

Choose the Best Definitions

Directions: For each sentence below and on page 43, choose the definition that matches the way the italicized word is used in the sentence.

1. **Senator Whistler took the *floor* to defend his position on the immigration bill.**

    a. to knock down

    b. upper or uppermost surface

    c. right to address an assembly

2. **Professor Watkins went to Australia to participate in the *dig*.**

    a. an archaeological site

    b. to learn or discover

    c. to break up, turn over, or remove

3. **My vigorous friend Audrey was a *rock* and stayed with me the entire time.**

    a. move back and forth; zigzag

    b. stable, firm, dependable one

    c. naturally formed mineral

4. **Attorney William Joseph's *opposite* in the case was Attorney Justine Modigliani.**

    a. one that is contrary to another

    b. located directly behind or ahead of

    c. sharply contrasting

5. **Catherine Laws, my sixth-grade teacher, *holds* a degree in music also.**

    a. to restrain; curb

    b. to possess

    c. to regard or consider

6. **When we went sailing Saturday, the seas were very *heavy*.**

    a. weighted down; burdened

    b. of great intensity

    c. violent, rough

7. **The argument between the two wealthy adversaries quickly became *heated*.**

    a. warm a building

    b. degree of warmth or hotness

    c. intense, angry

8. **The nomination committee decided to *block* the investigation of their decisions.**

    a. to impede the passage of

    b. to support or strengthen

    c. to indicate broadly; sketch

Choose the Best Definitions *(cont.)*

9. The gardener was *broadcasting* grass seed on the football field.

    a. making known over a wide area

    b. sowing widely, especially by hand

    c. transmitting by air

10. One *feature* of the agreement was hotly debated in the House of Representatives.

    a. prominent article in a newspaper

    b. publicize or make outstanding

    c. distinctive quality or element

11. One requirement of the equestrian class is that you must *groom* your horse.

    a. to make neat and trim

    b. to clean and brush

    c. to coach or tutor

12. The official began to *hedge* when he was pressed for details.

    a. to enclose with hedges

    b. to protect against monetary loss

    c. to purposely make an indefinite statement

13. The two countries approved a *joint* agreement to regulate trade.

    a. formed by united action

    b. a place where two or more things are joined together

    c. a cut of meat for roasting

14. Mahoud stood on the shore and could do nothing as he watched the yacht *keel*.

    a. to fall as from fainting

    b. to capsize

    c. to lean to one side; tilt

15. A *local* custom was to meet at the general store to discuss the weekend's events.

    a. widespread; throughout the country

    b. pertaining to a particular place

    c. making many stops on a route

16. My parents began teaching us *moral* behavior when my brother and I were quite young.

    a. concerning the state of mind of a person

    b. established standards of right and wrong

    c. teaching principles by stories or events

17. The townspeople found the actions of the newcomer *quaint*.

    a. unfamiliar or unusual

    b. delightfully pretty

    c. a trait or characteristic

Words for Specialized Areas

There are many words for specialized areas of study that ended in **-ology**. The suffix -ology means "the science of" or "the study of" something. For example, mineralogy is the study of minerals. Many of these words are used when studying social studies and science.

A. Match the specialized areas with the definitions below.

-ology Words	**Definitions**
1. _____ meteorology	A. study of insects
2. _____ biology	B. study of fruit
3. _____ cytology	C. study of poisons
4. _____ dermatology	D. study of ancestors
5. _____ pomology	E. study of cells
6. _____ genealogy	F. study of life
7. _____ entomology	G. study of weather
8. _____ sociology	H. study of skin
9. _____ toxicology	I. study of society

B. Write the name of the specialist that matches the described field of study. You may use the words listed below to aid you.

1. An _____ studies the eyes.

2. A _____ studies newborn babies.

3. An _____ studies criminal behavior.

4. An _____ studies birds.

5. A _____ studies minerals.

6. An _____ studies the mind.

7. An _____ studies word origins.

8. A _____ studies living tissues.

9. A _____ studies radiation.

mineralogist	etymologist	radiologist	histologist
neonatologist	ornithologist	ophthalmologist	psychologist
criminologist			

Vocabulary Venue

Directions: Using precise vocabulary can clarify your writing. It can be tempting to write the way we and others talk. Rewrite the following paragraphs. Replace the underlined phrases with vivid, precise words.

A. It is very important for <u>everyone</u> to learn how to read. Learning to read can be very difficult. It is <u>like frustrating</u> for some people. Some people don't learn to read because they have learning disabilities. Some people don't think that it <u>is cool</u> to learn to read. Finally, some people are never taught how to read.

_____

_____

_____

_____

_____

_____

B. I am <u>like so excited</u> about going on the trip over spring break. It is like going to be <u>so awesome</u>. My friends all think <u>hanging out</u> at the beach will be cool. We were <u>so looking forward</u> to a week off of school work. The first thing I do when I get to the ocean is jump right in. I don't even care if I have my swim suit on. All I really care about is feeling the breeze on my face and the salt water on my back.

_____

_____

_____

_____

_____

_____

Cause and Effect

Directions: Draw a line to match each cause to its effect. Then create two sentences for each of the first matched pairs. (One sentence should mention the cause first. One sentence should mention the effect first.)

Causes	Effects
• Ruth ate two bags of cotton candy.	• I gave him a round of applause.
• Kevin helped his dad make a cake.	• She got a very bad stomachache.
• Trudy practiced running every morning.	• His dad was proud.
• Zechariah sang a song with his dog.	• She won second place in the marathon race.

1. (Cause mentioned first)

   _____

   _____

   (Effect mentioned first)

   _____

   _____

2. (Cause mentioned first)

   _____

   _____

   (Effect mentioned first)

   _____

   _____

Cause and Effect *(cont.)*

Directions: Now create two sentences for each of the two remaining matched pairs on page 46. (One sentence should mention the cause first. One sentence should mention the effect first.)

3. (Cause mentioned first)

_____

_____

(Effect mentioned first)

_____

_____

4. (Cause mentioned first)

_____

_____

(Effect mentioned first)

_____

_____

Extra Credit: Compose four original sentences of cause and effect. After writing each one, rewrite it, reversing the order of cause and effect as you did for the previous four sentences.

_____

_____

_____

_____

_____

_____

Cause and Effect: Wayne the Victor

I used to miss school a lot. I'd be gone from school one or two days a week, and I really didn't have any excuses. Some days I was just tired or I didn't feel like going to school, so I didn't. Other times, I was mad at my teacher, or I felt like a failure and so I stayed home. When I was missing lots of school I didn't like school. It was hard to get to know people, and my teachers were frustrated with me. I was confused all the time and felt like I didn't belong. I felt like I'd never learn what people wanted me to learn.

Then I realized that I didn't like school because I was gone so much—I didn't give myself a chance to like school. I wasn't giving myself a chance to get to know people or figure out what was going on in my classes. I felt sad and mad inside. I realized I was giving up on myself and failing myself. I decided I was no longer going to give up on myself.

I chose to work on my school attendance first. I decided that no matter what, I was going to go to school every day. I told my brother about my new decision and he said he didn't care. I told my mom about my new decision and she said, "Okay, that's nice, Wayne," but I don't think she really cared either. I started feeling bad inside again because they didn't act proud or anything. So I told myself about my new decision, and then I told myself, "I am proud of you, Wayne! You can do it!" It may sound silly but it did make me feel better! I told myself that no matter how I felt or what my family or teachers thought, I had to make myself go to school every day.

I wrote myself this reminder with big letters on a piece of notebook paper: **Go to school, Wayne! Don't give up on yourself! I am proud of you!** Then I taped it to the wall beside my bed so I'd see it every night and every morning. I made another sign just like it and taped it on the wall in the corner, close to the floor. I decided I would put my book bag in that corner every day when I came home from school and then it'd be easy to find each morning so I could take it to school with me. I had decided that I was going to quit giving up on myself and I was doing things to help myself be a victor.

Cause and Effect: Wayne the Victor *(cont.)*

Directions: Read "Wayne the Victor" carefully. Complete the chart below. The left side of the chart is for "causes." The right side of the chart is for "effects." Make sure that your answers make sense.

Cause	Effect
1. Some days Wayne was tired or just did not feel like going to school.	1. _____ _____ _____
2. _____ _____ _____	2. Wayne did not like school and it was hard to get to know people.
3. Wayne decided he was no longer going to give up on himself.	3. _____ _____ _____
4. _____ _____ _____	4. Wayne started feeling bad inside again.
5. Wayne told himself, "I am proud of you!"	5. _____ _____ _____.

Games with a History

Checkers is one of the most popular board games in the world. The oldest form of the game of checkers began in Egypt in 1400 B.C. and was called alquerque. Checkers is related to another ancient game called draughts. International draughts has a 100-square board. English draughts, also known as checkers in the United States, uses a 64-square board. In 1756, William Payne, an English mathematician, wrote the first book in English about checkers. It is not known when checkers was brought to the United States.

Monopoly® began as a game called The Landlord Game. The Landlord Game was invented in 1903 by a young Quaker woman named Elizabeth Magie. She wanted to teach people about the evils of landlords, who have an unfair advantage over renters. Charles Darrow redesigned The Landlord Game and sold it to Parker Brothers, a popular game manufacturer. According to Parker Brothers, Darrow was the world's first game designer to become a millionaire.

Monopoly® is the best-selling game in the world. Over 200 million copies in 80 countries and in 26 languages have been sold. A Braille edition of Monopoly® was produced in the 1970s. In 1978, a chocolate version of the board game sold for $600. The favorite game piece is the racecar, and the newest game piece is a money sack.

Scrabble® is a very popular game in the United States and Canada. Scrabble® appears in one out of three homes in America. It was invented during the Great Depression by Alfred Butts. He called it Crisscross Words.

Although the first attempts to sell Crisscross Words failed, Butts and his partner did not give up. They eventually trademarked the name Scrabble® in 1948 and produced the game themselves. By the 1950s, it had become so popular that it had to be rationed in the stores because the small factory could not keep up with customer orders. In 1972, the Selchow and Righter Company, a game distributor, bought the trademark rights to Scrabble®. The rest, as they say, is history!

Games with a History *(cont.)*

Directions: After reading the story, answer the questions. Circle the letter before each correct answer.

1. **According to the article, what is the best-selling game in the world?**
   a. draughts
   b. Monopoly®
   c. checkers
   d. Scrabble®

2. **The answer to which of these questions would help you understand the history of games?**
   a. How were games invented?
   b. Why is Monopoly® so popular?
   c. Where was Scrabble® invented?
   d. How many people play checkers?

3. **This passage is arranged by. . .**
   a. newest game to the oldest game.
   b. the history of different games.
   c. the manufacturers of each game.
   d. alphabetical order by inventor.

4. **For this sentence, choose the word that means that Monopoly is a well-liked game.**
   Monopoly® is a very _____ game for Parker Brothers, who have sold over 200 million copies of it in 80 countries and 26 languages.
   a. recent
   b. complicated
   c. successful
   d. expensive

5. **Which of these best combines the two sentences into one?**
   Jacks and dominoes were once popular games.
   Electronic games are more popular today.
   a. Jacks and dominoes were popular, and electronic games are more popular.
   b. Once, jacks and dominoes were games, but today they are electronic games.
   c. Jacks and dominoes were once popular; then electronic games.
   d. Jacks and dominoes were once popular games, but electronic games are more popular today.

6. **When Pong® was introduced by Atari in 1977, the machine was big, the animation was slow, and the game was simple. Today, video games are hand held, the action is fast, and the games are complicated. From this information, you can infer that . . .**
   a. some video games seem smarter than humans.
   b. I do not like video games, because I prefer the outdoors.
   c. video games have improved greatly in the last 30 years.
   d. the invention of video games was a good thing.

The History of Pockets

When people put their hands in their pockets, they rarely realize they are using an invention that is only a few hundred years old. For several thousand years, human clothing did not have pockets of any kind. People cut a circle out of cloth or leather and put their money, keys, or other objects in the middle of the circle. Then they gathered up the edges and bunched the circle into a loose bag or purse. They tied a string, usually of leather, around the neck of this purse to keep objects from falling out.

These purses were usually tied onto belts. They dangled by their strings. Thieves would try to cut these strings to steal the purses. Near the end of the 1500s, men began to ask for slits in their trousers exactly where we have side pockets in pants today. A man still tied the strings of his purse to his belt, but then he pushed the purse through the side slit in his trousers. This made it more difficult for a thief to steal the purse.

These purses were also known as pockets even though they were not yet attached to trousers. We don't know who figured out how to sew this pocket into the side seam and make it a permanent part of the trousers. The invention made it easier and quicker to get something from the pocket. No longer did a man have to untie a purse from his belt and then undo the string around it.

Shortly after the pocket became a permanent part of trousers, people began to want pockets in other garments as well. Both women and men asked for them in cloaks and coats. At first, these pockets were attached near the lower hems of long capes and cloaks. A person had to pull up the garment and keep holding it up while reaching into the pocket. This took two hands. Eventually, people asked for pockets at the hip so that it would only take one hand to use the pocket.

Travelers in the days of the first sewn-in pockets had to journey from town to town in horse-drawn carriages. They began to ask for secret pockets so they could hide small valuables from the robbers who often held up coaches. The robbers could not always find a secret pocket sewn inside a piece of clothing. Today, business jackets for both men and women still have these inner pockets to protect valuables.

Modern travelers sometimes still use purses like those of long ago. Today tourists can buy small, flat bags for their passports and money. These are worn around the neck or waist and are kept out of sight, beneath the clothes. Then, even if thieves steal briefcases or women's handbags, tourists will still have the most important papers and emergency money that they kept tucked out of sight.

Three purposes have shaped the history of pockets. The first is safety. To prevent theft, pockets have evolved inside business jackets as secret places for valuables. Pockets also developed because people wanted to reach money, keys, pens, tissues, and other items quickly and easily. The third purpose of pockets was the last one to develop. Only in the last 150 years have people figured out that pockets offer a good way to keep hands warm in cold weather!

The History of Pockets *(cont.)*

Directions: After reading the story, answer the questions. Circle the letter before each correct answer.

1. **What is this passage mostly about?**
   a. how travelers protected valuable papers
   b. how pockets developed over time
   c. how tailors hide pockets in clothing
   d. how people used to carry purses

2. **Which of these statements shows that people use purses today in a way similar to how they were used in the past?**
   a. They are worn around the neck and are sometimes kept out of sight, beneath the clothes.
   b. The robbers could not always find a secret pocket sewn inside a piece of clothing.
   c. Both women and men asked for them in cloaks and coats.
   d. The third purpose of pockets was the last one to develop.

3. **The original pockets were probably sewn near the lower hem of capes and cloaks because . . .**
   a. robbers wouldn't think to look there.
   b. this was where valuables would fit.
   c. hems provide extra fabric needed to make a pocket.
   d. this was a convenient place for people to access.

4. **Why did people start sewing pockets permanently into trousers?**
   a. Permanent pockets allowed people to warm their hands.
   b. The leather used to make purses was hard to find.
   c. This made it easier to get to the pocket without having to unfasten the purse.
   d. It was less expensive to sew the pocket into trousers than to make purses.

5. **Why did people begin putting their small purses in side slits in their trousers?**
   a. This made it harder for the purses to be stolen.
   b. The purses were less likely to be lost.
   c. They didn't like the weight of the purses hanging from their belts.
   d. The purses didn't get in their way.

6. **Pockets kept people's belongings safe. What is another reason people liked pockets?**
   a. They were fashionable.
   b. They could hold more than purses.
   c. They were easy to make.
   d. They were easier to use.

Satellites

After World War II ended, people found new ways to use the things developed for the war. Radar had been invented to track enemy planes. Police started using radar to watch for speeding cars. The people who report our weather used radar to track storms. For years, radar was the only thing that watched the skies.

Then President Kennedy decided that an American should land on the moon. He provided funds to NASA (National Aeronautics and Space Administration) to run the space program. In addition to space flights, NASA has put many satellites into orbit. Satellites stay at a specific height and move at a specific speed as they circle our planet. The Earth's gravity holds them in orbit. We rely on these satellites every day.

Six kinds of satellites orbit our planet. Earth observation satellites keep track of the conditions of oceans, icebergs, volcanoes, and deserts. They also track forest fires and animal herds. Spy satellites watch military movements. Weather satellites record cloud movements and wind speeds. Global Positioning System (GPS) satellites let cars, planes, and ships know their **precise** position on the Earth. Astronomy satellites keep track of the sun, stars, and comets.

Communications satellites get signals from computers, telephones, and TV cameras. Then they send these signals to another computer, phone, or TV. They handle e-mails and long-distance phone calls. They let you watch what's happening in another part of the world while it's happening.

Out in space the sun always shines because there is no night or clouds. So satellites use solar cell power. The solar cells collect the sun's rays and change them into electricity. Solar cells work for many years, and astronauts on the space shuttle can go up and fix them if there is a problem.

Satellites *(cont.)*

Comprehension Questions

Directions: After reading the passage answer the questions. Circle the letter before each correct answer.

1. **Which is not a kind of satellite?**

   a. solar

   b. weather

   c. communications

   d. spy

2. **On a historical timeline, what happened third?**

   a. President Kennedy provided funds to NASA.

   b. Satellites were put into orbit.

   c. Radar was used to forecast the weather.

   d. Astronauts learned how to repair satellites.

3. **Which is an example of a naturally occurring satellite?**

   a. Halley's comet

   b. the sun

   c. one of Jupiter's moons

   d. an asteroid

4. *Precise* **means . . .**

   a. approximate.

   b. general.

   c. exact.

   d. closest.

5. **A satellite's solar cells receive energy . . .**

   a. from alkaline batteries.

   b. only during daylight hours.

   c. a different number of hours each season.

   d. 24 hours every day.

6. **Picture a satellite. What is it made of?**

   a. canvas

   b. aluminum

   c. marble

   d. wood

7. **Would you like to be one of the astronauts who fixes satellites out in space? Explain.**

   _____

   _____

   _____

Mission to Mars

On July 4, 1997, space exploration took a huge step. On that day, a spacecraft called *Pathfinder* landed on Mars. The National Aeronautics and Space Administration (NASA) sent *Pathfinder* to discover new information about the Red Planet.

The mission was a complete success. After landing, *Pathfinder* sent a small rover, *Sojourner*, onto the planet's surface. *Sojourner* explored more than 250 square meters of Mars. Together, *Pathfinder* and *Sojourner* took more than 16,000 photos of the rocky landscape. Engineers designed *Sojourner* to last for only seven days, but the little vehicle ran twelve times longer! *Pathfinder* surprised scientists, too. It sent back information for almost three months. That was three times longer than it was built to last.

Because *Pathfinder* and *Sojourner* ran for so long, scientists got more information than they ever dreamed of getting. For one thing, they discovered that Mars is very sandy. Pictures of sand dunes around the landing site hint that Mars once had water. Scientists know that water means life. Was there ever life on Mars? We don't know yet.

In addition, the *Pathfinder* mission told scientists that Mars is dusty. Huge "dust devils" on Mars spit enormous amounts of dust into the Martian air. *Pathfinder* also recorded frosty Martian temperatures at 200 degrees below zero Fahrenheit. At that temperature, a glass of water would freeze solid in just a few seconds.

In October, scientists lost *Pathfinder's* signal because the spacecraft's battery had run down. They tried to revive the signal but had no luck. The mission officially ended on November 4.

Scientists hope to use the knowledge from these missions to better understand how life on Earth began. They'll also use it to plan future Mars missions.

56

Mission to Mars *(cont.)*

Directions: After reading the passage, answer the questions. Circle the letter before each correct answer.

1. **What did NASA do to get information about Mars?**

   a. NASA sent the spacecraft *Sojourner* to Mars.

   b. NASA sent engineers on a three-month space mission.

   c. NASA sent the spacecraft *Pathfinder* to Mars.

   d. NASA sent astronauts to run tests for seven days.

2. **According to the passage, how much longer did the *Sojourner* last than expected?**

   a. Seven days

   b. Twelve times longer

   c. 250 days

   d. Three times longer

3. **What was the main reason NASA considered the *Pathfinder* mission a success?**

   a. Scientists found out that Mars is very cold and dusty.

   b. Scientists got more information than they ever dreamed of getting.

   c. Scientists learned that Mars definitely had water at one time.

   d. Scientists found out that there was once life on Mars.

4. **This article gives you reason to believe that NASA. . .**

   a. thinks missions to Mars cost more than they are worth.

   b. will not send other missions to Mars.

   c. will be sending future missions to Mars.

   d. has all the information it needs about Mars.

5. **You can tell from this passage that . . .**

   a. dust devils on Mars made the photographs hard to see.

   b. Martian temperatures caused *Pathfinder's* battery to fail.

   c. scientists suspect that life on Earth began on Mars.

   d. scientists will look for signs that life existed on Mars.

6. **Based on information in this passage, the reader can conclude that . . .**

   a. *Sojourner* took more photographs than *Pathfinder* did.

   b. scientists will plan a mission to replace the spacecraft's battery.

   c. conditions on Mars are harsher than conditions on Earth.

   d. engineers designed *Sojourner* to last as long as *Pathfinder*.

Danger Is Their Business

Most animals try to play it safe. They know that there is always another animal that would like to have them for dinner—and not as a guest! So animals find ways to stay one step ahead of their enemies. Some animals, like deer, try to outrun danger. Bigger animals, like moose, rely on their great size and strength for protection. Animals like the grouse, a small woodland bird, have special coloring that makes them difficult to see. There is still one more way that animals can protect themselves. Just like in the old saying "fight fire with fire," some animals find protection by walking right into the jaws of danger.

For example, a little bird called a plover makes a living cleaning the mouths of crocodiles. Small, swimming animals called leeches, which look like snakes with suction cups for heads, swim into crocodiles' mouths and attack their gums. Even though crocodiles are very strong creatures, they are helpless against the leeches. So, the crocodiles let the plovers help them. A crocodile that wants to get the leeches out of its mouth climbs onto dry land and opens its jaws wide. A little plover fearlessly hops into the reptile's mouth and eats the leeches. The crocodile needs the leeches removed, so it doesn't attack the little bird, and the plover gets an easy meal.

Other animals find similar ways to use danger to their advantage. An ocean fish called the clown fish lives inside the poisonous branches of a creature called the sea anemone. The sea anemone looks like a small bush, but its branches are really poisonous tentacles. The anemone uses the tentacles as defense and to trap food. The clown fish is immune to the sea anemone's poison, so it makes its home inside the sea anemone's tentacles. This way, the brightly-colored clown fish doesn't have to hide. No matter how hungry the other fish get, they can't touch the clown fish without getting stung by the sea anemone.

Some insects also survive by living in a dangerous place. One species of mosquito actually lives inside a predator's stomach! The pitcher plant is a meat-eating plant. It uses sweet smells to attract insects. The insects land on the plant and slip down its sides into a long tube. The tube leads to a bowl (the pitcher plant's "stomach") full of liquid that kills and digests the insects. Some types of baby mosquitoes, or larvae, are able to swim freely in this liquid without harm. By living in such a dangerous place, these young mosquitoes stay safe from other hungry insects that might otherwise eat them.

These animals all use danger to their advantage. It just goes to show that jumping out of the frying pan and into the fire is sometimes the best way to survive!

Danger Is Their Business *(cont.)*

Directions: After reading the passage, answer the questions. Circle the letter before each correct answer.

1. **The passage is mostly about . . .**
   a. how animals help each other.
   b. using fire to defend yourself against dangerous animals.
   c. why leeches are dangerous.
   d. how some animals survive in dangerous environments.

2. **Insects are probably attracted to the pitcher plant because . . .**
   a. its leaves rustle and sound like other insects.
   b. they know there are mosquitoes inside.
   c. the color of the plant appeals to them.
   d. they are looking for fragrant nectar.

3. **Why can the plover live safely around crocodiles?**
   a. The plover is poisonous to the crocodile.
   b. The crocodile needs the plover to get the leeches out of its mouth.
   c. The crocodile depends on the plover to scare off predators.
   d. The plover hides inside the crocodile's mouth.

4. **The author links "jumping out of the frying pan and into the fire" to. . .**
   a. hitting predators with frying pans.
   b. jumping out of the way of predators.
   c. using danger to avoid dangerous situations.
   d. scaring animals off with fire.

5. **In what way is the crocodile helpless?**
   a. It cannot protect itself from leeches.
   b. It likes to eat small birds.
   c. It cannot resist the taste of leeches.
   d. It is not very strong.

6. **Read the following sentence:**
   The clown fish is immune to the sea anemone's poison.
   What does *immune* to mean?
   a. attracted to
   b. afraid of
   c. unaffected by
   d. unaware of

Diving In

Josh stepped to the edge of the platform. As he looked down, he thought the water seemed as though it was a thousand feet below. This was the third time he had come up here, and for the third time he turned around and walked back to the ladder, afraid to make the dive from the high platform. As he turned, Josh could feel the stares from his classmates, friends, and teachers on the back of his head. He knew what they would say when he got down. They would say he'd better make the dive the next time.

Josh wasn't sure there would even be a next time. He was just too scared to dive from that high platform. It wasn't like it was really that important. This was just an intramural diving team that had been put together by the swimming coach at the junior high school. Josh had made good dives at lower levels, he thought. Mr. Barry, the coach, had even said that if he didn't want to dive from that height, he didn't have to.

He wanted to do it, though. He had wanted to feel like a part of the team ever since that first afternoon when he had seen the other swimmers at practice. He enjoyed the water himself, and he was a good swimmer. When the diving team was started, he leaped at the opportunity to join. When tryouts were posted, his name was the first on the list.

Standing on the ground, Josh stared up at that high-dive platform that now seemed to be so far above him. He looked around the pool at the other swimmers, who were either waiting at the ladder to try their own dives or talking to Mr. Barry about the one they had just completed. Josh was sure that none of them had a problem looking down at the distant water from high on that platform. He figured that since he had never seen anyone else hesitate, only he was afraid.

Suddenly, Mr. Barry began walking toward him. "How are you doing, Josh?" he asked.

"I'm all right, Mr. Barry. I just got a little scared up there, that's all," Josh said.

"Don't worry about it, Josh. You know, when I was young, I got scared up there too," Mr. Barry said.

"So how did you ever get up the nerve to dive from up there, Mr. Barry?" Josh asked.

"I decided that I had to stop thinking about it. And I figured if I could get myself off the board just once, I would be a lot closer to success. So one day I just climbed up the ladder, ran to the end, closed my eyes, and jumped off the board."

Josh suddenly remembered exactly what it was like to be up there, when it seemed like a thousand feet above the water. Then, almost immediately, he thought about the feeling he would get in his stomach when he actually stepped from the platform, and how the water might look, rushing toward him so fast. He thought about how it might feel like he was flying and the way the air would turn silent as he fell.

Josh took a deep breath, turned around, and started walking back to the ladder that led to the high dive platform. He knew it was something he would have to do. Even if it wasn't today, he would do it someday.

Diving In *(cont.)*

Directions: After reading the story, answer the questions. Circle the letter before each correct answer.

1. The author says that Josh was the first name on the tryout list to show that . . .
   a. he was very eager to be on the team.
   b. there were few people on the team.
   c. he was scared to dive.
   d. he was in junior high.

2. Which of these statements is true about the diving team according to the story?
   a. Diving from the high dive was required.
   b. The coach was an Olympic champion.
   c. The team practiced every afternoon.
   d. It was a junior high intramural team.

3. What did Josh do before he walked back to the high dive for his next attempt?
   a. He signed up for tryouts for the diving team.
   b. He watched a teammate dive.
   c. He practiced on a lower diving board.
   d. He spoke with his coach about his fear.

Here is a story about diving. Some words are missing. For Numbers 4 through 6, choose the word that best fills each blank in the paragraph.

Diving is an (4) activity. The sport is a (5) of gymnastic and swimming skills. In the seventeenth century, gymnasts would move their equipment to the beach. The gymnasts would perform their exercises over the water. This (6) activity became the diving that we enjoy today.

4.
   a. enthusiastic
   b. exciting
   c. effective
   d. annoying

5.
   a. definition
   b. combination
   c. congestion
   d. solution

6.
   a. common
   b. reserved
   c. severe
   d. unusual

Letter Club

One day, Tasha got some mail from her friend who recently moved to the other side of the country. Tasha loves getting mail and was very excited. When she opened the envelope, she found a short letter and a list of ten names with addresses. It was an invitation to join a letter-sending club.

Dear Friend:

Welcome to the Letter Club! Copies of this letter have been going around the world for many years now. This letter helps inquisitive people find out about other places. By following the steps below, one young girl got letters from all seven continents—even from Antarctica! Be sure to ask your parents for permission before you join the Letter Club. Then send out your letters today! You, too, can learn about places that interest you and that you want to know more about.

What to do:

1. Look at the list of ten names.

2. Send a postcard or letter to the person whose name is at the top of the list.

3. Remove the name of the person you sent a postcard to from the list.

4. Recopy the remaining nine names and addresses and add your own to the bottom.

5. Send a copy of this letter and the new list to ten people you know, but not to anyone on the list.

6. Start checking your mail for exciting postcards and letters!

How it works:

1. The ten people you send this letter and your list to will send a postcard or letter to the person whose name is first on the list.

2. Then, they will remove that name from the list, add their name to the bottom, and send copies of this letter and their new list to ten people they know.

3. After a while, your name will work its way to the top of the list. When this happens, you will start getting letters from all over world! It usually takes a couple of months before you begin receiving letters.

Because your name will soon appear on so many people's lists, you might receive hundreds of postcards or letters from many different and exciting locations!

Some hints for getting exciting letters:

If you want to get letters from interesting places, try sending this letter and your list to people you know who live far away from you. For example, maybe your grandparents live in another state, or you have a friend who moved out of town. If you try to send this letter and your list as far away as possible, you will be sure to get letters from faraway places, too!

Letter Club *(cont.)*

Directions: After reading the story, answer the questions. Circle the letter before each correct answer.

1. **In order to get letters from all over the world, the passage suggests that Tasha . . .**

    a. write to a young girl who got letters from all seven continents.

    b. send out letters only to people in her hometown.

    c. send letters to ten of her friends.

    d. write a letter back to her friend.

2. **In order to participate in the Letter Club, Tasha should . . .**

    a. find the names of ten people she doesn't know to send letters to.

    b. decide what countries she wants to get mail from.

    c. send a postcard to all the people listed in the letter from her friend.

    d. ask her parents for permission to join the club.

3. **When this letter talks about inquisitive people, it means people who are . . .**

    a. unusual.

    b. curious.

    c. boring.

    d. careful.

4. **According to the letter, copies of the letter . . .**

    a. first came from a girl in Antarctica.

    b. have been going around the world for a long time.

    c. need to go to all seven continents.

    d. should be signed by your parents.

5. **In what way does the welcome letter to the Letter Club try to interest the reader in joining?**

    a. By telling the reader about other countries

    b. By suggesting the reader might get lots of mail

    c. By indicating that the Letter Club is a new idea

    d. By telling the reader letters will start arriving in a few days

6. **As a result of receiving the letter, Tasha will probably . . .**

    a. travel to ten faraway places.

    b. follow the instructions in the letter.

    c. put her name at the top of the list.

    d. return the letter and list to her friend.

School Reporter

Damaras was in the school cafeteria eating lunch when she spied her friend Anna. "Hey, Anna. Guess what? My article is going to be in the next issue of the school newspaper!"
Anna gave her a big smile. "That's so wonderful. I can't wait to read it."
Damaras was a new reporter on the school paper. For her first assignment she had covered the upcoming school play. Damaras had interviewed both the lead actress and the lead actor. She had researched the history of the play, which had been written by a man from London. She had spoken with the director, Mr. Clausen, who was also a social studies teacher, and she had sat in on rehearsals to see what it was like to be in the play.

Another student, Troy, who was sitting at the same cafeteria table, overheard them. He asked, "You wrote a story for the paper?"
Damaras nodded. "It will be printed this Thursday. I think it's going to be the lead story!"
Later that day, as Damaras was waiting for her English class to start, another student, Jeff, turned around in his chair and called over, "Hey, Damaras. I heard you wrote the lead story for the next school paper."
Damaras said, "Yes, I did, but how did you know?"

"Troy told me," Jeff replied.
Their teacher, Mr. Kim, overheard them. He looked at Damaras. "You wrote a lead story? That's wonderful, Damaras."
Then the whole class started talking about it. Some students raised their hands and asked how they could be a part of the school newspaper.

Jeff quizzed Damaras, "Are you going to be a reporter when you grow up? Is that your plan?"
Damaras blushed. She was not used to getting so much attention.
On Thursday, when the paper came out, Damaras ran to find a copy of it as soon as she got to school. She went to the classroom that served as the newspaper office. She picked up a copy and looked at the first page. It was not her article at all! Damaras was disappointed that her story was not on the first page. Then she skimmed the rest of the paper and realized her article was not even in the paper at all! "Oh no!" Damaras cried in dismay. "Now everybody will think I wasn't telling the truth!"

She put the newspaper in her book bag and walked to her locker. As she walked, she kept wondering why her article was not in the paper. The newspaper was put together by students with the supervision of an English teacher, Mr. Kline. Damaras started thinking that maybe one of the editors had not liked her story. Maybe Mr. Kline had not thought that her story was well written. Damaras saw her friend Anna down the hall and quickly reversed directions. She did not know what to tell Anna or anybody else if they asked why her story was not in the paper. She dreaded her English class because everyone there thought she was going to be published.

There were still ten minutes before school started, so Damaras sought out Mr. Kline in his classroom. He greeted Damaras warmly. "Ah, one of our fine reporters!" Damaras could not smile back. She was thinking she should offer to quit the school paper, because they did not like her work. Finally, she asked, "Why didn't my story make the paper? I worked really hard to research and write it."
Mr. Kline looked surprised. "Of course it made the paper," he said. "We all loved it. We're running it as the lead story of next week's paper."
Damaras looked confused. "Next week's paper? I thought I submitted it for this week's issue."
Mr. Kline then reminded Damaras that production time for the paper made it necessary to submit articles at least one week before the issue in which they were scheduled to appear. Damaras had been so excited to see her story in the paper, she had confused the publishing schedule!
"Oh no!" Damaras laughed, relieved to hear they liked her work. "Now how will I explain that to everybody?"

School Reporter *(cont.)*

Directions: After reading the story, answer the questions. Circle the letter before each correct answer.

1. **What does the phrase "She sat in on rehearsals" mean?**
   a. Damaras sat on the stage during the rehearsals.
   b. Damaras watched the rehearsals for the play.
   c. Damaras wrote about the play rehearsals.
   d. Damaras tried out for the play during rehearsals.

2. **Why did Damaras think that her article would be running in this week's issue of the newspaper?**
   a. She knew that she was the best writer in the school.
   b. The school play was going to be over by next week's issue.
   c. New reporters always wrote an article during their first week.
   d. She submitted the article before this week's issue was published.

3. **Which of these explains what Mr. Kline probably meant when he said upon seeing Damaras, "Ah, one of our fine reporters!"?**
   a. He was complimenting Damaras for writing a good article for the paper.
   b. He was being sarcastic because Damaras had missed the deadline.
   c. He was trying to make Damaras feel good since her article was not in the paper.
   d. He was talking to somebody else who was in the room at the same time.

4. **According to your answer for Number 3, how might Mr. Kline describe Damaras?**
   a. eager
   b. disorganized
   c. conceited
   d. careful

5. **Part of the humor in this story is the fact that the news of Damaras's newspaper article spreads quickly around the school. Choose the action which best demonstrates this event.**
   a. The whole English class talked about being part of the school newspaper.
   b. Damaras interviewed Mr. Clausen, the director of the school play, for her article.
   c. Jeff asked Damaras if she is going to be a newspaper reporter when she grows up.
   d. Jeff heard about Damaras's article from Troy, who overheard Damaras and Anna talking.

6. **Which of these sounds most like something that Damaras would do?**
   a. Damaras takes credit for the school cafeteria article.
   b. Damaras argues with Mr. Kline for not publishing her article.
   c. Damaras does not confuse the deadlines for the newspaper again.
   d. Damaras writes a story without doing research.

Poetry: This is Me!

Phrase poetry can describe an item or person without using complete sentences! Write a phrase poem using the example poem as a guide. End your phrase poem with a word that describes the subject of the poem.

Morgan
Rides a bike
loves spaghetti
chats on the phone
kicks the soccer ball
loves babies
Alive!

Subject:

Phrase 1 _____

Phrase 2 _____

Phrase 3 _____

Phrase 4 _____

Phrase 5 _____

One Word:

I Am What I Am

Fill in the blanks below and you will have a poem about the person you know best—you!

I am _____

And _____

But I am not _____

Or _____

I like _____

And _____

But I don't like _____

Or _____

I feel _____

But I don't feel _____

Poetry Patterns

Alphabet

by Jima Dunigan   by _____

Carefree   _____

Dolphins   _____

Even   _____

Flip   _____

Gracefully   _____

Acrostic

by Jima Dunigan   by _____

Fierce   **C** _____

Righteous   **O** _____

Energetic   **O** _____

Dude   **L** _____

Concrete (special shape or design)
by Jima Dunigan   by _____

Dizzy LEAVES FALL

to the ground.

Quatrain (four-line stanza with rhyming lines)

Ghost Town 1
by Jima Dunigan

Not far west of Wyoming there lies

A little town that men despise.

The streets that once glittered with gold

Now are barren, dusty and cold.

by _____

_____

_____

_____

_____

Definition (not necessary to rhyme, any length)

Friendship	**Homework**	**Caterpillar**	by
by Jima Dunigan	by Jima Dunigan	by Jima Dunigan	
fun	hard	crawly	_____
laughing	tedious	creepy	_____
work	boring	leggy	_____
entertaining	learning	long	_____
company	mastering	fuzzy	_____
forever	confidence	frightening	_____

Poetry Patterns *(cont.)*

Cinquain (five lines)

	Blankets	**Soup**
One-word title	by Jima Dunigan	by _____
Two describing words	Snuggly, soft	_____
Three action words	Heating, comforting, cuddling	_____
Four feeling words	Warming body and soul	_____
One synonym for the title	Comforter	_____

Limerick (five lines)

	Boy from Rome	**Girl from Spain**
	by Jima Dunigan	by _____
Lines 1, 2, 5 rhyme	There once was a boy from Rome	_____
Lines 3, 4 rhyme	Who could not find a home.	_____
	He searched and he tried	_____
	'Til he found a bride.	_____
	They made a home of their own.	_____

Haiku (three lines giving a general impression)

	Footprints	_____
	by Jima Dunigan	by _____
Line 1—five syllables	See the red berries	_____
Line 2—seven syllables	fallen like little footprints	_____
Line 3—five syllables	on the garden snow.	_____ .

5 Ws

	My Dog	**Please Write**	**My Friend**
	by Jima Dunigan	by Jima Dunigan	by _____
Who:	My dog	Teacher	My friend
What:	curls up	says write	_____
When:	every night	each day	_____
Where:	on my bed	in school	_____
Why:	because I let him.	to master the art.	_____

Autobiographical Writing

Write a personal history of your life so far. Use the framework below to help you orginize your information.

My Memories

Hi! My name is _____

I was born in _____

A funny story about me is _____

_____

_____

When I was a baby, I used to play with _____

_____

_____

This year, I want to learn how to _____

_____

_____

Some of my friends are_____

_____

_____

My favorite foods are _____

_____

_____

My pets are _____

_____

_____

Some of my talents include _____

_____

_____

Something that I like about me is _____

_____

_____

Autobiography/Biography Planner

Auto = self   *Bio* = life   *Graph* = write or draw

Choose a person for whom you wish to write a biography. He or she can be a famous person with materials and research available, or someone you know. It may be you. If you choose to write about yourself, it is an autobiography. Use the chronologically sequenced boxes below to create an autobiography.

1. Birth

Name _____
Boy _____ Girl _____
Date of birth _____
Length at birth_____
Weight at birth _____
Place of birth_____
Mother_____
Father _____
Sister _____
Brother _____

2. Firsts

First Word _____
First Birthday _____
_____
_____
_____

3. Relatives

_____
_____
_____
_____
_____

4. Preschool Experiences

_____
_____
_____
_____
_____
_____
_____

5. Kindergarten

_____
_____
_____
_____
_____
_____

6. First Grade Experiences

_____
_____
_____
_____
_____

(For more, continue on the back of this page.)

Example of a Business Letter

Directions: Read the sample business letter below. Use this example to help you write your own letter on the next page.

3122 East Broadway Street
Edington, MD 21014
January 11, 2000

Ms. Alice Christfield, Editor
The Town Crier
2119 South Main Street
Edington, MD 21014

Dear Ms. Christfield:

I am a student at the Winstone Academy School, and I am concerned about a particular issue in our community. Every time I go to Rockfield Park, the community playground, there is trash all over the grass surrounding the play area. Whenever I go to the park, there are fast-food wrappers, empty soda cans, napkins, and plastic cups scattered on the ground. I would like to appeal to the citizens of our town and ask them to clean up when they leave the park.

There are many reasons to clean our community playground. First, if we don't clean up, we could attract wild animals like foxes and opossums to the playground. This could make the play area unsafe for small children. Second, if we don't clean up, the police or other town officials may come to clean up. This may mean they will need to add personnel to their staff and eventually our taxes will go up. Finally, if we don't clean up, our town will get a reputation as a messy town. When visitors come, they will think that we don't take pride in our community. I don't think we want to send that message.

My request is simple. If you use the community park, clean up your trash. There are trashcans next to the picnic area and next to the play area. If you get to the park and there is trash on the ground, take a few moments with your family to clean it up. We all need to work together on this, so that after awhile the park is always clean and no one will accept trash on the ground.

Ms. Christfield, thank you in advance for printing my message in *The Town Crier*.

Sincerely,

Anna Wintergate

Anna Wintergate

Business Letter Frame

Directions: Use this writing frame to write the rough draft of your business letter. Be certain to include the heading, inside address, greeting, body, closing, and signature.

_____

_____

_____

_____

_____

_____

Dear _____:

_____

_____

_____

_____

_____

_____

_____

_____

_____

_____

_____

Sincerely,

_____

_____

Narrative Paragraph

One kind of paragraph is called *narrative*. A narrative paragraph gives the details of an experience or event in story form. It explains what happens in a natural time order. You have probably written a narrative paragraph before, but you just didn't know what to call it. You have definitely spoken a narrative paragraph. On the first day of school, you probably went home and told someone all about it in chronological order. In each of the paragraphs below, choose one of the main ideas in parentheses or use one of your own. Use another piece of paper if you need more room.

The first time I ever (*rode a bike*, *cooked*, *baby-sat*) was a total disaster.

First, _____

_____

Next, _____

_____

Then, _____

_____

Finally, _____

_____

I had never been (*more embarrassed*, *more angry*, *more excited*) in my life!

_____

_____

_____

On (*my first day at school*, *my last birthday*, *my last vacation*), I

_____

_____

_____

_____

Narrative Writing Questionnaire

Plan a narrative about a personal experience. Answer these questions to help you write a personal narrative.

Event: _____

Where did the event take place?

_____

Who was with you?

_____

What happened? Describe it in detail.

_____

_____

_____

_____

What happened that was exciting, scary, funny, or interesting?

_____

_____

_____

How did the experience end?

_____

_____

How did you feel at the end?

_____

_____

_____

Story Map

Use this story map to help you plan a narrative story. Follow the arrows to the next step.

Setting (where and when the story takes place)

Characters (people/animals in the story)

Conflict/Problem (What is wrong in the story?)

Action/Events (What happens?)

Resolution (How does the story end?)

Expository Paragraph Model

> Automobiles are expensive to own. After buying a car you have to
> have money for insurance that the law says you must have in case of an
> accident. Cars, even new ones, need occasional costly repairs. Even if
> you drive carefully, you will sometimes make mistakes and might get a
> ticket, which you must pay for or your license will be taken away. Even
> if you never get in an accident or get a ticket, you have to fill the car
> with gas, and prices are at an all-time high.

- Why is the topic sentence a good one? _____

- Do the supporting sentences explain the controlling idea?_____

- Are all the sentences related? _____

- Underline your choice of the following for a concluding sentence to this paragraph.

    1. Owning a car will cost the owner plenty of money.

    2. Also, you could get in trouble driving without a license.

    3. Commercials on television tell you that you must have insurance.

- Why didn't you pick either of the other two? _____

Directions: Choose one of the following topics and write a clear expository paragraph.

   1. fast-food restaurants   2. horror movies   3. any sport

_____

_____

_____

_____

_____

_____

_____

Writing Expository Introductory Paragraphs

Below you will find several facts which could be used to open an essay. Your job is to write at least two more sentences for each. *The middle sentence(s) should give some examples* that can be used to support the first sentence. *The last sentence,* we know, *must state an opinion or attitude.* (You can change the sentences below if they do not serve your paragraph well.)

1. All schools can use improvement, and ours is no different.
2. Almost all students look forward to summer vacation.
3. Eating continuously at fast-food restaurants can cause problems.
4. Computer training is important for the future.

Use the space below to write one introductory paragraph.

Mixed-Up Stories

All stories need a *setting, characters, conflict*, and a *resolution*. Select one item from each group to use in a story. You can add other characters, settings, objects, and situations to your story.

A.	B.	C.	D.
a phone call	a playground	a child	a dog
an argument	a circus	a teacher	a jump rope
a letter	a classroom	a nurse	a purse
an accident	a swimming pool	a firefighter	a book

_____

_____

_____

_____

_____

_____

_____

_____

_____

_____

_____

_____

_____

_____

_____

The Five-Paragraph Essay

Beginning: Start with an attention-getting device. The introductory sentence tells the main topic of the essay and names the three sub-topics. TR = use a transitional word. ¶ = indent for a new paragraph.		

Middle: Body paragraphs begin with a Who or What sentence. The next two boxes will tell When, Where, How, or Why. The last sentence of each paragraph is an example or incident sentence.		

¶ Who or What is the subject?	¶ Who or What is the subject?	¶ Who or What is the subject?
When, Where, How, or Why	When, Where, How, or Why	When, Where, How, or Why
When, Where, How, or Why	When, Where, How, or Why	When, Where, How, or Why
Example or Incident (little story)	Example or Incident (little story)	Example or Incident (little story)

Ending: The conclusion paragraph (1) summarizes, (2) re-states the main topic, or (3) comes to a conclusion based on the evidence presented. The concluding paragraph lets the reader know the essay is finished.		
¶		

Generic Essay Writing Frame

Introductory Paragraph

(Introduces the topic and sub-topic ideas.)

_____

_____

_____

_____

_____

_____

_____

_____

_____

_____

_____

Body

(Body paragraph one gives details about the first sub-topic—minimum 75 words.)

_____

_____

_____

_____

_____

_____

_____

_____

_____

_____

_____

_____

Generic Essay Writing Frame *(cont.)*

Body *(cont.)*

(Body paragraph two gives details about the second sub-topic—minimum 75 words.)

_____

_____

_____

_____

_____

_____

_____

(Body paragraph three gives details about the third sub-topic—minimum 75 words.)

_____

_____

_____

_____

_____

_____

_____

Conclusion

(The conclusion summarizes the ideas of the essay or draws a conclusion point based on the information presented within the essay—minimum 30 words.)

_____

_____

_____

_____

_____

_____

Adding Signed Numbers

Sample

-4	Step 1: Start at 0.
$+ +5$	Step 2: Go left 4 spaces for -4.
$+1$	Step 3: From -4, go right 5 spaces.
	Step 4: Answer = $+1$

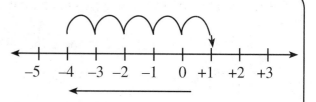

Directions: Use a long strip of paper to make a longer number line to help you. Complete the strip to positive 25 (+25) and to negative 25 (−25). Use your number line to help you solve these addition problems. Remember, always start at zero (0) when adding on the number line.

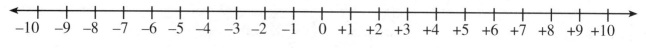

1. $\begin{array}{r} -4 \\ + -6 \\ \hline \end{array}$ 2. $\begin{array}{r} -6 \\ + -2 \\ \hline \end{array}$ 3. $\begin{array}{r} +3 \\ + +4 \\ \hline \end{array}$

4. $\begin{array}{r} -9 \\ + -7 \\ \hline \end{array}$ 5. $\begin{array}{r} -12 \\ + -9 \\ \hline \end{array}$ 6. $\begin{array}{r} -16 \\ + -8 \\ \hline \end{array}$

7. $\begin{array}{r} -23 \\ + +10 \\ \hline \end{array}$ 8. $\begin{array}{r} +24 \\ + -14 \\ \hline \end{array}$ 9. $\begin{array}{r} +18 \\ + -16 \\ \hline \end{array}$

10. $\begin{array}{r} -25 \\ + +12 \\ \hline \end{array}$ 11. $\begin{array}{r} +13 \\ + -19 \\ \hline \end{array}$ 12. $\begin{array}{r} -19 \\ + +17 \\ \hline \end{array}$

13. $\begin{array}{r} +20 \\ + -13 \\ \hline \end{array}$ 14. $\begin{array}{r} -7 \\ + -17 \\ \hline \end{array}$ 15. $\begin{array}{r} -13 \\ + +9 \\ \hline \end{array}$

16. $\begin{array}{r} -11 \\ + -12 \\ \hline \end{array}$ 17. $\begin{array}{r} +15 \\ + +10 \\ \hline \end{array}$ 18. $\begin{array}{r} -18 \\ + +15 \\ \hline \end{array}$

19. $\begin{array}{r} -18 \\ + -7 \\ \hline \end{array}$ 20. $\begin{array}{r} +5 \\ + -20 \\ \hline \end{array}$ 21. $\begin{array}{r} +6 \\ + -27 \\ \hline \end{array}$

Adding Signed Numbers *(cont.)*

To add numbers with the *same* sign, add the numbers and keep the sign.

$$
\begin{array}{r} +23 \\ + \ +14 \\ \hline +37 \end{array}
\qquad
\begin{array}{r} -40 \\ + \ -15 \\ \hline -55 \end{array}
$$

To add numbers with *different* signs, subtract the number with the smaller absolute value from the number with the larger absolute value. Then use the sign of the number with the higher absolute value.

$$
\begin{array}{r} +40 \\ + \ -20 \\ \hline +20 \end{array}
\qquad
\begin{array}{r} -70 \\ + \ +35 \\ \hline -35 \end{array}
\qquad
\begin{array}{r} +80 \\ + \ -40 \\ \hline +40 \end{array}
$$

Directions: Use a number line to help you check your work. The first one is done for you.

1. $\begin{array}{r} +25 \\ + \ -19 \\ \hline +6 \end{array}$
   2. $\begin{array}{r} +19 \\ + \ -23 \\ \hline \end{array}$
   3. $\begin{array}{r} +23 \\ + \ -7 \\ \hline \end{array}$

4. $\begin{array}{r} -34 \\ + \ -25 \\ \hline \end{array}$
   5. $\begin{array}{r} +56 \\ + \ -45 \\ \hline \end{array}$
   6. $\begin{array}{r} -67 \\ + \ +54 \\ \hline \end{array}$

7. $\begin{array}{r} -98 \\ + \ +76 \\ \hline \end{array}$
   8. $\begin{array}{r} +76 \\ + \ -45 \\ \hline \end{array}$
   9. $\begin{array}{r} +76 \\ + \ -99 \\ \hline \end{array}$

10. $\begin{array}{r} -100 \\ + \ +78 \\ \hline \end{array}$
    11. $\begin{array}{r} +124 \\ + \ -145 \\ \hline \end{array}$
    12. $\begin{array}{r} +200 \\ + \ -234 \\ \hline \end{array}$

13. $\begin{array}{r} -99 \\ + \ -11 \\ \hline \end{array}$
    14. $\begin{array}{r} -231 \\ + \ +199 \\ \hline \end{array}$
    15. $\begin{array}{r} +145 \\ + \ -201 \\ \hline \end{array}$

16. $\begin{array}{r} -238 \\ + \ +198 \\ \hline \end{array}$
    17. $\begin{array}{r} +900 \\ + \ -450 \\ \hline \end{array}$
    18. $\begin{array}{r} -456 \\ + \ -123 \\ \hline \end{array}$

19. $\begin{array}{r} +932 \\ + \ -756 \\ \hline \end{array}$
    20. $\begin{array}{r} -1000 \\ + \ +999 \\ \hline \end{array}$
    21. $\begin{array}{r} +789 \\ + \ -987 \\ \hline \end{array}$

Adding and Subtracting Integers

Directions: Solve each problem. Use the letters next to the problems to solve the riddle at the bottom of the page. Many letters will be used more than once while other letters will not be used at all.

II. $7 + (-5) =$ _____   **Q.** $-7 - (-3) =$ _____   **Z.** $(6 - 2) - (-4) =$ _____

Q. $-8 + 4 =$ _____   **X.** $-15 + (-6) =$ _____   **N.** $6 - [2 - (-3)] =$ _____

D. $4 + (-6) =$ _____   **S.** $-19 - (-18) =$ _____   **M.** $6 + [2 - (-4)] =$ _____

B. $-15 + (-3) =$ _____   **A.** $7 - 16 =$ _____   **I.** $10 + 22 + (-7) + (-30) =$ ____

F. $-28 + 28 =$ _____   **V.** $-2 - (-8) =$ _____   **P.** $-31 + 62 + (-9) =$ _____

G. $|-9| - |2| =$ _____   **U.** $8 - (-3) =$ _____   **T.** $9 + 24 + (-5) + (-25) =$ _____

O. $6 + -9 =$ _____   **E.** $-9 + (-7) =$ _____   **R.** $-5 + -6 + -9 =$ _____

W. $-7 + -8 =$ _____   **Y.** $-2 + 7 =$ _____   **L.** $|-20| + |-19| - 2 =$ _____

K. $-2 + (-4) =$ _____   **J.** $-18 + (-3) =$ _____   **C.** $5 \times 3 - (8 - 6) =$ _____

Riddle: Why did the dentist decide to join the army?

‾‾ ‾‾   ‾‾ ‾‾ ‾‾ ‾‾ ‾‾ ‾‾ ‾‾
2 -16   3   2 -3 11   7   2   3

‾‾ ‾‾   ‾‾ ‾‾ ‾‾ ‾‾ ‾‾
2 -16   -15 -3 11 -41 -2

‾‾ ‾‾   ‾‾   ‾‾ ‾‾ ‾‾ ‾‾
-18 -16   -9   7 -3 -3 -2

‾‾ ‾‾ ‾‾ ‾‾ ‾‾
-2 -20 -5 -41 -41

‾‾ ‾‾ ‾‾ ‾‾ ‾‾ ‾‾ ‾‾ ‾‾ .
-1 -16 -20   7 -16 -9   1   3

Evaluations Exponents

Directions: Evaluate these expressions by determining the value of the exponents. The first one is done for you.

1. 6^2

   $6 \times 6 = 36$

   __**36**__

2. 3^2

   _____

3. 5^2

   _____

4. 2^2

   _____

5. 10^2

   _____

6. 11^2

   _____

7. 5^3

   _____

8. 6^3

   _____

9. 9^2

   _____

10. 8^3

    _____

11. 7^2

    _____

12. 10^3

    _____

13. 7^3

    _____

14. 13^2

    _____

15. 2^3

    _____

16. 3^4

    _____

17. 2^4

    _____

18. 9^3

    _____

19. 5^3

    _____

20. 2^5

    _____

21. 14^2

    _____

22. 1^3

    _____

23. 15^2

    _____

24. 20^2

    _____

25. 30^2

    _____

26. 40^2

    _____

27. 50^2

    _____

Multiplying with Exponents

> A number multiplied by itself can be written as an exponent.
>
> The **exponent** tells how many times to multiply the base number by itself.
>
> 5^2 is 5 squared or "5 to the second power." 5^3 is "5 cubed" or "5 to the third power."
>
> $5^2 = 25$ $5^3 = 5 \times 5 \times 5$
>
> $5 \times 5 = 25$
>
> $25 \times 5 = 125$
>
> $5^3 = 125$

Directions: For each of the terms below, write an equation and solve it. The first one is done for you.

1. 3^2 _3_ x _3_ = _9_

2. 7^2 ___ x ___ = ___

3. 4^2 ___ x ___ = ___

4. 9^2 ___ x ___ = ___

5. 2^2 ___ x ___ = ___

6. 8^2 ___ x ___ = ___

7. 10^2 ___ x ___ = ___

8. 6^2 ___ x ___ = ___

9. 11^2 ___ x ___ = ___

10. 12^2 ___ x ___ = ___

Directions: For each of the terms below, write two equations and solve them. The first one is done for you.

11. 2^3 _2_ x _2_ = _4_

        _4_ x _2_ = _8_

    $2^3 =$ _8_

12. 3^3 ___ x ___ = ___

        ___ x ___ = ___

    $3^3 =$ ___

13. 5^3 ___ x ___ = ___

        ___ x ___ = ___

    $5^3 =$ ___

14. 7^3 ___ x ___ = ___

        ___ x ___ = ___

    $7^3 =$ ___

15. 4^3 ___ x ___ = ___

        ___ x ___ = ___

    $4^3 =$ ___

16. 6^3 ___ x ___ = ___

        ___ x ___ = ___

    $6^3 =$ ___

17. 10^3 ___ x ___ = ___

        ___ x ___ = ___

    $10^3 =$ ___

18. 9^3 ___ x ___ = ___

        ___ x ___ = ___

    $9^3 =$ ___

19. 11^3 ___ x ___ = ___

        ___ x ___ = ___

    $11^3 =$ ___

20. 12^3 ___ x ___ = ___

        ___ x ___ = ___

    $12^3 =$ ___

Multiplying with Signed Numbers

Directions: Compute the positive and negative values indicated in the problems below.

> ### Reminders
> - A negative times a negative is a positive.
> - A positive times a negative is a negative.
> - A negative divided by a negative is a positive.
> - A positive divided by a negative is a negative.
> - A negative divided by a positive is a negative.

1. Jill owes $4 to Jennifer, $4 to Michelle, and $4 to Eileen. How much does she owe altogether?
   _____

2. Joey owes $5 to 4 different friends. How much money does he owe altogether? _____

3. What is the product of ⁻7 and ⁻6? _____

4. The total bill at a restaurant was $49 to be split evenly among 7 friends. How much money did each friend owe? _____

5. How much is ⁻81 divided by 9? _____

6. How much is ⁻100 divided by ⁻10? _____

7. A group of 18 patrons each owe $15 at a restaurant. What is the total amount owed by all 18 customers? _____

8. What is the product of ⁻12 and ⁻13? _____

9. How much is ⁻16 times 4? _____

10. What is the quotient when ⁻45 is divided by ⁻9? _____

11. A group of 15 teenagers owes $75 at a pizza parlor. If they split the bill evenly, how much will each person owe? _____

12. How much is ⁻200 divided by ⁻10? _____

Multiplying by Using the Commutative Property

In multiplication the order of the factors does not affect the answer.

Examples

5 x 8   =   8 x 5   90 x 60   =   60 x 90

5 x 8 = 40   *(or)*   8 x 5 = 40   90 x 60 = 5,400   *(or)*   60 x 90 = 5,400

Remember, a x b = b x a.

Directions: Use the information above to solve these multiplication problems.

1. 9 x 8	**2.** 8 x 9	**3.** 7 x 6
4. 6 x 7	**5.** 10 x 8	**6.** 8 x 10

7. 10 x 17	**8.** 17 x 10	**9.** 19 x 10
10. 10 x 19	**11.** 20 x 30	**12.** 30 x 20

13. 50 x 40	**14.** 40 x 50	**15.** 80 x 60
16. 60 x 80	**17.** 40 x 70	**18.** 70 x 40

19. 90 x 30	**20.** 30 x 90	**21.** 60 x 70
22. 70 x 60	**23.** 75 x 55	**24.** 55 x 75

25. 45 x 25	**26.** 25 x 45	**27.** 23 x 67
28. 67 x 23	**29.** 42 x 17	**30.** 17 x 42

Multiplying by Using the Associative Property

In multiplication the factors may be grouped in any order. The answer will be the same.

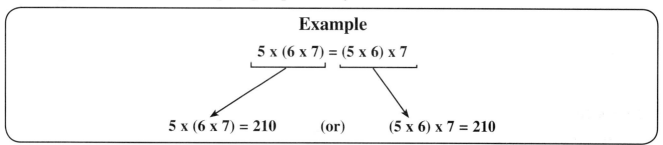

Example

5 x (6 x 7) = (5 x 6) x 7

5 x (6 x 7) = 210   (or)   (5 x 6) x 7 = 210

Remember, a x (b x c) = (a x b) x c.

Directions: Use the information above to help you solve these multiplication problems.

1. 7 x (8 x 9) = _____

2. (7 x 8) x 9 = _____

3. 6 x (5 x 10) = _____

4. (6 x 5) x 10 = _____

5. (12 x 10) x 5 = _____

6. 12 x (10 x 5) = _____

7. (10 x 20) x 30 = _____

8. 10 x (20 x 30) = _____

9. 20 x (50 x 80) = _____

10. (20 x 50) x 80 = _____

11. (90 x 80) x 25 = _____

12. 90 x (80 x 25) = _____

13. 15 x (25 x 10) = _____

14. (15 x 25) x 10 = _____

15. (25 x 41) x 12 = _____

16. 25 x (41 x 12) = _____

17. (25 x 15) x (44 x 23) = _____

18. 25 x (15 x 44) x 23 = _____

19. (44 x 14) x (33 x 13) = _____

20. 44 x (14 x 33) x 13 = _____

Using Two-Digit Multipliers with Three-Digit Multiplicands

Step by Step

1. Multiply 409 times 8 which equals 3,272.

2. Place an automatic zero (placeholder) in the ones place when multiplying 409 times 3 (tens) which equals 12,270.

3. Add the two partial products (3,272 + 12,270 = 15,542). Don't forget to add a comma every three digits starting from the ones place.

$$
\begin{array}{r}
409 \\
\times\ \ 38 \\
\hline
3,272 \\
+\ 12,270 \\
\hline
15,542 \\
\end{array}
$$

Directions: Use the information above to help solve the problems on this page. The first one is done for you.

1.
$$
\begin{array}{r}
507 \\
\times\ 37 \\
\hline
3,549 \\
+\ 15,210 \\
\hline
18,759 \\
\end{array}
$$

2.
$$
\begin{array}{r}
609 \\
\times\ 58 \\
\hline
\end{array}
$$

3.
$$
\begin{array}{r}
706 \\
\times\ 76 \\
\hline
\end{array}
$$

4.
$$
\begin{array}{r}
108 \\
\times\ 25 \\
\hline
\end{array}
$$

5.
$$
\begin{array}{r}
607 \\
\times\ 45 \\
\hline
\end{array}
$$

6.
$$
\begin{array}{r}
304 \\
\times\ 39 \\
\hline
\end{array}
$$

7.
$$
\begin{array}{r}
107 \\
\times\ 98 \\
\hline
\end{array}
$$

8.
$$
\begin{array}{r}
509 \\
\times\ 76 \\
\hline
\end{array}
$$

9.
$$
\begin{array}{r}
608 \\
\times\ 88 \\
\hline
\end{array}
$$

10.
$$
\begin{array}{r}
706 \\
\times\ 99 \\
\hline
\end{array}
$$

11.
$$
\begin{array}{r}
405 \\
\times\ 55 \\
\hline
\end{array}
$$

12.
$$
\begin{array}{r}
407 \\
\times\ 66 \\
\hline
\end{array}
$$

13.
$$
\begin{array}{r}
231 \\
\times\ 78 \\
\hline
\end{array}
$$

14.
$$
\begin{array}{r}
289 \\
\times\ 65 \\
\hline
\end{array}
$$

15.
$$
\begin{array}{r}
578 \\
\times\ 93 \\
\hline
\end{array}
$$

16.
$$
\begin{array}{r}
374 \\
\times\ 69 \\
\hline
\end{array}
$$

Multiplying Decimals

Keys to Multiplying Decimals
- Line up the numbers. You don't need to line up the decimal points, however.
- Multiply the numbers as you would multiply whole numbers.
- Count the number of decimal places in both numbers that are being multiplied. Make sure the decimal places in the product equal the number of decimal places in the problem.

Directions: Multiply to solve each problem.

1. $46.98
   x   2

2. $1.49
   x   3

3. $21.06
   x   5

4. $9.99
   x   7

5. $1.57
   x   34

6. $105.13
   x   4

7. $45.03
   x   13

8. $17.10
   x   15

9. 0.84
   x 3.15

10. 2.08
    x 0.9

11. 0.28
    x 9.51

12. 0.0076
    x 0.30

13. $10.50
    x 0.60

14. 47.8
    x 0.1

15. 14.2
    x 9.7

16. $5.75
    x 0.24

17. $5.58
    x 1.5

18. 0.14
    x 0.87

Using One-Digit Divisors with Two-Digit Dividends

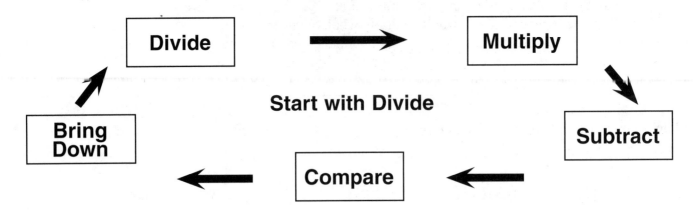

Start with Divide

Directions: Solve the division problems below. The first one is done for you.

1.
$$\begin{array}{r} 11\ \text{R}1 \\ 7\overline{)78} \\ -7\downarrow \\ \hline 08 \\ -7 \\ \hline 1 \end{array}$$

2. $5\overline{)84}$

3. $2\overline{)26}$

4. $6\overline{)67}$

5. $3\overline{)86}$

6. $4\overline{)99}$

7. $9\overline{)81}$

8. $1\overline{)34}$

9. $6\overline{)78}$

10. $9\overline{)96}$

11. $5\overline{)56}$

12. $4\overline{)57}$

13. $2\overline{)33}$

14. $3\overline{)56}$

15. $8\overline{)90}$

16. $4\overline{)67}$

17. $1\overline{)23}$

18. $7\overline{)46}$

19. $5\overline{)44}$

20. $6\overline{)56}$

21. $9\overline{)90}$

22. $7\overline{)35}$

23. $3\overline{)38}$

24. $4\overline{)87}$

25. $2\overline{)47}$

Dividing with Two-Digit Divisors

Follow these steps when solving long division problems.

Sample

1. Because the first digit (6) in the dividend cannot be divided by 12, divide 66 by 12. The closest multiple of 12 to 66 is 12 x 5 = 60. Place 5 in the quotient.
2. Multiply 12 x 5 and write the number 60 below 66.
3. Subtract 60 from 66. The answer is 6.
4. Because the number 6 is less than the divisor 12, bring down the 0 and divide 60 by 12.
5. Multiply 12 x 5. The answer is 60. Place 5 in the qoutient.
6. Subtract 60 from 60. The final answer is 55.

$$\begin{array}{r} x55 \\ 12\overline{)660} \\ -60\downarrow \\ \hline 60 \\ -60 \\ \hline 0 \end{array}$$

Directions: Use the sample above to help you do these problems. The first one is done for you.

1.

$$\begin{array}{r} x21\ R17 \\ 22\overline{)479} \\ -44\downarrow \\ \hline 39 \\ -22 \\ \hline 17 \end{array}$$

2. $31\overline{)975}$

3. $23\overline{)748}$

4. $21\overline{)661}$

5. $33\overline{)497}$

6. $41\overline{)453}$

7. $21\overline{)887}$

8. $33\overline{)715}$

9. $22\overline{)519}$

10. $31\overline{)428}$

11. $24\overline{)534}$

12. $22\overline{)721}$

Dividing and Multiplying

Directions: Write the division problem and solve. Multiply to check the answer. The first one is done for you.

1. 8,400 cookies divided into 40 boxes **Check:** $\begin{array}{r} 210 \\ 40\overline{)8400} \\ -80 \\ \hline 40 \\ -40 \\ \hline 00 \end{array}$ $\begin{array}{r} 210 \\ \times 40 \\ \hline 000 \\ +8,400 \\ \hline 8,400 \end{array}$	2. 41,916 pieces of bubble gum divided into 28 cartons **Check:**	3. 33,320 decks of playing cards divided into 136 cases **Check:**
4. 3,600 marbles placed into 90 pouches **Check:**	5. 8,928 potato chips placed into 9 gigantic bowls **Check:**	6. 28,917 game pieces for 81 board games **Check:**
7. 35,620 paper clips placed into 260 canisters **Check:**	8. 180,930 ants in 37 colonies **Check:**	9. 8,840 peanuts for 65 elephants **Check:**

94

Decimals: Multiplication and Division

Sweet Buggy Bites is a company that creates unusual kinds of candy. They make chocolate-covered ants, grasshopper kisses, sweet 'n' sour crickets, beetle bites, and other candy-coated bugs. Use your knowledge of multiplication and division with decimals to compute these answers.

Reminders

- Count all of the places to the right of the decimal in the multiplication problems and have the same number of places to the right of the decimal in the answer.

- If the divisor has a decimal, move it to the right of the divisor and move the decimal in the dividend the same number of places to the right.

Example: $3.1 \times 0.4 = 1.24$

Example: $.12\overline{)24.36}$ to $12.\overline{)2436.}$ with quotient 203

---

1. A bag of beetle bites weighs 1.47 lbs. There are 7 candies in each bag. How much does each bite weigh? _____

2. A box of chocolate-coated ants weighs 8.35 ounces. How much do 12 boxes weigh? _____ _____

3. A bag of sweet 'n' sour crickets weighs 9.81 ounces and holds 9 candies. How much does each candy weigh? _____

4. A large box of grasshopper kisses weighs 18.36 ounces. Each candy weighs 1.8 ounces. How many candies are in the box? _____

5. A super-sized bag of beetle bites weighs 2.255 lbs. What is the weight of 20 bags? _____

6. A mini-box of chocolate-covered ants weighs 4.025 ounces. Each ant weighs .05 ounces. How many chocolate-covered ants are in each box? _____

7. A large box of sweet 'n' sour crickets weighs 13.467 ounces. How much do 72 boxes weigh? _____

8. A regular box of grasshopper kisses costs $4.83 for 21 candies. What is the cost for each candy? _____

9. A regular box of sweet 'n' sour crickets costs $9.50 for 25 candied crickets. What is the cost for each cricket? _____

10. A box of beetle bites weighs 1.095 lbs. How much does a carton of 144 boxes weigh? _____ _____

Dividing Decimals

Directions: Solve the division problems. Round to the nearest hundredth.

1. $\dfrac{.7}{.14} =$

6. $\dfrac{9.2}{230} =$

11. $\dfrac{45.6}{8} =$

2. $\dfrac{6}{43.2} =$

7. $\dfrac{8}{27.2} =$

12. $\dfrac{.258}{6} =$

3. $\dfrac{4}{.3704} =$

8. $\dfrac{\$30}{.04} =$

13. $\dfrac{3.43}{.7} =$

4. $\dfrac{3}{.0048} =$

9. $\dfrac{\$42}{.24} =$

14. $\dfrac{7.2}{.09} =$

5. $\dfrac{.8}{60} =$

10. $\$65 \div \dfrac{4}{5} =$

15. $\dfrac{60}{1.2} =$

Directions: Change each decimal to a fraction or a mixed number. Reduce to the lowest terms.

16. .35 =

20. 18.33 =

24. .318 =

17. .064 =

21. 4.625 =

25. .0625 =

18. 3.4 =

22. .0084 =

26. 4.25 =

19. 3.125 =

23. 66.75 =

27. 1.10 =

Directions: Change each fraction to a decimal. Round to the nearest hundredth.

28. $\dfrac{4}{5} =$

30. $\dfrac{2}{3} =$

32. $\dfrac{5}{6} =$

34. $\dfrac{1}{3} =$

29. $\dfrac{3}{8} =$

31. $\dfrac{7}{9} =$

33. $\dfrac{5}{8} =$

35. $\dfrac{7}{10} =$

Using Square Roots

The **square root** of a number is another number that multiplied by itself will equal the first number.

The square root of 9 is 3 because 3 x 3 = 9.

This radical symbol $\sqrt{}$ indicates that you need to find the square root.

$$\sqrt{25} = 5 \qquad\qquad \sqrt{36} = 6$$

Directions: Use the samples above to help solve these problems. Use a calculator to help you check the answers on the more difficult problems.

1. $\sqrt{4}$ = _____

2. $\sqrt{16}$ = _____

3. $\sqrt{49}$ = _____

4. $\sqrt{81}$ = _____

5. $\sqrt{100}$ = _____

6. $\sqrt{64}$ = _____

7. $\sqrt{121}$ = _____

8. $\sqrt{144}$ = _____

9. $\sqrt{169}$ = _____

10. $\sqrt{225}$ = _____

11. $\sqrt{196}$ = _____

12. $\sqrt{400}$ = _____

13. $\sqrt{900}$ = _____

14. $\sqrt{4900}$ = _____

15. $\sqrt{6400}$ = _____

16. $\sqrt{1600}$ = _____

17. $\sqrt{490{,}000}$ = _____

18. $\sqrt{640{,}000}$ = _____

19. $\sqrt{160{,}000}$ = _____

20. $\sqrt{810{,}000}$ = _____

21. $\sqrt{250{,}000}$ = _____

22. $\sqrt{90{,}000}$ = _____

23. $\sqrt{360{,}000}$ = _____

24. $\sqrt{10{,}000}$ = _____

25. $\sqrt{9{,}000{,}000}$ = _____

26. $\sqrt{81{,}000{,}000}$ = _____

27. $\sqrt{25{,}000{,}000}$ = _____

28. $\sqrt{36{,}000{,}000}$ = _____

29. $\sqrt{49{,}000{,}000}$ = _____

30. $\sqrt{64{,}000{,}000}$ = _____

Math

Calculating Square Roots

A number multiplied by itself is *squared*. Look at the examples below. The number 3 squared is 9. The square root of 9 is 3. The number 4 squared is 16. The square root of 16 is 4.

$$3^2 = 3 \times 3 = 9 \qquad\qquad 4^2 = 4 \times 4 = 16$$
$$\sqrt{9} = 3 \qquad\qquad\qquad\qquad \sqrt{16} = 4$$

Directions: Use your knowledge of multiplication facts to calculate the square root of each of the following problems.

1. $\sqrt{16}$ = _____ 2. $\sqrt{36}$ = _____ 3. $\sqrt{144}$ = _____ 4. $\sqrt{25}$ = _____

5. $\sqrt{64}$ = _____ 6. $\sqrt{81}$ = _____ 7. $\sqrt{121}$ = _____ 8. $\sqrt{1}$ = _____

9. $\sqrt{9}$ = _____ 10. $\sqrt{100}$ = _____ 11. $\sqrt{49}$ = _____ 12. $\sqrt{4}$ = _____

You can calculate the square root of some very large numbers using the grid and your knowledge of the multiples of 10. For example, the square root of 100 is 10 because 10 times 10 equals 100. The square root of 10,000 is 100 because 100 times 100 equals 10,000. The square root of 1,000,000 is 1,000 because 1,000 times 1,000 equals 1,000,000. The square root of 3,600 is 60 because 60 times 60 equals 3,600.

Directions: Compute the square root of each of the numbers listed here. Look for a pattern. Check your answers with a calculator.

13. $\sqrt{2,500}$ = _____ 14. $\sqrt{3,600}$ = _____ 15. $\sqrt{400}$ = _____

16. $\sqrt{100}$ = _____ 17. $\sqrt{6,400}$ = _____ 18. $\sqrt{4,900}$ = _____

19. $\sqrt{900}$ = _____ 20. $\sqrt{16,900}$ = _____ 21. $\sqrt{8,100}$ = _____

22. $\sqrt{1,600}$ = _____ 23. $\sqrt{14,400}$ = _____ 24. $\sqrt{12,100}$ = _____

25. Describe the pattern you discovered.

Order of Operations

Reminder

Evaluate expressions in this order: PEMDAS

1. <u>P</u>arentheses: Do these operations first

2. <u>E</u>xponents: Find these values next

3. <u>M</u>ultiply and <u>D</u>ivide: In order from left to right

4. <u>A</u>dd and <u>S</u>ubtract: In order from left to right

Directions: Evaluate these expressions. Be sure to follow the order of operations listed above. The first one is done for you.

1. $4^2 + 9 - (3 \times 5)$

$4^2 + 9 - 15$

$16 + 9 - 15 = 10$

$\underline{\qquad 10 \qquad}$

2. $6^2 - (9 \times 2) + 12$

$\underline{\qquad\qquad}$

3. $10 + (8 \times 3) - 3^2$

$\underline{\qquad\qquad}$

4. $(8 \times 8) - 4^3 + 1$

$\underline{\qquad\qquad}$

5. $8^2 + (4 \times 5) - 21$

$\underline{\qquad\qquad}$

6. $(9 \times 5) - 2^3 + 16$

$\underline{\qquad\qquad}$

7. $15 \div 5 + 7 - 2^2$

$\underline{\qquad\qquad}$

8. $(9 + 11) - 3^2 + 7$

$\underline{\qquad\qquad}$

9. $(6 \times 5) - 14 - 4^2$

$\underline{\qquad\qquad}$

10. $12^2 - 9 \times 12 - 4^2$

$\underline{\qquad\qquad}$

11. $13^2 - (11 \times 9) + 16$

$\underline{\qquad\qquad}$

12. $13 + (6 \times 8) - 5^2$

$\underline{\qquad\qquad}$

13. $17 - (9 + 8) + 2^3$

$\underline{\qquad\qquad}$

14. $9^2 - (27 + 13) - 6^2$

$\underline{\qquad\qquad}$

15. $44 - 7 \times 6 + 4^2$

$\underline{\qquad\qquad}$

PEMDAS: Easy Applications

The acronym for this order of operations is PEMDAS.

Parentheses   **E**xponents   **M**ultiplication   **D**ivision   **A**ddition   **S**ubtraction

A popular expression for remembering this is **P**lease **E**xcuse **M**y **D**ear **A**unt **S**ally.

Directions: Find the numerical value of the following expressions using the correct order of operations.

1. $9 \times 5 - 4 + 3 \times 4 =$ _____

2. $12 + 8 \times 6 \div 2 \times 8 =$ _____

3. $3 + 6 \times 8 - 5 \times 2 =$ _____

4. $7 + 8 \div 4 + 3 - 2 =$ _____

5. $22 \div 11 + 12 - 3 =$ _____

6. $9 \times 8 - 6 \times 3 + 7 =$ _____

7. $13 + 5 \times 6 \div 2 + 10 =$ _____

8. $35 \div 7 \times 8 + 2 - 4 \times 2 =$ _____

9. $(100 \div 5) \times 5 + 4 - 9 =$ _____

10. $88 \div 11 + 56 \div 8 + 12 - 5 =$ _____

Remember the following facts:
- The fraction bar (—) means division.
- The raised dot (•) means multiplication.
- Numbers written next to parenthesis or parentheses next to each other also require multiplication.

Directions: Find the numerical value of these expressions.

11. $5(8) - \dfrac{30}{5} + 4 \times 3 =$ _____

12. $(7)(9) + \dfrac{9}{3} - 20 \times 3 =$ _____

13. $8(9) + 10 \cdot 5 + 8 \cdot 2 =$ _____

14. $3 + 8 \cdot 10 - 13 \times 3 =$ _____

15. $17 + 5 - 6 \cdot 4 + \dfrac{12}{3} =$ _____

16. $9 + \dfrac{44}{4} - 8 \times 2 + 20 - 3 =$ _____

PEMDAS: Parentheses and Exponents

Sample

Read the problem.	$3 + (2 \times 4) - 2^2 + 3 = ?$
Do the work in the parentheses first.	$3 + 8 - 2^2 + 3 = ?$
Get the numerical value of the exponent next.	$3 + 8 - 4 + 3 = ?$
Add and subtract in order from left to right.	$11 - 4 + 3 = ?$
	$7 + 3 = ?$
Record your answer.	$3 + (2 \times 4) - 2^2 + 3 = 10$

Directions: Find the numerical value of each expression.

1. $(2 \times 3) + 3^2 - 5 \times 3 = $ _____

2. $10^2 - (3 \times 30) + 8 = $ _____

3. $4 + (2 \times 10) - 2^2 = $ _____

4. $8 + (5 \times 5) - 3^2 = $ _____

5. $4^2 - 13 + (12 \times 2) = $ _____

6. $7^2 + 3(2 \times 4) - 3 = $ _____

7. $3 + 5^2 - (12 + 3) = $ _____

8. $9 + 4^2 - (5 \times 5) + 2 = $ _____

9. $11 - 2^2 + (3 \times 2) - 4 = $ _____

10. $2(4 \times 5) + 3^2 - 2^2 = $ _____

11. $18 - (3 \times 4) + 5^2 - 2 = $ _____

12. $7(4 \times 2) - 4^2 + (2 \times 9) = $ _____

13. $10^2 - 3 \times 4 + (6 \times 4) - 5 = $ _____

14. $12^2 + 3 - 2(2 \times 4) - 5^2 + 11 = $ _____

15. $(15 + 7) \times 2 \times 3 - 6(4 \times 3) + 12 = $ _____

16. $(12 - 5) + (2 + 13) - 2^2 + 30 = $ _____

Adding and Subtracting Fractions

To add fractions with the same denominator, add the numerators and write the sum over the same denominator. To subtract fractions with the same denominator, subtract the numerators and write the difference over the same denominator. Always write the sum or difference in lowest terms.

1. $\dfrac{5}{6} - \dfrac{3}{6} =$ _____ 2. $\dfrac{4}{7} + \dfrac{2}{7} =$ _____ 3. $\dfrac{7}{12} - \dfrac{4}{12} =$ _____ 4. $\dfrac{5}{16} + \dfrac{3}{16} =$ _____

To add or subtract fractions with different denominators, first write equivalent fractions with a common denominator. Then add or subtract. Write the sum or difference in lowest terms.

5. $\dfrac{3}{5} + \dfrac{2}{8} =$ _____ 6. $\dfrac{3}{5} + \dfrac{5}{7} =$ _____ 7. $\dfrac{7}{9} - \dfrac{1}{2} =$ _____ 8. $\dfrac{4}{5} - \dfrac{3}{4} =$ _____

To add or subtract mixed numbers, determine if the fractions have to be changed to equivalent fractions. First change the fractions to equivalent fractions and then proceed with the addition or subtraction.

Sometimes the mixed number will have to be renamed. Change the whole number to a fraction equal to one and add it to the fraction portion, resulting in an improper fraction.

Proceed with the addition or subtraction. Write the sum or difference in lowest terms.

Directions: Add or subtract. Then write the answer in lowest terms.

9. $\dfrac{7}{10}$
$-\dfrac{5}{10}$
_____

10. $\dfrac{3}{8}$
$+\dfrac{5}{12}$
_____

11. $\dfrac{3}{4}$
$-\dfrac{1}{5}$
_____

12. $\dfrac{5}{16}$
$+\dfrac{3}{8}$
_____

13. $4\,^{3}/_{4} + 5\,^{5}/_{6}$ = _____

14. $9\,^{7}/_{8} - 6\,^{2}/_{4}$ = _____

15. $5\,^{2}/_{3} - 2\,^{4}/_{9}$ = _____

Adding and Subtracting Fractions

Directions: Compute the answers for these problems.

1. $\frac{2}{5} + \frac{1}{4} =$

2. $\frac{1}{4} + \frac{1}{2} =$

3. $\frac{3}{4} + \frac{1}{8} =$

4. $\frac{4}{6} - \frac{1}{2} =$

5. $\frac{7}{9} - \frac{1}{3} =$

6. $\frac{8}{12} + \frac{1}{4} =$

7. $\frac{5}{8} + \frac{1}{4} =$

8. $\frac{4}{5} + \frac{1}{10} =$

9. $\frac{5}{9} + \frac{1}{3} =$

10. $\frac{2}{5} + \frac{1}{3} =$

11. $\frac{11}{20} - \frac{2}{5} =$

12. $\frac{1}{8} + \frac{1}{6} =$

Directions: After adding or subtracting, be sure to simplify (reduce) your answers to these problems, if necessary.

13. $\frac{4}{7} + \frac{2}{3} =$

14. $\frac{5}{6} + \frac{5}{8} =$

15. $\frac{5}{9} + \frac{4}{6} =$

16. $\frac{5}{8} - \frac{5}{12} =$

17. $\frac{7}{9} - \frac{5}{12} =$

18. $\frac{4}{9} - \frac{2}{8} =$

19. $\frac{5}{6} + \frac{4}{7} =$

20. $\frac{4}{12} + \frac{7}{8} =$

21. $\frac{9}{10} - \frac{3}{4} =$

22. $\frac{7}{9} + \frac{3}{6} =$

23. $\frac{5}{10} + \frac{5}{12} =$

24. $\frac{11}{15} + \frac{1}{10} =$

Multiplying Fractions

Sample: $\frac{3}{4} \times \frac{1}{6} = ?$

   Step 1 → Multiply the fractions.

   Step 2 → Write the fraction in simplest form by dividing the numerator and denominator by the greatest common factor, which in this case is 3.

$\frac{3}{4} \times \frac{1}{6} = \frac{3}{24}$

$\frac{3 \div 3}{24 \div 3} = \frac{1}{8}$

Sample: $\qquad \frac{3}{5} \times \frac{10}{24} = \frac{\cancel{3}^{1}}{\cancel{5}_{1}} \times \frac{\cancel{10}^{2}}{\cancel{24}_{8}} = \frac{2}{8} = \frac{1}{4}$

Directions: Compute the answers to these problems. Remember to cancel whenever possible. Reduce answers to simplest terms.

1. $\frac{2}{9} \times \frac{3}{8} =$

2. $\frac{5}{9} \times \frac{6}{8} =$

3. $\frac{1}{4} \times \frac{8}{9} =$

4. $\frac{3}{9} \times \frac{4}{12} =$

5. $\frac{4}{15} \times \frac{10}{16} =$

6. $\frac{6}{8} \times \frac{11}{18} =$

7. $\frac{7}{9} \times \frac{3}{21} =$

8. $\frac{4}{7} \times \frac{21}{28} =$

9. $\frac{5}{12} \times \frac{8}{10} =$

10. $\frac{4}{8} \times \frac{3}{9} =$

11. $\frac{6}{8} \times \frac{9}{12} =$

12. $\frac{9}{21} \times \frac{14}{10} =$

13. $\frac{6}{10} \times \frac{6}{9} =$

14. $\frac{10}{25} \times \frac{4}{6} =$

15. $\frac{8}{12} \times \frac{8}{20} =$

Directions: Compute the products. Cancel as often as possible. The first one is done for you.

16. $\frac{2}{5} \times \frac{5}{9} \times \frac{3}{4} = \frac{\cancel{2}^{1}}{\cancel{5}_{1}} \times \frac{\cancel{5}^{1}}{\cancel{9}_{3}} \times \frac{\cancel{3}^{1}}{\cancel{4}_{2}} = \frac{1}{6}$

17. $\frac{5}{6} \times \frac{3}{7} \times \frac{4}{12} =$

18. $\frac{4}{7} \times \frac{11}{8} \times \frac{21}{5} =$

19. $\frac{2}{3} \times \frac{4}{5} \times \frac{9}{16} =$

20. $\frac{7}{8} \times \frac{6}{21} \times \frac{3}{16} =$

21. $\frac{1}{3} \times \frac{3}{5} \times \frac{5}{2} =$

More Multiplying Fractions

Directions: Multiply the fractions. Remember to write the answer in simplest form when possible.

1. $\frac{1}{2} \times \frac{3}{4} =$

2. $\frac{2}{3} \times \frac{1}{7} =$

3. $\frac{3}{8} \times \frac{3}{5} =$

4. $\frac{1}{5} \times \frac{6}{7} =$

5. $\frac{1}{2} \times \frac{1}{3} =$

6. $\frac{2}{3} \times \frac{1}{4} =$

7. $\frac{1}{3} \times \frac{6}{7} =$

8. $\frac{4}{9} \times \frac{1}{2} =$

9. $\frac{1}{2} \times \frac{1}{2} =$

10. $\frac{1}{2} \times \frac{3}{2} =$

11. $\frac{1}{3} \times \frac{3}{4} =$

12. $\frac{2}{9} \times \frac{3}{4} =$

13. $\frac{3}{8} \times \frac{2}{5} =$

14. $\frac{5}{8} \times \frac{7}{9} =$

15. $\frac{1}{2} \times \frac{1}{2} \times \frac{1}{2} =$

16. $\frac{1}{2} \times \frac{1}{4} \times \frac{4}{5} =$

17. $\frac{1}{2} \times \frac{2}{3} \times \frac{3}{5} =$

18. $\frac{5}{9} \times \frac{3}{7} \times \frac{14}{15} =$

19. $\frac{6}{7} \times \frac{7}{8} \times \frac{4}{5} =$

20. $\frac{11}{15} \times \frac{10}{11} \times \frac{3}{4} =$

21. $\frac{9}{10} \times \frac{1}{4} \times \frac{8}{9} =$

22. $\frac{5}{6} \times \frac{14}{15} \times \frac{2}{21} =$

23. $\frac{20}{21} \times \frac{9}{16} \times \frac{4}{5} =$

24. $\frac{3}{4} \times \frac{5}{7} \times \frac{2}{11} =$

25. $\frac{11}{12} \times \frac{3}{4} =$

26. $\frac{7}{8} \times \frac{2}{14} =$

27. $\frac{4}{15} \times \frac{5}{13} =$

28. $\frac{3}{5} \times \frac{10}{21} =$

29. $\frac{121}{300} \times \frac{10}{11} =$

30. $\frac{125}{470} \times \frac{320}{1000} =$

31. $\frac{289}{1222} \times \frac{2}{17} =$

32. $\frac{14}{525} \times \frac{15}{320} =$

Dividing Fractions

To divide fractions, do the following steps:

1. Get the reciprocal by flipping the divisor upside down.
2. Change the sign to multiplication (x) and cancel where possible.
3. Multiply the numerators and then multiply the denominators.
4. Simplify answers where possible.

$$\frac{3}{4} \div \frac{1}{4} = \frac{3}{4} \times \frac{4}{1} = \frac{3}{\cancel{4}_1} \times \frac{\cancel{4}^1}{1} = \frac{3}{1} = 3$$

Directions: Compute the answers to these problems. The first one is done for you.

1. $\frac{2}{3} \div \frac{1}{3} = \frac{2}{\cancel{3}_1} \times \frac{\cancel{3}^1}{1} = \frac{2}{1} = 2$

2. $\frac{4}{5} \div \frac{2}{5} =$

3. $\frac{2}{5} \div \frac{1}{5} =$

4. $\frac{4}{3} \div \frac{1}{3} =$

5. $\frac{3}{9} \div \frac{1}{9} =$

6. $\frac{4}{6} \div \frac{1}{6} =$

7. $\frac{7}{8} \div \frac{1}{2} =$

8. $\frac{5}{9} \div \frac{2}{3} =$

9. $\frac{7}{12} \div \frac{1}{2} =$

10. $\frac{6}{10} \div \frac{1}{3} =$

11. $\frac{7}{8} \div \frac{1}{4} =$

12. $\frac{6}{9} \div \frac{2}{3} =$

13. $\frac{9}{12} \div \frac{1}{4} =$

14. $\frac{4}{7} \div \frac{1}{14} =$

15. $\frac{2}{9} \div \frac{2}{3} =$

More Dividing Fractions

Directions: Divide the fractions below.

1. $3\frac{2}{3} \div 4\frac{2}{3} =$

2. $4\frac{3}{7} \div 2\frac{4}{7} =$

3. $2\frac{1}{3} \div 3\frac{1}{6} =$

4. $5\frac{6}{7} \div 6\frac{3}{14} =$

5. $3\frac{3}{5} \div 5\frac{4}{5} =$

6. $\frac{5}{6} \div \frac{2}{3} =$

7. $\frac{1}{4} \div \frac{3}{8} =$

8. $\frac{5}{12} \div \frac{2}{24} =$

9. $\frac{3}{10} \div \frac{12}{30} =$

10. $\frac{1}{5} \div \frac{4}{15} =$

11. $\frac{13}{20} \div \frac{3}{10} =$

12. $\frac{2}{7} \div \frac{2}{3} =$

13. $\frac{1}{6} \div \frac{2}{5} =$

14. $\frac{4}{9} \div \frac{1}{2} =$

15. $\frac{8}{9} \div \frac{3}{4} =$

16. $\frac{3}{6} \div 1\frac{2}{3} =$

17. $2\frac{1}{3} \div \frac{3}{4} =$

18. $3\frac{3}{4} \div \frac{3}{5} =$

19. $6\frac{1}{2} \div \frac{2}{3} =$

20. $1\frac{1}{2} \div 6 =$

21. $\frac{5}{7} \div 3\frac{4}{5} =$

22. $\frac{1}{4} \div 3\frac{1}{5} =$

23. $2\frac{3}{8} \div \frac{4}{5} =$

24. $3\frac{3}{4} \div \frac{1}{9} =$

25. $\frac{2}{5} \div 3\frac{8}{9} =$

26. $\frac{3}{8} \div 12 =$

27. $15 \div \frac{1}{10} =$

28. $2\frac{3}{6} \div \frac{1}{3} =$

29. $3\frac{2}{3} \div \frac{9}{10} =$

30. $2\frac{1}{2} \div \frac{1}{4} =$

Fractions and Decimals

A *mixed number* is a fraction greater than 1, written as a whole number and a fraction. A fraction written with the numerator larger than the denominator is called an *improper fraction*. Improper fractions should be changed into proper fractions or mixed fractions. To change an improper fraction into a mixed fraction, divide the numerator by the denominator.

Example: $\dfrac{16}{5} = 3\dfrac{1}{5}$ $5\overline{)16} \quad \begin{array}{c} 3\,r1 \\ -15 \\ \hline 1 \end{array}$ or $3\dfrac{1\ (remainder)}{5\ (divisor)}$

Directions: Write the fraction as a mixed number or a whole number.

1. $\dfrac{25}{6}$ 2. $\dfrac{13}{4}$ 3. $\dfrac{40}{5}$ 4. $\dfrac{38}{7}$ 5. $\dfrac{27}{9}$

Directions: Write the mixed number as a fraction.

6. $3\dfrac{2}{7}$ 7. $5\dfrac{3}{5}$ 8. $7\dfrac{2}{9}$ 9. $4\dfrac{3}{8}$ 10. $2\dfrac{9}{10}$

Directions: Write the quotient as a mixed number. Write the fraction in lowest terms.

11. $5\overline{)11}$ 12. $8\overline{)38}$ 13. $5\overline{)48}$ 14. $8\overline{)74}$

Mixed numbers may be written as decimals. To write a mixed number as a decimal, first write the fraction as a decimal by dividing the numerator by the denominator. Then add the whole number and the decimal.

Example: $2\dfrac{3}{5}$ $\dfrac{3}{5} = 5\overline{)3.0}\ ^{0.6}$ $2 + 0.6 = 2.6$

Directions: Write the fraction or the mixed number as a decimal. Round to the nearest hundredth.

15. $\dfrac{2}{8}$ $8\overline{)2.0}$ 16. $\dfrac{3}{4}$ $4\overline{)3.0}$ 17. $6\dfrac{4}{20}$ $20\overline{)4.00}$

18. $\dfrac{1}{2}$ 19. $\dfrac{3}{8}$ 20. $\dfrac{15}{25}$ 21. $3\dfrac{6}{10}$

Converting Fractions to Percents

A fraction is converted to a percentage by dividing the denominator into the numerator.

numerator ⟶ $\frac{1}{4}$ $4\overline{)1.00}$ .25 $\frac{1}{2}$ $2\overline{)1.00}$ .50
denominator ⟶

Always place a decimal point and two zeros to the right of the numerator in the dividend. This converts the fraction to a decimal which is used to compute the percent.

Directions: Convert the fractions in these problems into decimals. Use the decimals to compute the percentages. The first one is done for you.

1. $\frac{1}{2}$ of 24 = ___12___

2. $\frac{3}{4}$ of 32 = _____

3. $\frac{5}{10}$ of 80 = _____

$2\overline{)1.00}$ .50

24
x .50
12.00

4. $\frac{1}{4}$ of 84 = _____

5. $\frac{3}{10}$ of 105 = _____

6. $\frac{9}{10}$ of 56 = _____

7. $\frac{1}{2}$ of 87 = _____

8. $\frac{3}{5}$ of 204 = _____

9. $\frac{1}{5}$ of 94 = _____

10. $\frac{3}{20}$ of 66 = _____

11. $\frac{7}{20}$ of 52 = _____

12. $\frac{7}{10}$ of 48 = _____

Directions: Some fractions need to be divided to three or more places. Round the answers to two places.

13. $\frac{5}{8}$ of 64 = _____

14. $\frac{7}{8}$ of 88 = _____

15. $\frac{1}{8}$ of 14 = _____

Working with Fractions, Decimals, and Percents

Directions: For problems 1–5, write the fraction as a decimal. For problems 6–10, write the decimal as a fraction. For problems 11–15, write the decimal as a fraction in lowest terms.

1. $\frac{7}{10}$ = _____

2. $\frac{2}{5}$ = _____

3. $\frac{3}{4}$ = _____

4. $\frac{3}{20}$ = _____

5. $1\frac{3}{4}$ = _____

6. 0.26 = _____

7. 0.03 = _____

8. 0.2 = _____

9. 0.78 = _____

10. 0.825 = _____

11. 0.05 = _____

12. 0.02 = _____

13. 0.125 = _____

14. 0.04 = _____

15. 6.9 = _____

Directions: Write each as a decimal and a percent.

	decimal	percent
16. six hundredths	_____	_____
17. seventy hundredths	_____	_____
18. 63 per hundred	_____	_____
19. 3 out of 100	_____	_____
20. thirty-one hundredths	_____	_____

Directions: Complete the table.

	percent	fraction	decimal
21.	25%		
22.	2%		
23.	0.5%		
24.	33%		
25.	40%		

Calculating Fractions, Decimals, and Percents

Math

Directions: Some states require that out-of-state businesses pay a shipping tax to send goods to state residents. Refer to this table to do the problems below. (Note: The shipping rates do not reflect the actual current rates.)

Some States' Shipping Taxes

State	Abbr.	Tax
Alabama	AL	8.00%
Maryland	MD	5.75%
Georgia	GA	4.00%
Illinois	IL	2.00%
Indiana	IN	5.00%
Kentucky	KY	6.00%
Missouri	MO	5.725%

1. Miguel lives in Maryland and purchased a sweater for $39.99 from a catalog. Add the shipping tax. What's the total cost of the sweater? _____
2. Mr. and Mrs. Wong paid a total of $200.00 for an entertainment center for their home in Chicago, Illinois. The salesperson said that a 2% shipping tax was already added to the final price. What was the price of the entertainment center before the tax was added? _____
3. Stuart lives in Alabama and recently joined a book club that will send a book to him every month. The books are $15.00 each. The book club billing will include the shipping tax. What is the total amount that Stuart will have to pay for each book? _____
4. The Middlebury High School band in Indiana is going to sell holiday ornaments to raise money for uniforms. Each ornament will cost $5.00. How much is the shipping price per ornament? _____
5. The Williams family live in Lexington, Kentucky. They recently purchased a computer for $1,295.00. What is the total price for the computer after the shipping tax was added? _____

Directions: Complete the table below.

	Fraction	Decimal	Percent
1.	$\frac{1}{10}$		
2.		.25	
3.			45%
4.			15%
5.	$\frac{4}{5}$		
6.	$\frac{5}{6}$		
7.		.77	
8.	$\frac{1}{20}$		
9.		.222	
10.			40%

Range, Mean, Median, and Mode

Tom picked these five numbers: 92, 36, 40, 52, 40. He knew that the difference between the greatest number and the least number is called the range.

> Example: The range between 92 and 36 is
> $92 - 36 = 56$

Tom knew that he had five numbers and their sum was equal to 260. If he divided the sum by the total numbers he had, he could find the mean.

> Example: $\dfrac{36 + 40 + 52 + 40 + 92 =}{5} \quad \dfrac{260}{5} = 52$

When Tom looked at the numbers after he listed them in order from least to greatest, he was able to find the median. The median is the number in the middle of the sequence (or the mean of the two middle numbers if there are an even number of items in the sequence).

> Example: 36   40   (40)   52   92

The mode is the number that appears most often.

> Example: 36   (40)   52   (40)   92

> The number 40 appears twice, so it is the mode.

Directions: Find the range, mean, median and mode for each set of numbers.

1. 25, 73, 12, 25, 35

   A. Order: ____ ____ ____ ____ ____

   B. Range: ____ – ____ = ____

   C. Mean: $\dfrac{\_\_\_ + \_\_\_ + \_\_\_ + \_\_\_ + \_\_\_}{5} = \dfrac{\_\_\_}{5} = \_\_\_$

   D. Median: _____

   E. Mode: _____

2. 100, 23, 49, 88, 30, 23, 51

   A. Order: ____ ____ ____ ____ ____ ____ ____

   B. Range: _____

   C. Mean: _____

   D. Median: _____

   E. Mode: _____

Range, Mean, Median, and Mode *(cont.)*

3. 18, 36, 24, 18

   A. Order: _____

   B. Range: _____

   C. Mean: _____

   D. Median: _____

   E. Mode: _____

4. 22, 70, 22, 84, 36, 42

   A. Order: _____

   B. Range: _____

   C. Mean: _____

   D. Median: _____

   E. Mode: _____

5. 170, 200, 305

   A. Order: _____

   B. Range: _____

   C. Mean: _____

   D. Median: _____

   E. Mode: _____

6. 45, 66, 89, 69, 77, 22, 66

   A. Order: _____

   B. Range: _____

   C. Mean: _____

   D. Median: _____

   E. Mode: _____

Working with Mode, Median, and Mean

It is important to recognize the **measures of central tendency** (*mode*, *median*, or *mean*), which is most representative of a set of data. Sometimes one of the measures is clearly the most useful. Sometimes two or three measures may be equally valuable.

- If all three numbers are identical or very close, you know the data is likely to be statistically valid.

> Daily high temperatures for a week: (79°, 80°, 81°, 78°, 79°, 82°, 77°)
> Mode: 79° Median: 79° Mean: 79° (79.4°, rounded off)

- A reading of 79° is clearly representative of this week's high temperatures.

Directions: Find the mode, median, and mean in each set of data. Indicate which measure or measures you think is most representative of the data.

1. Number of dots on selected ladybugs:

   (15, 0, 7, 9, 13, 2, 13, 15, 16, 13, 9, 13, 0)

   Mode: _____ Median: _____ Mean: _____

   Most representative measure: _____

   Reason: _____

2. Number of candy-coated chocolates in small bags:

   (22, 24, 25, 22, 21, 26, 23, 22, 23, 23, 25, 24)

   Mode: _____ Median: _____ Mean: _____

   Most representative measure: _____

   Reason: _____

3. Length of red worms (in centimeters):

   (10, 8, 6, 5, 12, 8, 7, 9, 11, 8, 6, 9, 10, 8, 8)

   Mode: _____ Median: _____ Mean: _____

   Most representative measure: _____

   Reason: _____

4. Number of drops of water that will fit on a penny:

   (21, 40, 46, 34, 56, 46, 99, 65, 48, 38, 69, 54, 50, 61)

   Mode: _____ Median: _____ Mean: _____

   Most representative measure: _____

   Reason: _____

5. Number of drops of water that will fit on a dime:

   (40, 38, 42, 16, 23, 28, 44, 25, 41, 23, 45, 30, 29, 27)

   Mode: _____ Median: _____ Mean: _____

   Most representative measure: _____

   Reason: _____

Outliers

Some sets of data include quantities that affect the mean so that the average seems not to represent the data correctly. These quantities, called **outliers**, usually are very different from the other quantities in the set. They can be much larger or smaller than most of the other numbers.

Look at Justin's reading grades.

When a teacher averages grades, she or he usually finds the mean.

mean grade: 95

> **Justin's Reading Grades**
>
> **vocabulary quizzes:** 98, 95, 96
>
> **comprehension tests:** 92, 90, 95
>
> **classwork:** 98, 95, 95, 96

Find Justin's other average grades.   **median grade:** 95   **mode grade:** 95

Grade Scale		
100 – 94		A
93 – 85		B
84 – 77		C
76 – 79		D
69 – 0		F

Justin has a high average at this point, as shown by the mean, median, and mode. But what if Justin does poorly on just one vocabulary quiz? Re-average Justin's grades, this time with an additional vocabulary quiz grade of 31.

mean grade: 89   **median grade:** 95   **mode grade:** 95

When the teacher averages Justin's grades, she or he will assign him a B even though he has earned an A on most of his class work. Justin's grades are better represented using the median and mode averages instead of the mean. In this set of data, 31 is an **outlier**.

Directions: Find the mean, median, and mode for each set of data below. Then, decide which number is the outlier for each set of data.

> **Average Number of Points Scored by the Byrd High School Cardinals Girls Basketball Team**
>
> | 64 | 62 | 78 | 64 | 70 |
> |---|---|---|---|---|
> | 65 | 66 | 64 | 72 | 63 |
> | 74 | 31 | 61 | 75 | 66 |

> **Average Number of Points Scored by the Byrd High School Cardinals Boys Basketball Team**
>
> | 73 | 78 | 80 | 76 | 74 |
> |---|---|---|---|---|
> | 74 | 48 | 80 | 78 | 74 |
> | 72 | 70 | 74 | 76 | 68 |

1. mean score _____

2. median score _____

3. mode score _____

4. outlier _____

5. mean score _____

6. median score _____

7. mode score _____

8. outlier _____

©Teacher Created Resources, Inc.   115   #3945 Mastering Sixth Grade Skills

Finding Median and Mode from Graphs

Directions: Use the graph as your source for data. Then, find the median and mode for each set of data.

Fourth- and fifth-graders read books as part of their reading program. The number of books each class reads in one week was totaled and graphed below.

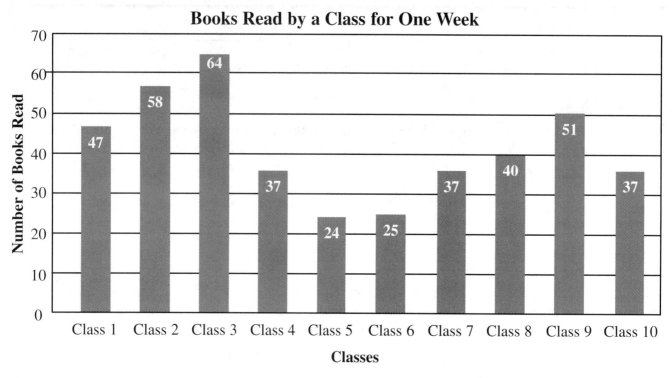

Books Read by a Class for One Week

1. What is the mode number of books read by the fourth- and fifth- grade classes? _____

2. What is the median number of books read by the fourth- and fifth- grade classes? _____

For each book read, students took a test. The results of their tests are seen below as percentages.

Hint: To find the number of tests for each score, multiply the number of tests taken by the percentage.

Scored 100: 30%

Scored 80: 30%

Scored 60: 20%

Scored 40: 10%

Scored 20: 5%

Scored 0: 5%

3. What percentage of students score 80 or 100? _____

4. Based on the percentages, if 100 tests were taken, how many students would score 60? _____

5. Based on the percentages, if 500 tests were taken, how many students would score 80 or 100? _____

6. What is the median score? _____

7. What is the mode score? _____

Math

Calculating Median and Mode with Stem-and-Leaf Plots

Stem-and-Leaf Plot
A stem-and-leaf plot may help you organize large sets of data to easily find the median and mode. To make a stem-and-leaf graph, list digits in the tens and higher place values in the stem. List the digits in the ones place value for each data in the leaf. For the number 72, the 7 is the stem and the 2 is the leaf. For the number 690, the 69 is the stem and the 0 is the leaf.

Directions: Use the information above to answer the questions below.

Rhonda's Garden Plan

beans – 12	celery – 16
carrots – 20	cherry tomatoes – 18
lettuce – 18	brussels sprouts – 8
tomatoes – 16	potatoes – 20
cucumbers – 20	leeks – 16
radishes – 30	onions – 20
peas – 20	watermelon – 30

Rhonda is planning her garden. She decides on the numbers of each vegetable shown on the chart. Create a stem-and-leaf plot on another sheet of paper to find the median and mode number of vegetables she plants.

1. Median number of plants _____

2. Mode number of plants _____

A new off-Broadway show runs for two weeks, for a total of 20 performances. The capacity of the theater is 870 patrons. Create a stem-and-leaf plot on another sheet of paper to determine the median and mode number of attendees.

Off-Broadway Show Attendance

performance #	1	2	3	4	5	6	7	8	9	10	11	12	13	14	15	16	17	18	19	20
attendance	870	870	851	845	863	831	846	828	799	856	789	779	800	842	863	865	789	850	870	870

3. During how many performances was the theater filled to capacity? _____

4. What was the median number of attendees? _____

5. What was the mode number of attendees? _____

6. If you were the producer of this play, would you extend its performance? Why or why not?

_____

_____

Look at these stem-and-leaf plots. What is the median? What is the mode?

Stem	Leaf
0	3 4 4 8
1	6 7 7 9
2	0 1 5 8 8
3	2 2 2 2 6
4	3 7

7. Median _____

8. Mode _____

Stem	Leaf
12	0 1 6 7
13	3 4 5 7
14	0 1 1 6

9. Median _____

10. Mode _____

Tables and Plots

This line plot illustrates a survey of hours spent during one week on computer-generated games by 29 sixth-grade students in one classroom. Study the plot and answer the questions below.

```
         X
         X                             X
Number   X             X               X
of       X X           X               X
Students X X X         X         X  X X X
         X X X X   X X   X   X   X X   X
        ─────────────────────────────────
         0         5         10        15
```

Hours Spent Weekly

Note: Each X represents one student.

1. How many students did not spend any time playing computer games?
   _____

2. How many students spent 3 hours a week playing computer games?
   _____

3. How many students spent 5 hours a week playing computer games?
   _____

4. How many students spent 15 hours a week playing computer games?
   _____

5. How many students spent 10 hours a week playing computer games?
   _____

6. How many students in the class spent 10 hours or more a week on games? _____

7. How many students in the class spent less than 10 hours a week on games? _____

8. How many students spent 13 hours a week on games? _____

This frequency table illustrates a survey of pets owned by sixth-grade students in one classroom. Study the table, complete the frequency totals, and answer the questions below.

Survey of Pets Owned by Sixth Grade Students

Pets	Tally	Frequency
Cat	////////	8
Dog	////////////	
Snake	//	
Bird	///	
Mouse	///	
Hamster	////	
Fish	///////	
Other	///	

9. How many more dogs are owned than cats?
   _____

10. What is the most frequently-owned pet?
    _____

11. What is the least frequently-owned pet?
    _____

12. How many more cats are owned than mice?
    _____

13. What is the total number of pets owned by these students? _____

14. How many four-legged animals are owned (that aren't in the 'other' category)? _____

Single Bar Graphs

This single bar graph shows the number of electoral votes for each of the 10 most-populated states. The states are labeled in blocks along the horizontal axis. The number of electoral votes is indicated on the vertical axis. There are 538 electoral votes distributed among the 50 states and the District of Columbia. They are elected by the people in each state to officially vote for the president of the United States. It takes 270 electoral votes to win an election.

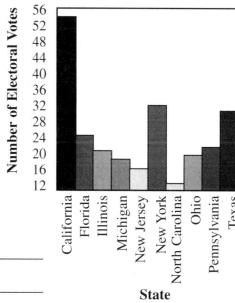

Directions: Use the information on the graph to answer these questions.

1. How many electoral votes does California have? _____

2. How many electoral votes does Texas have? _____

3. What is the interval between numbers on the scale? _____

4. How many electoral votes does New Jersey have? _____

5. What is the difference in the number of votes between Michigan and Illinois?

   _____

6. Which state has exactly one more electoral vote than Texas? _____

7. What is the total number of electoral votes of the 10 most-populated states?

   _____

8. How many electoral votes are distributed among the remaining 40 states and the District of Columbia? _____

9. Why would a candidate spend more time campaigning in California than in North Carolina? _____

10. How many more votes in addition to these 10 states would be needed to win a presidential election? _____

11. Which two pairs of states have the same number of electoral votes as California?

    _____

12. Why did the intervals start with 12 votes? _____

13. What could be misleading about this graph? _____

Double Bar Graphs

This double bar graph illustrates a survey of the relative popularity of soccer and football as participant sports for boys in the third through the eighth grades.

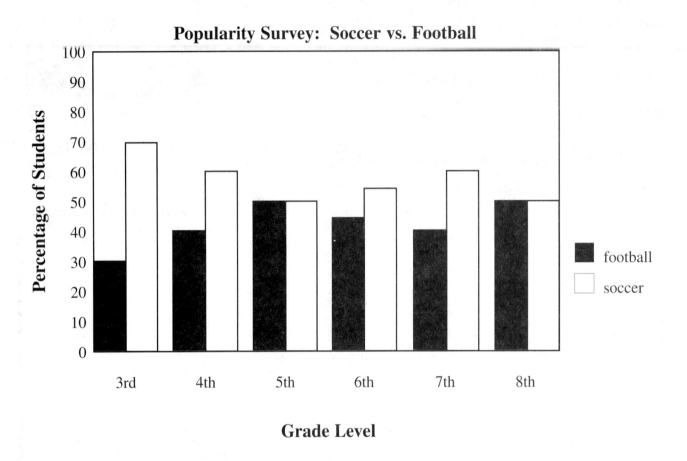

1. What percentage of third-grade boys preferred to play football? _____

2. In which two grades do boys like to play soccer and football equally well? _____

3. What percentage of boys in the fourth grade prefer soccer? _____

4. Is there any grade in which more boys prefer football? _____

5. What percentage of boys prefer football in the sixth grade? _____

6. What percentage of boys prefer football in the seventh grade? _____

Stem and Leaf Plot

Directions: Arrange the test scores below in a stem and leaf plot from least to greatest. After organizing all of the data in the plot, count the number of leaves per stem. Then look below the chart to find the letter which corresponds to the number of leaves. Find the answer to the following question by writing the correct letter on the appropriate line.

Question: Where do Australian children go to play? _____

Test Scores: 96, 81, 79, 79, 100, 100, 93, 87, 62, 67, 91, 80, 91, 83, 47, 98, 93, 88, 88, 70, 75, 63, 63, 100, 57, 58, 96, 74

Stems	Leaves

Number of Leaves	Letter

Letters

A=6	D=8	G=11	K=3	U=2
B=5	E=9	H=12	O=1	T=4
C=7	F=10	I=13		

Organizing Data

Directions: Arrange the following data (test scores) in the Frequency Table. Notice the frequency for each number, and find its corresponding letter in the Letter Bin. Write the letters in the letter column to find the first part of the answer to the riddle.

Question: Who did the vampire play with when he was younger? _____

Frequency Table			
Scores	**Tally**	**Frequency**	**Letter**
65			
68			
69			
78			
79			
85			
87			
88			
89			
90			
95			
97			
98			

Test Scores: 85, 85, 85, 85, 85, 79, 79, 79, 79, 87, 90, 90, 78, 78, 68, 69, 69, 85, 69, 68, 98, 90, 69, 68, 78, 68, 87, 97, 79, 69, 98, 90, 89, 89, 89, 97, 97, 68, 78, 78, 85, 69, 85, 65, 68, 68, 69, 87, 90, 85, 90, 88, 69, 88, 69, 78, 87, 97, 78, 90, 78, 90, 90, 79, 85, 97, 69, 90

Letter Bin

T = 1	**S** = 2
N = 3	**L** = 4
K = 5	**I** = 6
H = 7	**G** = 8
E = 10	**R** = 10
C = 0	

Using the same data, complete the chart below. Circle the letter that each number group reaches to find the last word of the riddle.

	1	2	3	4	5	6	7	8	9	10	11	12	13	14	15	16	17	18	19	20
60–69			X				J			G				P				D		
70–79		W			A			E					O	C		B				
80–89				Q				Z			F		Y					O		
90–99	M	N				H			L					K	R					

Creating Graphs

1. Create a line graph that shows how many Grand Slam sneakers were sold from week to week.

   - Week 1: 23 pairs
   - Week 2: 19 pairs
   - Week 3: 15 pairs
   - Week 4: 23 pairs

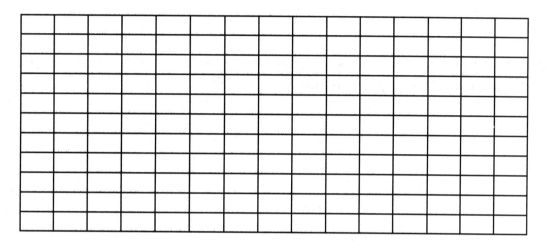

2. On a Monday each of 80 people purchased one item in the store. Create a circle graph that shows the amount of each item that was sold.

   - T-shirts: 20 sold
   - Sneakers: 40 sold
   - Athletic Posters: 10 sold
   - Other Athletic Equipment: 10 sold

Type of Shoe	Sold at Regular Price	Sold at Discount Pirce
Grand Slam	25 pairs	25 pairs
Metro	15 pairs	10 pairs
Neo Running Shoes	20 pairs	25 pairs

3. Use this information to create a double bar graph inside of the box below. Use a ruler.

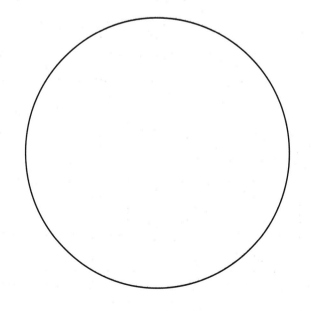

Math

Identifying Coordinate Points

Directions: Write the coordinates for each point.

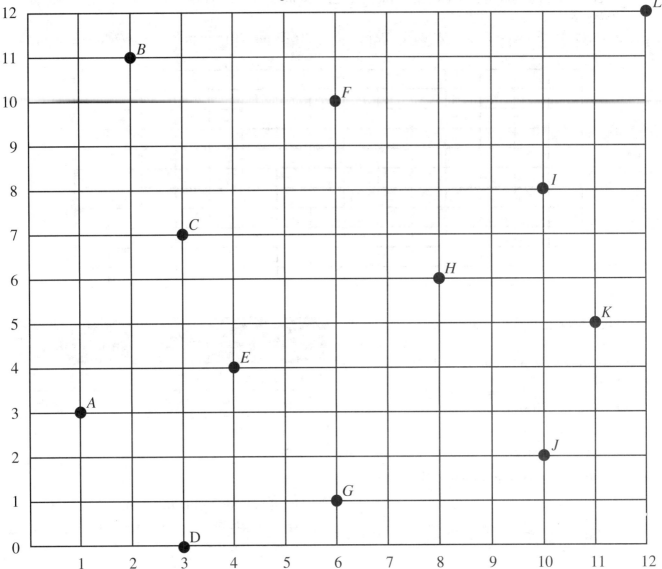

1. $K =$ _____   4. $L =$ _____   7. $H =$ _____   10. $C =$ _____

2. $D =$ _____   5. $E =$ _____   8. $B =$ _____   11. $A =$ _____

3. $G =$ _____   6. $I =$ _____   9. $F =$ _____   12. $J =$ _____

Cartesian Coordinates

How Do You Make a Hot Dog Stand?

The answer to this riddle is written in a special code at the bottom of this page. Each pair of numbers stands for a point on the graph. Write the letter shown at the point near the intersection of each pair of numbers. Read numbers across and then up. The letters will spell out the answer to the riddle.

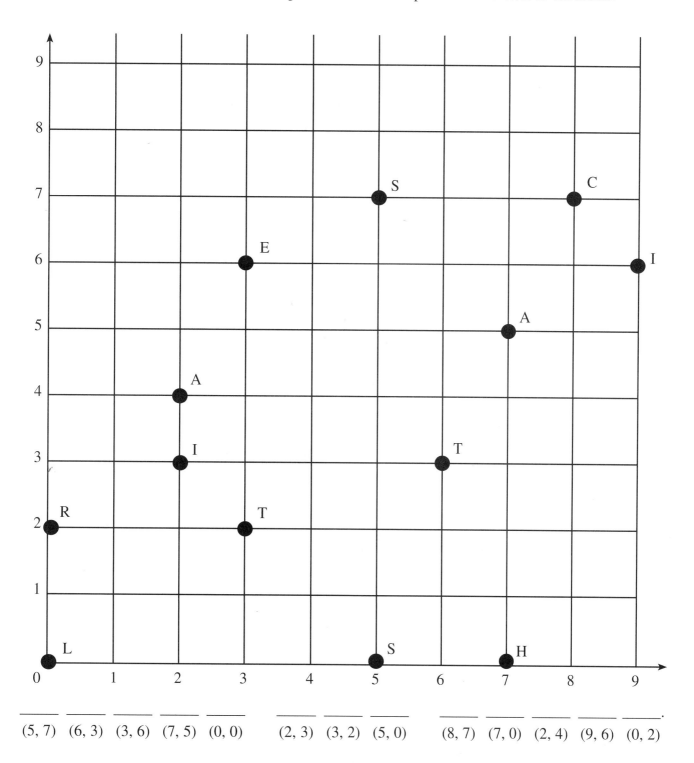

___ ___ ___ ___ ___   ___ ___ ___   ___ ___ ___ ___ ___ .
(5, 7) (6, 3) (3, 6) (7, 5) (0, 0)   (2, 3) (3, 2) (5, 0)   (8, 7) (7, 0) (2, 4) (9, 6) (0, 2)

Coordinates (Positive and Negative)

Coordinates must always be plotted using the *x* axis for the first number in a number pair and the *y* axis for the second number of each pair. (*Note:* Always go across before you go up or down.)

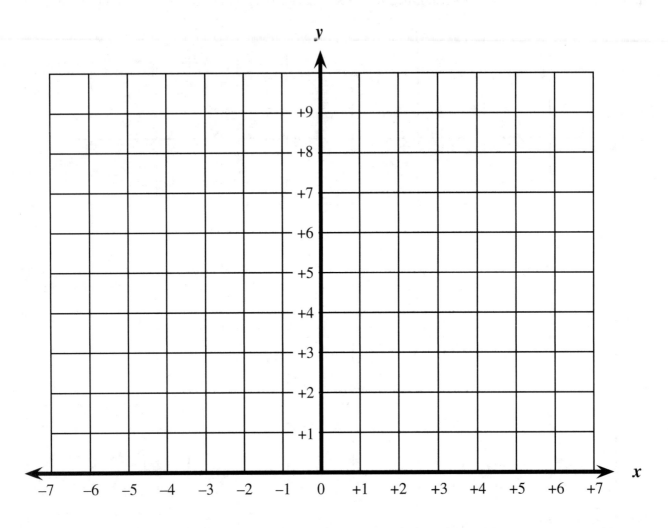

Directions: Graph these coordinate number pairs. Connect each dot with a ruler as you proceed. (**Note:** You will go over some line segments more than once.)

First Shape

      A. (+1, +3)   B. (+6, +3)   C. (+6, +8)   D. (+1, +8)   E. (+1, +3)

      F. (+6, +8)   G. (+1, +8)   H. (+6, +3)

Second Shape

      I. (−2, +2)   J. (−6, +2)   K. (−7, +5)   L. (−6, +8)   M. (−2, +8)

      N. (−1, +5)   O. (−2, +2)   P. (−6, +8)   Q. (−2, +8)   R. (−6, +2)

      S. (−7, +5)   T. (−1, +5)   U. (−4, +5)   V. (−4, +8)   W. (−4, +2)

Working with Four Quadrants

Coordinates must always be plotted using the *x* axis for the first number in a number pair and the *y* axis for the second number of each pair. (*Note:* Always go across before you go up or down.)

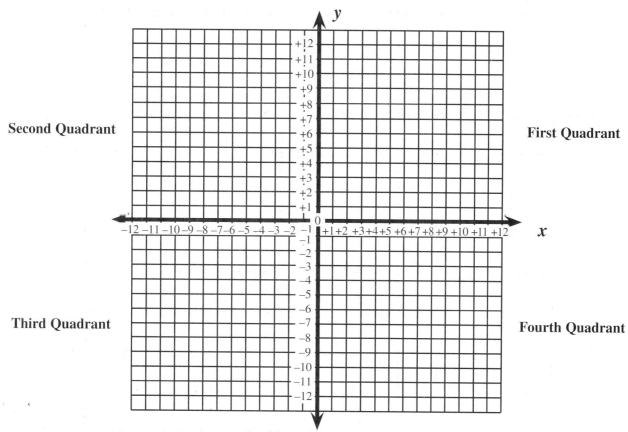

Directions: Graph these coordinate number pairs in each quadrant. Connect each dot within a quadrant with a ruler as you proceed. (Note: You will go over some line segments more than once.)

First Quadrant

A. (+9, +2)	B. (+9, +9)	C. (+2, +9)	D. (+2, +2)	E. (+3, +2)
F. (+8, +2)	G. (+8, +8)	H. (+3, +8)	I. (+3, +2)	J. (+9, +9)
K. (+2, +9)	L. (+8, +2)	M. (+9, +2)		

Second Quadrant

A. (−3, +1)	B. (−5, +4)	C. (−3, +7)	D. (−5, +10)	E. (−8, +10)
F. (−10, +7)	G. (−3, +7)	H. (−10, +7)	I. (−8, +4)	J. (−5, +4)
K. (−8, +4)	L. (−10, +1)	M. (−3, +1)		

Third Quadrant

A. (−4, −2)	B. (−4, −6)	C. (−3, −8)	D. (−3, −10)	E. (−9, −10)
F. (−9, −8)	G. (−8, −6)	H. (−8, −2)	I. (−4, −2)	J. (−2, −10)
K. (−10, −10)	L. (−8, −2)			

Fourth Quadrant

A. (+1, −2)	B. (+9, −2)	C. (+10, −11)	D. (+7, −8)	E. (+5, −11)
F. (+3, −8)	G. (0, −11)	H. (+1, −2)	I. (+5, −8)	J. (+9, −2)
K. (+5, −2)	L. (+1, −8)	M. (+9, −8)	N. (+5, −2)	O. (+3, −5)
P. (+7, −5)				

Coordinate Pairs

Use this grid to help you answer the questions on page 129.

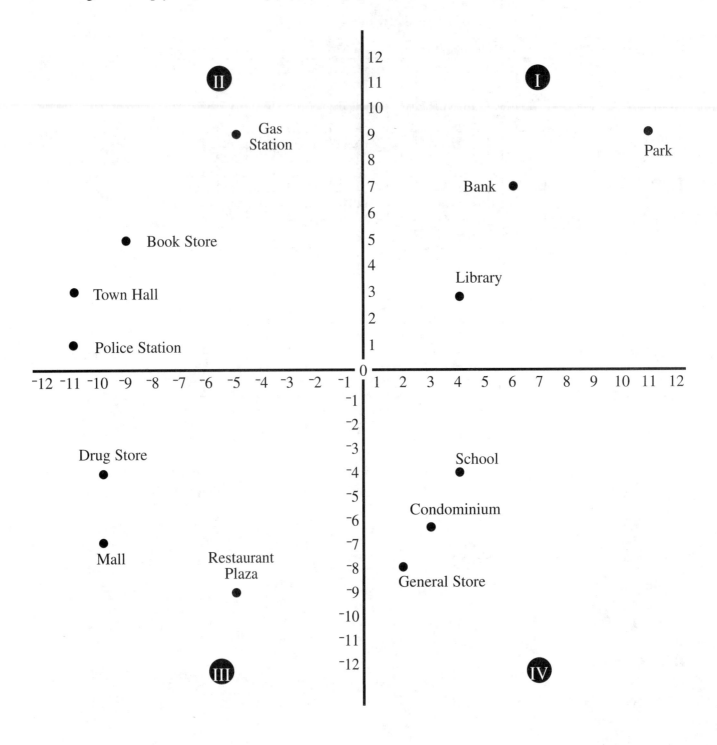

Coordinate Pairs *(cont.)*

Directions
- Study the grid shown on page 128.
- Notice where landmarks such as the school and library are located.
- Notice which numbers are positive and which are negative.
- Note how the four quadrants are labeled: I, II, III, and IV.
- Remember: Always go across before going up or down.
- Use the information to answer these word problems.

1. What building is located at coordinates (4, 3)?_____

2. What city building is located at coordinates ($^-$11, 3)? _____

3. Which business is located at ($^-$5, 9)?_____

4. What are the coordinates of the police station?_____

5. What are the coordinates of the school? _____

6. What are the coordinates of the restaurant plaza?_____

7. What public area is located at coordinates (11, 9)? _____

8. What are the coordinates of the mall?_____

9. What are the coordinates of the book store? _____

10. What is located at coordinates (2, $^-$8)? _____

11. What is located at coordinates ($^-$10, $^-$4)?_____

12. Which quadrant has all negative coordinates?_____

13. Which quadrant has only positive coordinates? _____

14. Which quadrant always begins with a negative number and concludes with a positive number?

_____

Graphing Coordinate Pairs

Directions: Graph each of the points on the graph paper on page 131. Connect the points as you go. You should have a picture when you are finished.

1. (-5.5, 17)	27. (-2, 8)	53. (0, -1)	79. (15, -20.5)
2. (-5, 16)	28. (-2, 6)	54. (5.5, -7.5)	80. (16, -21)
3. (-4.5, 15.5)	29. (-1.5, 5)	55. (5.5, -4.5)	81. (14.5, -19)
4. (-6, 12)	30. (-1, 3.5)	56. (5.5, -7.5)	82. (15, -17)
5. (-9, 9)	31. (-3, 3)	57. (6, -10)	83. (15, -14.5)
6. (-8.5, 8.5)	32. (-7, 3.5)	58. (7, -12)	84. (15.5, -12)
7. (-8, 8)	33. (-11, 0)	59. (1, -16)	85. (15.5, -9)
8. (-7, 8.5)	34. (-11, -3)	60. (0, -18.5)	86. (15, -7)
9. (-6.5, 8.5)	35. (-9, -3)	61. (1, -19)	87. (14, -5)
10. (-7, 8.5)	36. (-9, -2)	62. (2, -19)	88. (12, -3)
11. (-8, 8)	37. (-11, -2)	63. (3, -18.5)	89. (10, 0)
12. (-7, 7)	38. (-9, -2)	64. (3.5, -17.5)	90. (9, 2)
13. (-6, 7.5)	39. (-9, -1)	65. (3, -17)	91. (8, 4)
14. (-6, 8)	40. (-7.5, 0)	66. (9, -15)	92. (7.5, 6)
15. (-5, 8.5)	41. (-6, 2)	67. (11, -12)	93. (7, 8.5)
16. (-4, 9)	42. (-7.5, 0)	68. (13.5, -8)	94. (9.5, 7)
17. (-3, 10)	43. (-9, -2)	69. (13.5, -10)	95. (8, 10.5)
18. (-4, 10)	44. (-8, -5)	70. (13, -11)	96. (9, 10.5)
19. (-4.5, 10.5)	45. (-6, -6)	71. (12.5, -12)	97. (7, 15)
20. (-4, 10)	46. (-5.5, -5)	72. (12, -13)	98. (9, 16)
21. (-3, 10)	47. (-5.5, -4)	73. (11.5, -14)	99. (3, 18)
22. (-2, 10.5)	48. (-6.5, -3)	74. (11, -16)	100. (4, 20)
23. (-1.5, 12)	49. (-7, -3)	75. (11, -20)	101. (0, 18)
24. (-2, 10.5)	50. (-4, 0)	76. (13, -21)	102. (-4, 16)
25. (-3, 10)	51. (2, 0)	77. (13, -20.5)	103. (-5.5, 17)
26. (-2, 9)	52. (0, 0)	78. (15, -21)	

Graphing Coordinate Pairs *(cont.)*

Graph Paper

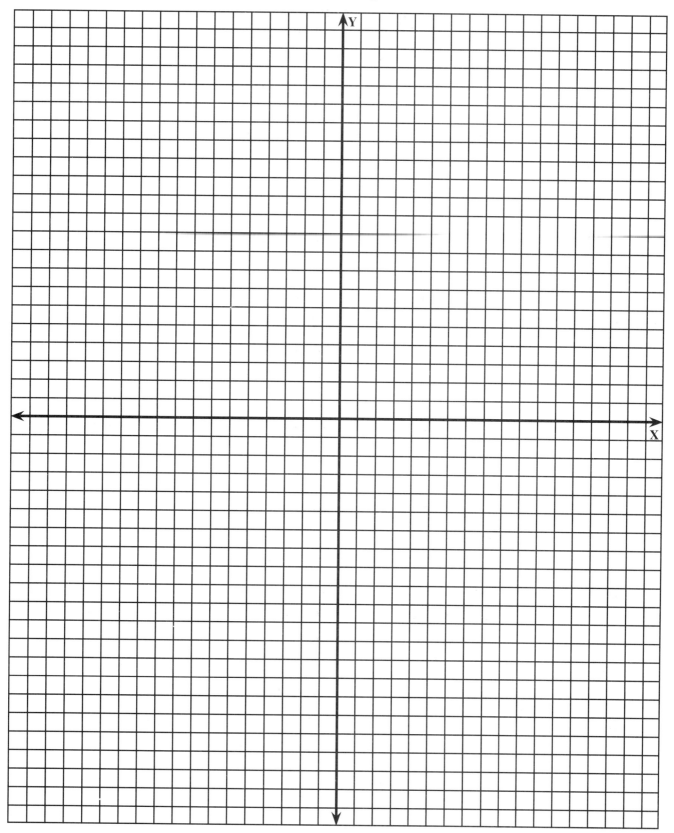

Converting Measurements

> **Equivalents**
> 12 inches = 1 foot
> 36 inches = 1 yard
> 3 feet = 1 yard

Directions: Write the number of inches.

1. 7 feet = _____ inches

2. 5 feet = _____ inches

3. 2 feet = _____ inches

4. 10 feet = _____ inches

5. 5 1/2 feet = _____ inches

6. 2 1/4 feet = _____ inches

7. 6 1/2 feet = _____ inches

8. 5 2/3 feet = _____ inches

Directions: Write the number of feet.

9. 96 inches = _____ feet

10. 12 inches = _____ foot

11. 24 inches = _____ feet

12. 48 inches = _____ feet

13. 68 inches = _____ feet

14. 6 inches = _____ foot

15. 30 inches = _____ feet

16. 54 inches = _____ feet

Directions: Write the number of yards.

17. 24 feet = _____ yards

18. 6 feet = _____ yards

19. 12 feet = _____ yards

20. 7 feet = _____ yards

21. 72 inches = _____ yards

22. 36 inches = _____ yard

Converting Fluid Ounces and Cups

Customary Units	
8 fluid ounces = 1 cup	4 cups = 1 quart
16 fluid ounces = 1 pint	128 fluid ounces = 1 gallon
2 cups = 1 pint	4 quarts = 1 gallon
32 fluid ounces = 1 quart	8 pints = 1 gallon
2 pints = 1 quart	

Directions: Use the information above to help you do these problems.

1. 1 cup = _____ fluid ounces

2. 2 cups = _____ fluid ounces

3. 4 cups = _____ fluid ounces

4. 6 cups = _____ fluid ounces

5. 8 cups = _____ fluid ounces

6. 9 cups = _____ fluid ounces

7. 1 quart = _____ fluid ounces

8. 2 quarts = _____ fluid ounces

9. 5 quarts = _____ fluid ounces

10. 3 quarts = _____ fluid ounces

11. How many quarts will a 1-gallon container hold? _____

12. How many quarts are equal to 4 gallons? _____

13. How many fluid ounces are in 1 gallon? _____

14. How many quarts are in a 15-gallon tank of gas? _____

15. How many fluid ounces are in a 15-gallon tank of gasoline? _____

16. 1 pint = _____ fluid ounces

17. 3 pints = _____ fluid ounces

18. 7 pints = _____ fluid ounces

19. 5 gallons = _____ pints

20. 11 gallons = _____ cups

21. 15 gallons = _____ pints

22. 10 gallons = _____ fluid ounces

23. 17 pints = _____ cups

Metric Measurement

Metric Measurement Tips:

• A *meter* (m) is about the length from your fingertips to the end of your opposite shoulder if your arms are extended outward from your shoulder.

• A *centimeter* (cm) is about the distance across the nail of your pinky.

• A *millimeter* (mm) is about the thickness of a dime.

• A *kilometer* (km) is the distance a person can walk in about 10–12 minutes.

Circle the best estimate.

1. length of a workbook   a. 35 m   b. 35 mm   c. 35 cm   d. 2 km

2. length of a bus   a. 2 km   b. 12 m   c. 50 cm   d. 6 ml

3. length of a new pencil   a. 20 kg   b. 20 mm   c. 20 cm   d. 20 m

4. distance on plane from NY to CA   a. km   b. kg   c. m   d. L

5. width of your hand   a. 12 cm   b. 1.2 cm   c. 120 m   d. 12 mm

Choose the most appropriate measurement: mm, cm, m, km

6. height of a tree   _____

7. diameter of Mars   _____

8. length of a small turtle   _____

9. width of a paper clip   _____

10. diameter of a penny   _____

11. height of a vase   _____

12. perimeter of a room   _____

13. Nile River   _____

Match the best estimate for each picture below. Remember that the width of your pinky is 1 cm.

14. lips   A. 4.5 cm

15. fish   B. 40 mm

                                C. 7 cm

16. pencil

Converting Metric Measurements

10 mm = 1 cm	1 L = 1000 mL
100 cm = 1 m	1 kg = 1000 g
1000 mm = 1 m	1 kL = 1000 L
1000 m = 1 km	1 g = 1000 mg

Complete the conversions.

1. 10 mm = _____ cm
2. 50 cm = _____ mm
3. 30 mm = _____ cm
4. 10 cm = _____ mm
5. 50 mm = _____ cm
6. 90 cm = _____ mm
7. 65 mm = _____ cm
8. 33 cm = _____ mm
9. 100 cm = _____ m
10. 1,000 m = _____ km
11. 600 cm = _____ m
12. 5,000 m = _____ km
13. 800 cm = _____ m
14. 7,000 m = _____ km
15. 753 cm = _____ m
16. 8,350 m = _____ km
17. 4 m = _____ cm
18. 3 km = _____ m
19. 7 m = _____ cm
20. 6 km = _____ m
21. 9 m = _____ cm
22. 10 km = _____ m
23. 6.8 m = _____ cm
24. 15.5 km = _____ m

Complete the equations.

25. 4 mL = _____ L
26. 7 mm = _____ m
27. 650 mm = _____ cm
28. 70 mm = _____ m
29. 650 mm = _____ m
30. 4 mL = _____ L
31. 650 cm = _____ m
32. 4 L = _____ mL
33. 4 g = _____ kg
34. 7.5 L = _____ mL
35. 4 kg = _____ g
36. 6,500 L = _____ kL
37. 225 g = _____ kg
38. 3.5 kL = _____ L
39. 225 kg = _____ g
40. 57 g = _____ kg

Perimeter of Polygons

> ### Reminder
> The perimeter of a parallelogram is computed by adding the length plus the width and multiplying the sum times two.
>
> **P = 2 x (l + w)**

Directions: Compute the perimeter of these shapes

1.

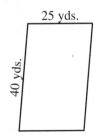

25 yds.

40 yds.

_____

2.

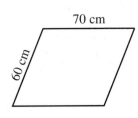

70 cm

60 cm

_____

3.

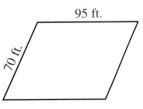

95 ft.

70 ft.

_____

4.

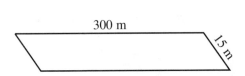

300 m

15 m

_____

5.

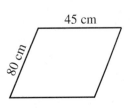

45 cm

80 cm

_____

6.

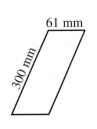

61 mm

300 mm

_____

7.

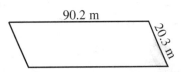

90.2 m

20.3 m

_____

8.

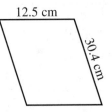

12.5 cm

30.4 cm

_____

136

Perimeter of Other Polygons

Directions: Compute the perimeter of each polygon.

1. 16 m

_____

2. 25 cm

_____

3. 31 yds.

_____

4. 35 mm

_____

5. 45 in.

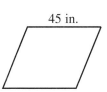

_____

6. 25 mm

_____

7.

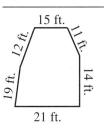

15 ft.   12 ft.   11 ft.   19 ft.   14 ft.   21 ft.   15 ft.

_____

8.

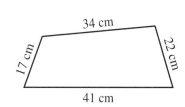

34 cm   17 cm   22 cm   41 cm

_____

9.

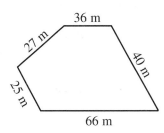

36 m   27 m   40 m   25 m   66 m

_____

10.

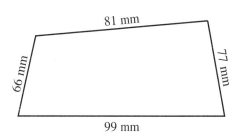

81 mm   66 mm   77 mm   99 mm

_____

Computing Circumference

> ## Reminder
> - The circumference is the distance around a circle.
> - pi = 3.14
> - The circumference is computed by multiplying 3.14 times the diameter.
>   **C = πd** (pi times the diameter)

Directions: Compute the circumference of each circle.

1.

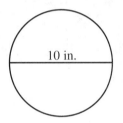

C = _____

2.

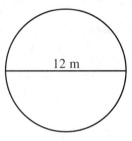

C = _____

3.

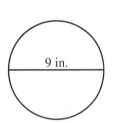

C = _____

4.

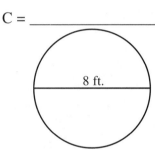

C = _____

5.

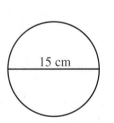

C = _____

6.

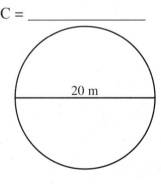

C = _____

7.

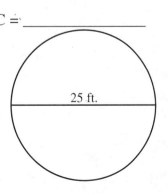

C = _____

8.

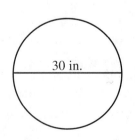

C = _____

Area of Rectangles and Squares

This rectangular figure is 8 meters long and 3 meters wide.

Area = length x width

A = 8 m x 3 m = 24 m^2

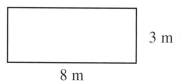

3 m

8 m

Directions: Use the information in the example above to compute the area for the problems below. Remember, answers must be expressed in square units.

1. l = 60 meters   A = _____

    w = 40 meters

40 m

60 m

2. l = 60 feet   A = _____

    w = 50 feet   50 ft.

60 ft.

3. s = 40 yards   A = _____

40 yds.

4. l = 70 centimeters   A = _____

    w = 40 centimeters

70 cm

40 cm

5. l = 60 millimeters   A = _____

    w = 30 millimeters

60 mm

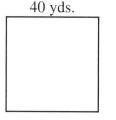

30 mm

6. l = 90 millimeters   A = _____

    w = 70 millimeters

90 mm

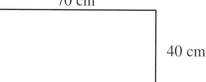

70 mm

7. A classroom is 7 meters long and 6 meters wide. What is the area? _____

8. A square house is 70 feet long on each side. What is the area of the house? _____

9. A warehouse is 92 feet long and 65 feet wide. What is the area? _____

10. A model of a city is 47 inches long and 32 inches wide. What is the area of the model? _____

Area of Parallelograms

Reminder

The area of a parallelogram is computed by multiplying the base times the height or A = b x h and then writing the total in square units.

Directions: Compute the area of each rectangle.

1.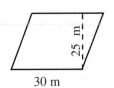
   30 m

   _____ m^2

2.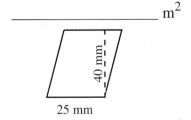
   25 mm

   _____ mm^2

3.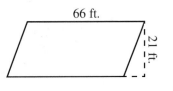
   66 ft.

   _____ ft.^{2}

4.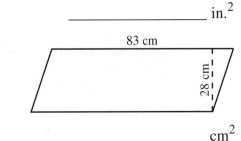
   123 in.

   _____ in.^{2}

5. 83 cm
   28 cm

   _____ cm^2

6. 9 m
   3.5 m

   _____ m^2

7. b − 56 mm
   h = 41 mm
   A = _____

8. b = 3.1 ft.
   h = 8 ft.
   A = _____

9. b = 300 in.
   h = 48 in.
   A = _____

10. b = 1.9 m
    h = 20 m
    A = _____

11. b = 121 mm
    h = 40 mm
    A = _____

12. b = 7.5 in.
    h = 3.1 in.
    A = _____

13. b = 6.2 m
    h = 3.2 m
    A = _____

14. b = 900 cm
    h = 68 cm
    A = _____

Area of Triangles

Reminder

- The area of a triangle is one-half the area of a parallelogram or a rectangle.
- To compute the area of a triangle, multiply the base times the height and divide by 2 or multiply 1/2 the base times the height or **A = 1/2 (b x h)** or **A = (b x h) ÷ 2**

Directions: Compute the area of each triangle.

1.

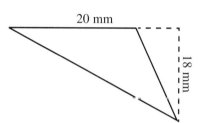

20 mm

18 mm

_____ mm²

2.

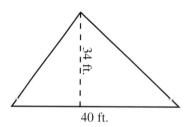

34 ft.

40 ft.

_____ ft.²

3.

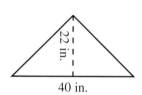

22 in.

40 in.

_____ in.²

4.

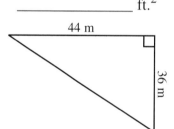

44 m

36 m

_____ m²

5.

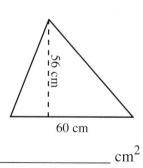

56 cm

60 cm

_____ cm²

6.

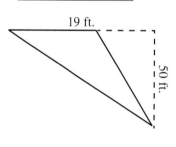

19 ft.

50 ft.

_____ ft.²

7.

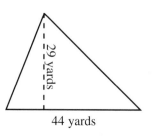

29 yards

44 yards

_____ yards²

8.

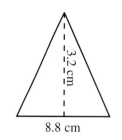

3.2 cm

8.8 cm

_____ cm²

Area of a Circle

<table>
<tr><td>

Reminder

- The area of a circle is computed by multiplying the radius times itself and that answer by 3.14.
- **A = πr²** (pi times the radius squared) (**Remember**, pi = 3.14)

</td></tr>
</table>

Directions: Compute the area of each circle.

1.

A = _____ in.²

2.

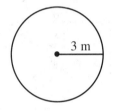

A = _____ m²

3.

A = _____ yards²

4.

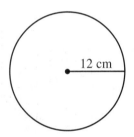

A = _____ cm²

5.

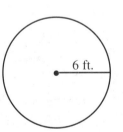

A = _____ ft.²

6.

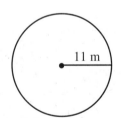

A = _____ m²

7.

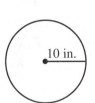

A = _____ in.²

8.

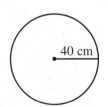

A = _____ cm²

Volume of a Rectangular Prism

Reminder

The volume of a rectangular prism is computed by multiplying the length times the width times the height of the prism or **V = l x w x h or V = lwh**

Directions: Compute the volume of each rectangular prism

1.

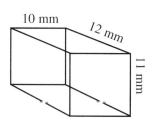

V = _____ mm^3

2.

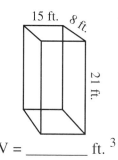

V = _____ ft.^{3}

3.

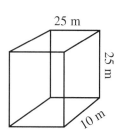

V = _____ m^3

4.

V = _____ cm^3

5.

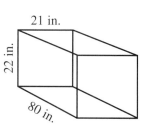

V = _____ in.^{3}

6.

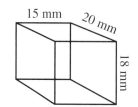

V = _____ mm^3

7.

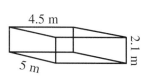

V = _____ m^3

8.

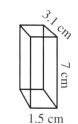

V = _____ cm^3

Volume of Cylinder

Reminder

The volume of a cylinder is computed by multiplying the height times the area of the base.

$$V = h \times \pi r^2$$

Directions: Compute the volume of each cylinder.

1.

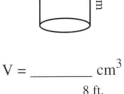

V = _____ cm^3

2.

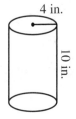

V = _____ in.^{3}

3.

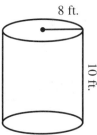

V = _____ ft.^{3}

4.

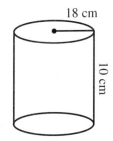

V = _____ cm^3

5.

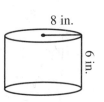

V = _____ in.^{3}

6.

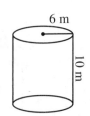

V = _____ m^3

7.

V = _____ mm^3

8.

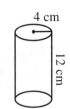

V = _____ cm^3

144

Volume of a Pyramid

Reminder

- The volume of a pyramid is 1/3 the volume of a prism with the same base.
- The volume of a pyramid is computed by multiplying 1/3 times the length times the width of the base times the height of the pyramid.

$$V = 1/3 \times l \times w \times h \text{ or } V = 1/3 \text{ (lwh)}$$

Directions: Compute the volume of each pyramid.

1.

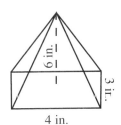

$V =$ _____ in.^{3}

2.

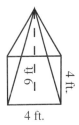

$V =$ _____ ft.^{3}

3.

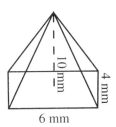

$V =$ _____ mm^3

4.

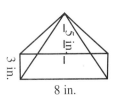

$V =$ _____ in.^{3}

5.

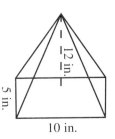

$V =$ _____ in.^{3}

6.

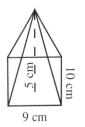

$V =$ _____ cm^3

7.

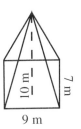

$V =$ _____ m^3

8.

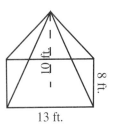

$V =$ _____ ft.^{3}

Math

Surface Area

Reminder

To compute the surface area of a rectangular prism, calculate the area of each face then add the six areas.

Directions: Compute the surface area of each rectangular prism.

1.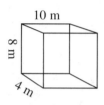
10 m
8 m
4 m

face 1_____
face 2_____
face 3_____
face 4_____
face 5_____
face 6_____
Total _____ m²

2.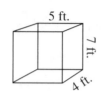
5 ft.
7 ft.
4 ft.

face 1_____
face 2_____
face 3_____
face 4_____
face 5_____
face 6_____
Total _____ ft.²

3.
5 cm
11 cm
10 cm

face 1_____
face 2_____
face 3_____
face 4_____
face 5_____
face 6_____
Total _____ cm²

4.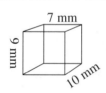
7 mm
9 mm
10 mm

face 1_____
face 2_____
face 3_____
face 4_____
face 5_____
face 6_____
Total _____ mm²

5.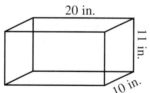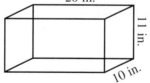
20 in.
11 in.
10 in.

face 1_____
face 2_____
face 3_____
face 4_____
face 5_____
face 6_____
Total _____ in.²

6.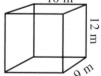
10 m
12 m
9 m

face 1_____
face 2_____
face 3_____
face 4_____
face 5_____
face 6_____
Total _____ m²

Probability

What is the probability of two heads landing when you flip two coins, a penny and a nickel, at one time?

Possible outcomes:

penny (heads); nickel (heads)
penny (tails); nickel (tails)
penny (heads); nickel (tails)
penny (tails); nickel (heads)

Probability of two heads: 1 in 4 or 1/4

Directions: List the possible outcomes for each problem. The first one is done for you.

1. What is the probability of a penny landing heads when you flip it?

   Possible outcomes: head or tail

   Probability of heads: 1 in 2 or 1/2

2. What is the probability of rolling a 4 with one die?

   Possible outcomes:_____

   Probability of rolling a 4: _____

3. What is the probability of rolling a 6 with one die?

   Possible outcomes:_____

   Probability of rolling a 6: _____

4. What is the probability of rolling a 4 or a 6 with one die?

   Possible outcomes:_____

   Probability of rolling a 4 or 6:_____

5. A black cloth bag holds one red marble, one green marble, one blue marble, and one black marble. All are the same size. Without looking into the bag, what is the probability of drawing a black marble from the bag?

   Possible outcomes:_____

   Probability of drawing the black marble:

   _____

6. What is the probability of drawing either the black or the blue marble from the bag?

   Possible outcomes:_____

   Probability of drawing the black or blue marble: _____

7. What is the probability of drawing a white marble?

   Possible outcomes:_____

   Probability of drawing a white marble:

   _____

8. What is the probability of drawing either the black, the green, or the blue marble from the bag?

   Possible outcomes:_____

   Probability of drawing the black, green, or blue marble: _____

9. What is the probability of one head and one tail landing when you flip two coins, a penny and a nickel, at the same time?

   Possible outcomes:_____

   Probability of one head and one tail:

   _____

Area and Probability

Look at the spinner below, next to the first set of questions. There are eight spaces. Each is the same size. Four spaces are dark. Four spaces are light.

What is the probability of landing on a dark space? The probability is 4/8 or 1/2 because half of the spaces on the spinner are dark.

Directions: Use the spinner on the left to answer these questions.

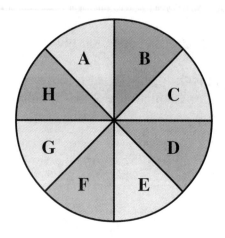

1. What is the probability of landing on space A? _____

2. What is the probability of landing on a light space? _____

3. What is the probability of landing on either space A or B? _____

4. What is the probability of landing on either space G or H? _____

5. What is the probability of landing on either a dark or light space? _____

6. What is the probability of landing on any space? _____

Directions: Use the dartboard on the right to answer these questions. Use fractions or percentages to express probability.

7. What is the probability of hitting space A on this dartboard? _____

8. What is the probability of hitting space C on this dartboard? _____

9. What is the probability of hitting space A or D on this dartboard? _____

10. What is the probability of hitting space B or C on this dartboard? _____

11. What is the probability of hitting space A, B, or C on this dartboard? _____

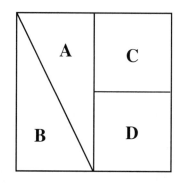

Directions: Use the dartboard on the left to answer these questions. Use fractions or percentages to express probability.

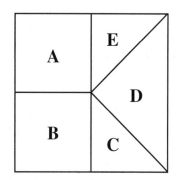

12. What is the probability of hitting space A on this dartboard? _____

13. What is the probability of hitting space D on this dartboard? _____

14. What is the probability of hitting space A or D on this dartboard? _____

15. What is the probability of hitting space C or E on this dartboard? _____

16. What is the probability of hitting space D, C, or E on this dartboard? _____

148

Showing Probability
with Fractions

Facts to Know

Directions: Read each situation. Think about the occurrence of each event. Then, write the probability of each occurrence as a fraction.

A bag has two green marbles, two blue marbles, and one yellow marble. If you were to reach into the bag, write as a fraction what the probability would be that you would randomly select a:

1. blue marble _____

2. green marble _____

3. yellow marble _____

4. red marble _____

Six children entered a drawing to win a bike. John's name is in the box three times. Karen's name is in the box two times. Roger's name is in the box once. Sarah's name is in the box twice. Joe's name is in the box once. Linda's name is in the box once. Write the children's names on the cards below as described and determine the probability that . . .

5. John's name will be randomly picked. _____

6. Sarah's name will be randomly picked.

7. Joe's name will be randomly picked. _____

8. a boy's name will be randomly picked.

9. a girl's name will be randomly picked. _____

10. Whose name is most likely to be randomly picked?_____

11. Should Linda expect to be the winner of the bike? Explain your answer._____

_____

_____

_____

Alphabet tiles are placed in a bag during a kindergarten lesson. Each student is asked to pull a tile at random to identify the letter, then, put it back. What is the probability that . . .

12. a vowel will be selected? _____   **15.** the Greek letter "Σ" will be selected? _____

13. a consonant will be selected? _____   **16.** a letter before "J" will be selected? _____

14. the letter "Y" will be selected? _____   **17.** a letter in the word "pig" will be selected? _____

Showing Probability with Decimals and Percents

You can show the numerical probability of an event occurring as a **decimal** or **percent**. To find the **decimal**, first find the fractional probability, then divide the numerator by the denominator.

Example: fractional probability = $\frac{2}{5}$ ⟶ $2 \div 5 = .40$

To find the **percent**, multiply the decimal by 100 and add a percent sign.

Example: decimal probability = .40 ⟶ $.40 \times 100 = 40\%$

Directions: Look at each situation below. Calculate the probability of each event as a decimal and percent.

Jake decided to color his picture by selecting crayons from the box at random. There were 10 crayons in the box: blue, red, yellow, orange, green, purple, white, brown, black, and gray. Write the probability for each event.

	Decimal	Percent
1. Jake will color the duck blue.	_____	_____
2. Jake will color the sky orange.	_____	_____
3. Jake will color the tree a primary color.	_____	_____
4. Jake will color the cloud a color that starts with the letter "b".	_____	_____

Gina went to the pet store to get a new puppy. When she got there, she couldn't decide which one to get. So she asked the storeowner to select one for her at random. Use the list of different kinds of puppies available to determine the probability of each event. (**Hint:** Drawing a picture might help. Draw one on the back.)

Puppies
2 puppies with black stripes, both male
3 tan puppies with white spots, 1 male, 2 female
2 white puppies with black spots, both female
1 black puppy, male
1 white puppy, male
1 tan puppy, female

	Decimal	Percent
5. Gina receives an all-white puppy.	_____	_____
6. Gina receives a male puppy.	_____	_____
7. Gina receives a female spotted puppy.	_____	
8. Gina receives a female striped puppy.	_____	_____
9. Gina receives a white female puppy with black spots.	_____	_____
10. Gina receives a puppy without any black.	_____	_____

Algebra: Solving Equations

An *equation* is a brief way of saying that two expressions are equal in value. Below are some examples of equations.

$$x + 3 = 7 \qquad\qquad n - 5 = 15 \qquad\qquad 2a = 20$$

You can use the axioms of equality to find the value of the unknown (represented by a letter such as x, n, or a) in an equation. The number added, subtracted, multiplied, or divided will leave the unknown on one side of the equation and the numerical value on the other side of the equation.

Steps

1. Decide which number to add or subtract from each side of the equation.
2. Find the numerical value of each unknown.
3. Check your answer by using it instead of the unknown in the equation.

$$
\begin{array}{r}
n - 5 = 15 \\
+5 \quad +5 \\
\hline
n = 20
\end{array}
$$

n (unknown) = 20 (numeral value)

$$20 - 5 = 15$$

Directions: Solve these equations. The first one is done for you.

1. $n + 9 = 20$

$$
\begin{array}{r}
-9 \quad -9 \\
\hline
n = 11
\end{array}
$$

Check: $11 + 9 = 20$

2. $n + 16 = 19$

3. $a + 12 = 16$

4. $n + 15 = 40$

5. $a + 10 = 25$

6. $n + 13 = 39$

7. $x - 17 = 10$

8. $n - 6 = 4$

9. $a - 5 = 15$

10. $n - 11 = 20$

11. $x - 10 = 15$

12. $a - 4 = 10$

13. $n + 6 = 30$

14. $a - 11 = 80$

15. $n + 14 = 41$

16. $a - 15 = 50$

17. $x + 22 = 60$

18. $n - 13 = 53$

Algebra: Working with Equations

You can find the value of the unknown quantity in an equation by using the axioms of equality. The number added, subtracted, multiplied, or divided will leave the unknown on one side of the equation and the numerical value on the other side of the equation.

Remember the following steps:

1. Decide the number by which to multiply or divide each side of the equation.
2. Find the numerical value of each unknown.
3. Check your answer by using it instead of the unknown in the equation.

Sample

Divide both sides of the equation by 3.
When $3a$ is divided by 3, the answer is a.
When 30 is divided by 3, the answer is 10.
So $a = 10$.
Check your answer.

$3a = 30$
$$\frac{3a}{3} = \frac{30}{3}$$
$a = 10$

$3 \times 10 = 30$

Directions: Solve these equations. The first one is done for you.

1. $4n = 20$
$$\frac{4n}{4} = \frac{20}{4}$$
$n = 5$

2. $6n = 66$

3. $7n = 21$

4. $8a = 32$

5. $5n = 35$

6. $12n = 120$

7. $10n = 50$

8. $12a = 72$

9. $6a = 90$

10. $\frac{n}{2} = 10$

11. $\frac{n}{2} = 30$

12. $\frac{a}{5} = 12$

13. $\frac{n}{4} = 4$

14. $\frac{n}{4} = 15$

15. $\frac{a}{8} = 8$

16. $\frac{n}{4} = 40$

17. $7a = 490$

18. $12n = 480$

Roman Numerals

The Seven Basic Roman Numerals	Value
I	1
V	5
X	10
L	50
C	100
D	500
M	1000

Roman Numerals 1–20			
I	1	XI	11
II	2	XII	12
III	3	XIII	13
IV	4	XIV	14
V	5	XV	15
VI	6	XVI	16
VII	7	XVII	17
VIII	8	XVIII	18
IX	9	XIX	19
X	10	XX	20

Directions: Study the tables above. Write the present-day number equivalent to each Roman numeral.

1. I = _____

2. IV = _____

3. VI = _____

4. X = _____

5. III = _____

6. V = _____

7. VIII = _____

8. XII = _____

9. VII = _____

10. IX = _____

11. XV = _____

12. XIII = _____

Directions: Using the chart above, write these numbers as Roman numerals.

13. 21 = _____

14. 22 = _____

15. 23 = _____

16. 24 = _____

17. 25 = _____

18. 26 = _____

19. 27 = _____

20. 28 = _____

21. 29 = _____

Directions: Write the value for each of these Roman numerals.

22. XXX = _____

23. XXVI = _____

24. XXXIII = _____

25. XXXV = _____

26. XXIX = _____

27. XXXVIII = _____

28. XXXIX = _____

29. XXXIV = _____

30. XXXVII = _____

Directions: Write these values as Roman numerals.

31. 45 = _____

32. 49 = _____

33. 48 = _____

34. 47 = _____

35. 16 = _____

36. 46 = _____

37. 27 = _____

38. 37 = _____

39. 29 = _____

40. Write your age in Roman numerals: _____

41. Write a friend's age in Roman numerals: _____

42. Write an older relative's age in Roman numerals: _____

Using Roman Numerals

Directions: Study the tables on page 153. Convert these Roman numeral dates to present-day numerals.

1. MM = _____

2. MMI = _____

3. MMV = _____

4. MCM = _____

5. MDCCC = _____

6. MDCCCIII = _____

7. MCMXII = _____

8. MCML = _____

9. MCMLXXXIII = _____

10. MDC = _____

11. MDCCXVIII = _____

12. MCMXCVIII = _____

Directions: Convert these dates to Roman numerals.

13. 2000 = _____

14. 2001 = _____

15. 2010 = _____

16. 1900 = _____

17. 1960 = _____

18. 1800 = _____

19. 1910 = _____

20. 1940 = _____

21. 1881 = _____

22. 1654 = _____

23. 1492 = _____

24. 1588 = _____

Directions: Determine the value of each of these Roman numerals.

25. V = _____

26. X = _____

27. L = _____

28. C = _____

29. D = _____

30. M = _____

31. MM = _____

32. CCC = _____

33. MD = _____

34. MDCC = _____

35. MMMDCL = _____

36. MDCLXVI = _____

Directions: Write these answers in Roman numerals.

37. What is the sum of XXXVIII and XXV? _____

38. What is the sum of LXXXVI and XI? _____

39. What is the sum of XC and CX? _____

40. What is the sum of XXIII and XXVII? _____

Base Two (The Binary System)

Using Base Two

Sticks	Eights	Fours	Twos	Ones
//	0	0	1	0
/// /	0	0	1	1
////	0	1	0	0
//// /	0	1	0	1

Base two has only two counting numbers or digits. They are 0 and 1.

The two sticks shown above would be represented this way in base two: 10_{two}. It is read as **1** two and **0** ones—base two.

The three sticks shown above would be represented this way in base two: 11_{two}. It is read as **1** two and **1** one—base two.

The four sticks shown above would be represented this way in base two: 100_{two}. It is read as **1** four with **0** twos and **0** ones—base two.

These five sticks shown above would be represented this way in base two: 101_{two}. It is read as **1** four, **0** twos, and **1** one—base two.

(Note: Notice how the base two groupings increase: ones, twos, fours, eights, sixteens, etc.)

Directions: Study the information above. Express the number of sticks indicated in each problem below in base two.

1. /

———— two

2. //

———— two

3. // /

———— two

4. ////

———— two

5. //// /

———— two

6. //// //

———— two

7. //// // /

———— two

8. ////////

———— two

9. ///////// /

———— two

Directions: Express the number of stars indicated in each problem below in base two.

10. ** *

———— two

11. **** *

———— two

12. **

———— two

13. ******** *

———— two

14. ****

———— two

15. **** **

———— two

16. **** ** *

———— two

17. *

———— two

18. ********

———— two

Charting Base Two

This chart illustrates the number of sticks shown here expressed in base two.

Sticks	Eights	Fours	Twos	Ones
//////// // /	1	0	1	1

Directions: Use the chart shown below to indicate the number of sticks shown expressed in base two.

	Sticks	Eights	Fours	Twos	Ones
1.	// /				
2.	//// /				
3.	//// //				
4.	//// // /				
5.	//				
6.	////				
7.	/				
8.	////////				
9.	//////// /				
10.	//////// // /				

Directions: Draw sticks to represent these base ten numbers. Then express the numbers in base two on the chart. The first one is done for you.

Base Ten Number		Sticks	Eights	Fours	Twos	Ones
11.	5	//// /	0	1	0	1
12.	3					
13.	4					
14.	7					
15.	8					
16.	2					
17.	6					
18.	9					
19.	11					
20.	10					
21.	12					
22.	15					
23.	14					
24.	13					

When Did It Happen?

If you have ever read about something that happened long ago, then you are probably familiar with the abbreviations BC or BCE and AD or CE. Buddha was born in 563 BCE. Muhammad died in CE 632. Both BC and BCE represent the years before the birth of Jesus Christ. CE and AD mean the years after the birth of Jesus. The abbreviations stand for the following:

BC = Before Christ   **BCE** = Before the Common Era
AD = Anno Domini (in the year of our   **CE** = Common Era
        Lord)

You have probably also read of events happening, for example, in the 5th century or even in the 5th century BCE. A century is 100 years. If people lived in the 1st century, they lived in the first 100 years CE, or in the first 100 years after the birth of Jesus. So, if we say something happened in the 19th century, we mean it happened during the years CE 1801–1900. The same rule applies to the centuries BCE, only we count backwards from the birth of Jesus. For example, Buddha was born in 563 BCE, which would mean he was born in the 6th century BCE.

Questions

Here are some practice questions. You will need to use the time line below and your math skills to find the answers.

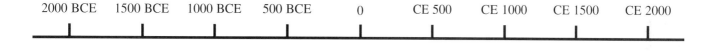

| 2000 BCE | 1500 BCE | 1000 BCE | 500 BCE | 0 | CE 500 | CE 1000 | CE 1500 | CE 2000 |

1. Who existed long ago, someone born in 1760 BCE or someone born in 1450 BCE?

   _____

2. How many years difference is there between CE 250 and 250 BCE?

   _____

3. How many years difference is there between CE 1524 and 1436 BCE?

   _____

4. You visit a cemetery. One of the tombstones reads: "Born in the 15th century, died in the 16th." Make up possible dates that this person may have been born and died.

   _____

5. In what century are you living now?

   _____

The Indus Valley Civilization

India's earliest known civilization originated on the fertile flood plains of the Indus River in northwestern India. The climate of this region in ancient times was much like it is today, hot and dry. Although only the lower valley receives much rainfall during the monsoon season, the monsoon rains caused the river to flood, creating rich deposits of silt for farming crops of wheat, barley, dates, and melons.

Around 5000 BCE primitive farmers began settling in scattered villages in the hilly region near the river. Each season they traveled down into the valley and cultivated the rich soil left by the river floods. They could not live in the valley itself because they could not protect their homes against the destructive flood waters. Eventually these people developed a technique to bake building bricks in an oven. Because these bricks were stronger than sun-dried bricks, people could move closer to the fertile grounds without fear of the floods.

With this discovery and migration into the valley, the civilization flourished. The farmlands were plentiful, the river supplied abundant water for drinking and irrigation, fish for food, and highways for travel and trade. The surrounding forests provided timber for building, fuel, and plentiful game animals. With such bountiful resources, larger towns soon grew, and some individuals turned to occupations like weaving, tanning leather, making pottery, or building furniture. The demand for luxury goods required cloth-dyers, bead makers, goldsmiths, and stone-cutters.

By about 2300 BCE the towns had grown into bustling cities. Elaborate governmental systems were designed to keep order, a writing system was developed, religious beliefs emerged, and advances were made in other technical and artistic skills. The Indus Valley Civilization grew to be larger than any other ancient empire, including those of Egypt and Mesopotamia. Its two great centers were the cities of Mohenjo-Daro and Harappa.

Until the early part of the twentieth century, few people knew anything about the Indus Valley Civilization. Only mounds of dirt, some as high as 60 feet, remained where the great cities once flourished. Between 1856 and 1919 bricks from ancient Harappan roads and walls were carried away to be used in Indian railway beds. Archaeological excavations of the Indus cities began during the 1920s and 1930s, and the great cities were unearthed, revealing carefully planned and constructed city formats.

In the center of each city was a fortress or citadel which was raised on a mud-brick platform about 400 by 200 yards (364 m x 182 m) in size. This citadel and other public buildings were surrounded by very thick walls of baked brick. Outside the walls, the town extended for at least one square mile (2.6 square km). Both Harappa and Mohenjo-Daro were divided into large rectangular blocks by wide streets with advanced drainage. The sewer systems of the Indus Valley Civilization are considered one of its greatest achievements, unequaled by any other ancient civilization until the time of the Romans.

Scholars believe that this great civilization disintegrated about 2000 BCE and have suggested several theories for its decline. The Indus people may have overgrazed their lands and cut down too many trees for fuel and building projects, leading to smaller harvests and a decrease in trade. In addition, they may have disrupted the natural habitat of native animals. Today the land around the Indus River is barren of forests and large game. Flooding or insufficient flooding of the river during a planting season may have caused a famine. Some of the Indus people may have migrated to other parts of India, like the Ganges River Valley, using their farming techniques to shift from wheat and grain cultivation to rice.

The Indus Valley Civilization *(cont.)*

Comprehension Questions

1. The Indus Valley is in which country?

a. United States

b. Egypt

c. India

d. Greece

2. What technique did people use to allow them to move closer to fertile grounds?

a. They built their homes on stilts.

b. They built their homes near a river.

c. They used cement to build their homes.

d. They baked building bricks in an oven.

3. Which of the following is an occupation that some people turned to when they migrated to the valley?

a. sewing

b. weaving

c. herding

d. cleaning

4. Archaeological excavations of the Indus Valley began in . . .

a. 5000 BCE.

b. 2300 BCE.

c. 1856.

d. the 1920s.

5. What is considered one of the Indus Valley Civilization's greatest achievements?

a. its sewer systems

b. its railroad systems

c. its communication systems

d. its farming systems

6. Which of the following is NOT a theory that scholars have of the decline of the Indus Valley Civilization?

a. Some of the Indus people may have migrated to other parts of India.

b. Flooding or insufficient flooding may have caused a famine.

c. A huge war may have wiped out many of the people in the valley.

d. The Indus people may have overgrazed the land and cut down too many trees.

The Origins of Hinduism

The Indus Valley Civilization

Look at the map of the Indus Valley on page 161. This area, now shared largely by Pakistan and a portion by India, is the birthplace of Hinduism. Hinduism is a complex faith with a history that can be traced back five thousand years to the people of the Indus Valley.

Most of what we know of the Indus people comes from archaeological findings. Surveys done with the help of satellites using modern technology such as infrared photography, and artifacts and relics dating back as early as 4000 BCE, tell the story of a civilization flourishing with craftsmanship, agriculture, and religious life. As you will see, many of these early practices and beliefs still shape Hinduism.

One such example is the Indus people's emphasis on cleanliness or ritual bathing. Mohenjo Daro, one of the major Indus cities, contained a huge water tank for public bathing. Old and famous Hindu temples are usually found in the places where water is naturally available.

Another lasting legacy of Hinduism is found in the abundance of terra-cotta figurines unearthed in the Indus Valley. Popular among these small ceramic statuettes were depictions of women. Among them is the Mother Goddess, which has many forms in the Hindu faith and thus plays many roles. She is viewed as the ultimate source of strength and as a symbol of fertility. The concepts of rebirth and continuity that the Mother Goddess represents are still very important to the Hindu religion. According to the teachings of Hinduism, when a person dies, it is only the body that dies while the Atma, the soul, is immortal.

Ceramic seals also tell us something about the Indus' religious beliefs. Among the most common designs is that of the bull. The bull is the means of transport of Lord Shiva, one of the most revered Hindu gods.

The inhabitants of the Indus Valley were an agricultural people, growing crops and raising animals. Being that thy lived on the banks of the Indus River and dependend on its nourishment and renewal, there was a deep reverence for water. Water still remains sacred to Hindus.

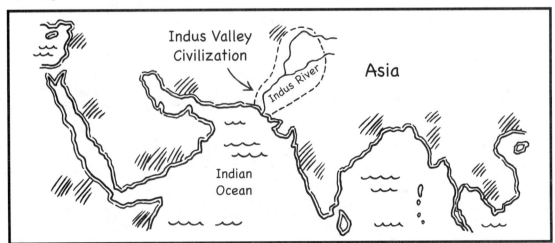

The Origins of Hinduism *(cont.)*

Comprehension Questions

1. How did researchers discover most of the information about the Indus people?

   _____

2. List two findings and briefly explain their links to Hinduism.

   _____

   _____

   _____

3. How did the Indus people survive? How does this relate to their religious worship?

   _____

   _____

   _____

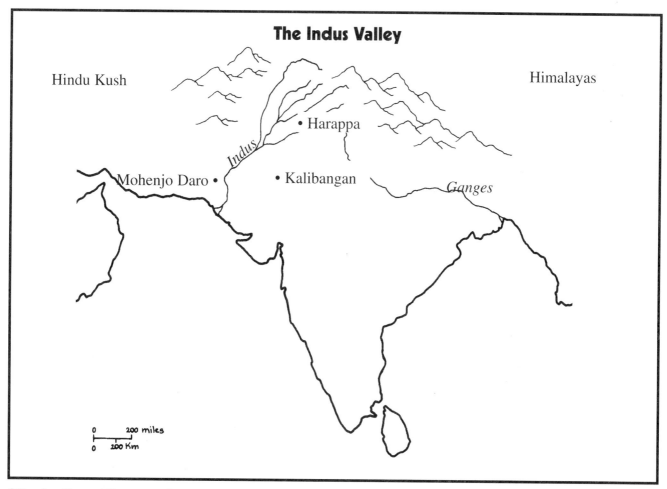

The Indus Valley

Hindu Kush

Himalayas

• Harappa

Indus

Mohenjo Daro •

• Kalibangan

Ganges

0   200 miles

0   200 Km

Social Studies

Egyptian Hieroglyphics

The Egyptians were one of the first civilizations to use written language, and their earliest writing dates back to 3100 BCE. They recorded information on temple walls, tombs, and papyrus scrolls. Hieroglyphics began as simple picture writing with a picture or sign representing a particular object. Slowly a method evolved for using hieroglyphs to represent ideas and actions. Eventually, it was expanded to use individual signs as sounds, much like our alphabet today. However, hieroglyphics comprises 750 signs compared to our 26 letters. Most of the hieroglyphs are pictures of people, animals, plants, or objects.

Use the code in the key below and the clues given to translate the message on page 163. Write the words on the lines provided. Hint: Some words are pictured phonetically, so letters may be missing.

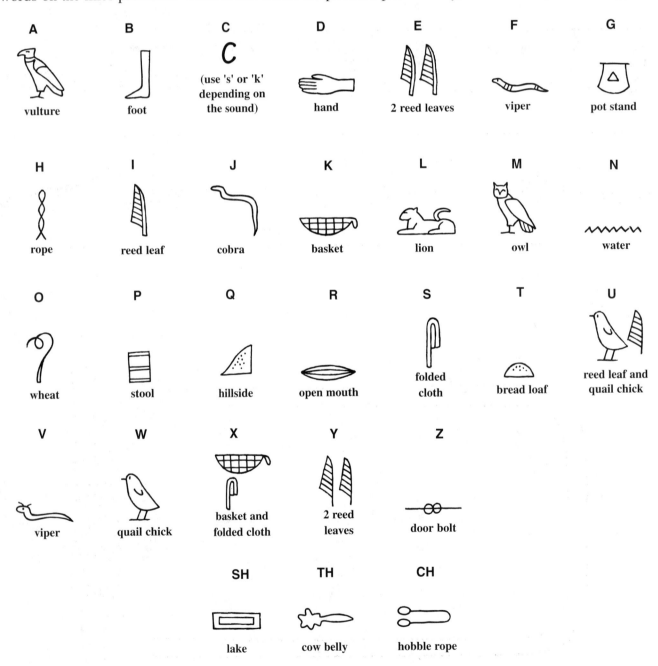

Hieroglyphics Code

The individual rulers of Ancient Egypt each had their own personal signature in the form of cartouches. A royal cartouches consisted of the name of the ruler written in hieroglyphics enclosed in a ring.

After translating the message, use the ring below to make your own cartouche. Use the code on page 162 to write your hieroglyphic name. Use pencil first, making the figures as large as possible. Then, trace over them in black ink and color the cartouche. Cut out your cartouche and glue it onto black paper.

O 〰〰 e   of the   ⌐ e 🐍 e 〰〰

_____   _____

🐦 o 〰〰 ✋ e 👄 ⌐ of the 🐦 o 👄 🐆 ✋

_____   _____

is the ▦ 𝄃𝄃𝄃 👄 🦅 🦉 𝄃 ✋ of 🗺 𓎢 🐦 𝄃 🪱 u

_____   _____

at ⬢ i 〜∞〜 a.   **Examples:**

_____

Examples:

Social Studies

The Nile in Ancient Egypt

Read the passage below and answer the questions.

Ancient Egyptian life centered around the life-giving waters of the Nile, the longest river in the world. Every Egyptian, from the poorest peasant to the pharaoh, depended on the Nile, as its banks contain the only land with soil able to grow crops.

The Egyptians took full advantage of the Nile River. People were able to live secure in the knowledge that they were safe from intruders who didn't dare cross the deserts that surrounded their fertile valleys. Because of the annual flooding, the Egyptians were able to establish a fairly regular cycle of planting and harvesting. Excess crops were then exported, making Egypt a wealthy nation. Animals thrived in the waters and surrounding land of the Nile. Goods were easily transported on barges and ferries. Probably the most valuable gift of the Nile was papyrus, a tall reed which grew along its banks. Papyrus was used to make paper, and Egypt was the sole supplier of this product until rag paper was invented in the twelfth century.

1. **Who depended on the Nile?**
   a. the pharaoh
   b. the farmers
   c. the peasants
   d. all of the above

2. **According to the passage, what did the Nile do that helped the Egyptians establish a farming cycle?**
   a. It ran into channels they had created to water their crops.
   b. It flooded each year.
   c. It dried out each year so the farmers could use the riverbed for farming.
   d. It kept the farm animals alive.

3. **According to the passage, how did the Nile help make the Egyptians wealthy?**
   a. The Egyptians could produce enough crops to sell to other countries.
   b. The Egyptians could produce enough crops to feed their families.
   c. The Egyptians could pan for gold in the Nile.
   d. The Egyptians bottled the water from the Nile and sold it.

4. **According to the passage, probably the most valuable gift of the Nile was . . .**
   a. water.
   b. the animals who lived on the Nile.
   c. papyrus.
   d. the crops that the Nile produced.

Animals of the Nile

Read the paragraph below. Find and circle the bold-faced animal names in the word search puzzle. Names may be up, down, across, or diagonal, and may be forward or backward.

A wide variety of animals thrived in the deserts and flood plains of ancient Egypt. **Lions, wild bulls, antelopes,** and **gazelles** were plentiful in the desert east and west of the Nile Valley. **Hyenas, rams, jackals,** and **oxen** also inhabited those areas. Birds of all kinds made their home in the papyrus thickets beside the Nile. Nests of **pintail ducks, pelicans, geese,** and **cormorants** could be found there. **Hippos** and **crocodiles** roamed along the banks of the Nile as well as in the river itself. Among the fish population were **perch** and **catfish**. **Cats** roamed freely and sometimes lived in Egyptian homes.

```
p e l i c a n s h g i m y n w a m e i s r h
r i k a n d i h a a e v e a i g i r l f r s
i e n d w h o i s z a e b e l a u t i f u i
l g i r l i o n s e y e s a d t r i p t o f
h a w a i i i i l p h i e b l j u h n b t
l h o k i j n h y l h y t g u b g c k i l a
p c c i u y t r e e j h g f l p c r k i u c
h y t r r f v g h s x o i u l n h o y g t g
f r e d e n h i p p o s n l s h y c v s f r
e d c d w p w r o k i h m n y f r o m s b g
c k i j u g t g d r m j u l c i k d b a g y
k i u y h t g y t r e k i k i k i i h n y h
b g t g b g t g b g c d g f r t g l v e g t
a a b p i n t a i l d u c k s c d e e y f g,
n h i j k l m n o p q r a t y u y s h h m j
t m r j j u y h g t f v m k l r j i u g t r
e g d r a h u i k o s t a c v d a l o p i u
l h s t f c h n g b f o u t s w e m g r f s
o n h j u k k l p o n n e x o t f f s d y e
p d i g o r d a i c o r m o r a n t s v o l
e l e y b a l l s u r f i n g i s a s p c
s r t t h a t i s s d a n g e r o u s o k
```

Building the Pyramids

The Egyptians were an advanced civilization of people highly knowledgeable in math, science, and the arts. Some of their most astounding skills can be seen in their magnificent architecture, especially the pyramids.

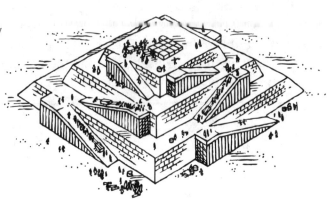

Egyptians buried their pharaohs in elaborate tombs to ensure that the body would be kept safe for all eternity, and the pharaoh's spirit would have a happy afterlife. The pharaoh King Menes, was buried in a tomb called a mastaba, which in Arabic means bench. It was like a house with many rooms. King Zoser was the first pharaoh who had a pyramid for a tomb. Imhotep, the pharaoh's chief architect, designed the tomb with a mastaba as a base, but then built five more mastabas on top of it. Each succeeding mastaba was slightly smaller than the one beneath it, and the six together reached a height of nearly 2,000 feet. He called his new style of tomb a step pyramid. It was thought that the pyramid was built as a stairway for the pharaoh's ba, or spirit, to reach heaven.

In order for the foundation of the pyramids to be level, the Egyptians used water to fill the base where the foundation would be laid. When any type of container is filled with water, the surface of the water is level. Once the Egyptians filled the area with water and it found its natural level, they marked the water line and drained the water. How accurate was this form of measuring? The base of King Khufu's Great Pyramid was off level by only five-eighths of an inch!

While the site of the pyramid was being prepared and marked, stonemasons worked in limestone quarries to cut the slabs using metal chisels and saws, and wooden mallets, hammers, and wedges. The slabs were then mounted on sleds or rollers and dragged into place by laborers pulling them up ramps along the sides of the pyramid. This was very dangerous work, and hardly a day went by when someone was not killed or injured. Many of the pyramids were built by slaves, but there were also farmers who helped out for three or four months each year when the Nile flooded their fields. They were paid for their services with food, oil, and cloth. The farmers hoped that by helping with the preparation of the pyramid, they would please the gods and be rewarded in the next world.

Most of the slabs fit together so well that no mortar was needed to hold them in place. Some of the joints between the slabs were so tight that you couldn't even slide the blade of a knife between them. The very last stone to be put into place was called the capstone. The very top level of the pyramid has a hole. A plug was carved on the underside of the capstone. The plug fit into the hole and held the capstone in place. The sides of the pyramid were then smoothed and polished. The stonemasons worked downward from the top, removing the dirt ramps as they worked toward the base. Finally, the work was complete.

166

Building the Pyramids *(cont.)*

Comprehension Questions

1. **Who was the first Egyptian pharaoh to have a pyramid for a tomb?**

    a. King Menes

    b. King Zoser

    c. King Khufu

    d. King Tutankhamen

2. **What did the Egyptians do to ensure a level foundation for a pyramid?**

    a. They used water to find its natural level and then marked the water line.

    b. They used the horizon line.

    c. They used a ruler.

    d. They used a protractor and a compass.

3. **According to the passage, the slabs for the pyramids were made from . . .**

    a. granite.

    b. quartz.

    c. limestone.

    d. concrete.

4. **Farmers helped with the preparation of the pyramids in hopes that . . .**

    a. they would please the pharaoh and be rewarded with more land.

    b. they would please the architects and be rewarded with more money.

    c. they would please their families and be rewarded with food, oil, and cloth.

    d. they would please the gods and be rewarded in the next world.

5. **The last stone to be put into place on a pyramid was called the . . .**

    a. topstone.

    b. pointed stone.

    c. finishing stone.

    d. capstone.

6. **Which of the following is the final part of finishing a pyramid?**

    a. The foundation was marked by the water line and made level.

    b. The stonemasons cut the slabs out of limestone.

    c. The stonemasons smoothed and polished the sides of the pyramid.

    d. The laborers pulled the slabs up ramps along the sides of the pyramid.

Mummies in Ancient Egypt

Thousands of years ago people in Ancient Egypt thought that dead people needed their bodies after death. They believed that the people continued to live in a place called the afterlife. So they found a way to keep dead bodies from rotting. They figured out how to turn dead people into mummies. They **preserved** most of their kings and queens this way.

It was a lot of work to make a mummy. First, priests washed the dead body. Then they removed all of the organs—even the brain! They put a kind of salt all over the body. After six weeks, the body completely dried out. Next, they stuffed the body with sand, sawdust, or cloth. This made the body look full again. Then they rubbed spices and oils into the skin. Finally the priests wrapped cloth strips tightly around each part of the body. Wrapping the body took about two weeks. Lastly, they put the body into a coffin. On its cover the coffin had paintings and sometimes gems.

The most famous mummy is King Tut. He was still a teenager when he died over 4,000 years ago. He was put into a secret tomb. Scientists found this tomb in 1922. His family had put all sorts of gold, gems, and other riches into his tomb. Inside, King Tut's mummy lay in a solid gold coffin. Even his sandals were made of solid gold.

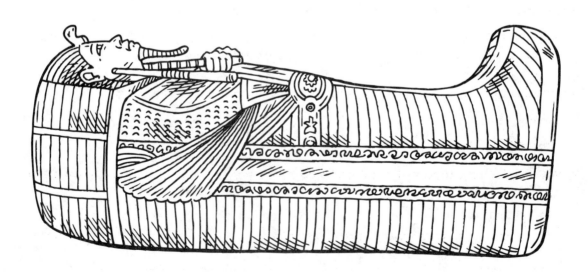

Mummies in Ancient Egypt *(cont.)*

Comprehension Questions

Circle the best answer. You may look back at the story.

1. Ancient Egyptians believed dead kings and queens . . .
   a. would use their belongings after they died.
   b. should be burned instead of buried.
   c. would send good luck to their people.
   d. would return to their throne after they died.

2. What did the priests do last when making a mummy?
   a. They washed the body.
   b. They removed the organs.
   c. They wrapped the body.
   d. They stuffed the body.

3. Egyptians mummified their rulers because . . .
   a. they thought it would make the rulers look better in the afterlife.
   b. they thought the rulers needed their bodies in the afterlife.
   c. they wanted to use the rulers' organs.
   d. they hoped the rulers would be found years later.

4. The opposite of *preserved* is . . .
   a. kept.   c. ruined.
   b. worshipped.   d. changed.

5. Today most people who believe in an afterlife call it . . .
   a. a funeral home.   c. a pyramid.
   b. a graveyard.   d. heaven.

6. Picture discovering a mummy's tomb. What don't you see inside?
   a. gold dishes   c. silver jewelry
   b. a gold watch   d. diamonds

7. Do you think that mummies' tombs should be opened so that the world can see their treasures? Explain.

_____

_____

_____

Trade Routes of Ancient Egypt

1. Name at least three places one could travel for exotic animals or skins.

   _____

2. What spices can be found in Punt?

   _____

3. If you started at the Egyptian delta, then traveled east on the Mediterranean Sea, what direction would you need to go to get to the Hittite Empire?

   _____

4. Using specific directions, describe one way to get from Egypt to India.

   _____

5. Name four places Egyptians could travel to using only waterways.

   _____

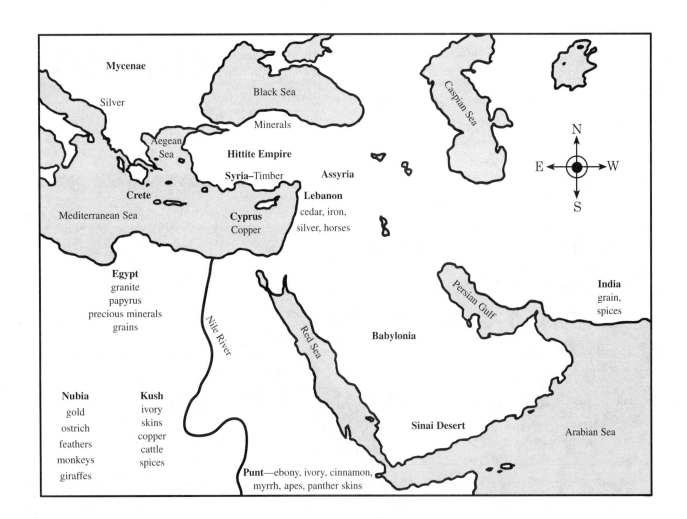

Egyptian Religion

Religion played a very important role in the daily lives of Ancient Egyptians. They believed that by worshiping their gods in special ways they could protect themselves from their enemies, sickness, evil spirits, and the forces of nature.

The Ancient Egyptians practiced polytheism, or the worship of many gods. Their first gods represented the natural elements that affected their daily lives, such as the sun, storms, river, and death. Each had to be encouraged and thanked in order for the people to prosper. Animals, both fierce and helpful, were also worshiped to help protect the people. During the New Kingdom, the pharaoh Akhenaten made his people worship only one god—the sun disc, Aten. But once Akhenaten died, the people destroyed most of the temples and returned to polytheism.

Ancient Egyptians believed that the pharaoh was the gods' son on Earth, and was therefore owed much respect and honor. It was his duty to feed and protect the gods, as well as keep everything in proper order for them. In every temple was a picture of the pharaoh making his daily offerings. Temples symbolized the world; the lower portion represented the earth and the ceiling symbolized heaven. Each temple was built on the spot where the god was believed to be dwelling.

Over time, the Egyptians began to think of the gods as having human qualities, and therefore, they were depicted with human shapes. But some of the gods retained the head of an animal. Each region in Egypt had it own special god, although gradually a few of these were worshiped throughout the land as universal gods.

Answer the following questions in complete sentences.

1. What is polytheism?

   _____

   _____

2. What were the Egyptians protecting themselves from when they prayed to the gods?

   _____

   _____

3. What was the duty of the pharaoh to the gods?

   _____

   _____

Buddhism

Many centuries ago in a peaceful kingdom in the foothills of the Himalaya mountains, there lived a king and queen who longed for a son to take the throne. One night the queen had a wonderful dream. A beautiful white elephant with six golden tusks came to her, gently touching her right side with a lotus flower. In the center of the lotus blossom glittered a brilliant jewel. Upon waking, she described the dream to her husband and the wise men of the kingdom. They all agreed that the dream foretold a miracle. The wise men explained that a son would soon be born, a boy of great importance and promise. If the boy remained in the royal household, he would grow up to be a magnificent king and rule the world. However, if he ventured out, he would find the Truth and become a holy man set on becoming the savior of the world. This prophecy alarmed the king, for holy men at the time were poor beggars who wandered the land spreading their word. This was not a suitable future for his noble son, and he vowed to shelter the boy from life outside the kingdom walls.

Soon the prediction came true. One afternoon while the queen strolled through the royal gardens, the earth began to shake and quiver. The queen quickly grasped the branch of a nearby flowering tree as a baby boy emerged from her right side. Heavenly water rained down on the infant, bathing his head, and lotus blossoms fell from the skies. The boy was named Siddhartha, meaning "every wish fulfilled."

Siddhartha grew up surrounded by luxury and showered with love. At the age of 16, Siddhartha married a beautiful princess. The king had three exquisite palaces built for the couple to ensure that Siddhartha would remain in the kingdom and fulfill his destiny as a great ruler. For 13 years Siddhartha lived in the most splendid surroundings with a loving wife tending to his every need, but he still grew more and more restless. He yearned to see what lay beyond in the big world.

One day he commanded his chariot driver to carry him outside the kingdom. As they slipped beyond the palace gates, Siddhartha saw on the street an old man, a sick man, and a dead man. For the first time in his life, he witnessed human suffering.

The next day Siddhartha, filled with curiosity, slipped away again. On this journey he met a monk in a saffron robe who seemed completely at peace and free from suffering. Siddhartha commanded his driver to stop so he could speak with the monk. "Who are you?" he asked, "How can you be content with the knowledge of this world around you?" The monk explained to the prince that he was a seeker of Truth, a seeker of life over death. To seek the Truth he had given up everything on this Earth. Siddhartha decided that he, too, would seek the Truth in order to find peace. He would leave his riches, his family, and his protected life to follow in the monk's footsteps.

Along his journey he met with many monks and sought their wisdom, but none could teach him how to find the Truth of life over death and reach the state of absolute peace. Siddhartha met five hermits who denied their bodies any comfort in order to rise above earthly concerns. He remained six years with these men, eating very little and practicing rituals that caused him great pain. Close to starvation and death, he realized that he was still no closer to understanding the Truth. He decided that the Truth cannot be found in the mind or in the body but only in the innermost core of the heart which is connected to all existence. It was then that he decided to follow a middle path.

The hermits left Siddhartha in disgust for his weakness, and Siddartha traveled on in his quest. He accepted food from villagers and bathed in the river. Finally, he came to a large Bodhi tree. A cowherd offered him eight handfuls of grass to sit upon. Siddhartha spread the grass beneath the tree and vowed, "Even if my blood dries up and my skin and bones waste away, I will not leave this seat until I have found the Truth of life over death, the end of suffering for myself and for all people." Mara, the evil one, heard this vow and called on his army of demons to defeat Siddhartha's enlightenment. He plagued the prince with doubts and fears and called forth winds, rain, and lightening. No matter what evils the anti-god threw at him, Siddhartha remained pure in mind and meditated for 49 days.

Social Studies

Buddhism (cont.)

At dawn on the fiftieth day, Siddhartha opened his eyes and glimpsed the last fading star. It was perfectly peaceful and the horizon glowed. At that moment Siddhartha became enlightened. Finally he could see the entire cycle of life and understand all of its mysteries. He saw the whole of existence within himself and himself the whole of existence. Rivers, once dry, began to flow, while flowers blossomed in the morning light. The animals danced and the birds all sang. Spirits, angels, and heavenly protectors were revealed with the scent of incense. At the age of 35, Siddhartha had ended his search. He had become Buddha, the enlightened one.

After becoming enlightened, the Buddha travled and taught his Truth of life after death. He taught meditations that helped purify body, speech, and mind. Eventually he had hundreds of followers from every walk of life, for he preached that anyone could reach enlightenment if he or she could find the path in his or her heart.

Buddha returned to his father's kingdom where he performed miracles to prove to the king that this was his chosen path. Many people in the kingdom, including his wife and son, were so moved that they left the comforts of the kingdom to follow him.

As in Hinduism, reincarnation, the idea that the soul lives on after the body dies and is reborn in the body of another human or living form, and karma are central Buddhist beliefs. During each lifetime, the soul suffers and strives to reach enlightenment. The good or bad deeds performed within a lifetime, called karma, travel with the soul into the next life and determines one's fate. Good karma puts one closer to enlightenment while bad karma inflicts more suffering. This cycle is finally broken when one reaches enlightenment, like the Buddha. The soul then enters the state of nirvana, or highest bliss, and never returns to Earth again.

At the age of 80, after preaching for 45 years, the Buddha knew it was his time to die. Believing in reincarnation, he knew that the cycle of birth, suffering, death, and rebirth continues until enlightenment is gained. Most people travel through many lifetimes seeking this enlightenment. Siddhartha Gautama, the Buddha, had finally accomplished this feat and was finally free from further rebirth and earthly suffering. He had reached *nirvana*.

Answer the following questions in complete sentences.

1. What aspects of Buddhism seem similar to Hinduism?

_____

_____

What aspects are different?

_____

_____

2. Why did Siddhartha part ways with the hermits?

_____

_____

3. Describe the cycle of reincarnation.

_____

_____

Ancient Greece: The Minoans

The earliest Greek settlers arrived on the island of Crete around 6000 BCE. They most likely came by boat from Asia Minor. For thousands of years they lived peacefully in caves and simple huts, isolated from the rest of the world. Gradually they developed more sophisticated skills, until they grew to be a major power in the area. Two major factors contributed to the growth and prosperity of the Minoan civilization. One was the sea; the other was the land. The calm waters of the Mediterranean Sea that surround the island proved to be excellent fishing grounds. The Minoans also constructed a large naval and merchant fleet of ships. They traded their wares as far off as Syria and Egypt.

Their trading abilities allowed the Minoans to import materials they did not have locally. From imported gold, silver, other metals, and fabrics, Minoan craftsmen created delicate jewelry, elaborate clothing, and ornaments. Minoan potters were regarded as the best in the world, and their wares were much sought after throughout the Mediterranean region.

Women had special status because they were responsible for bearing the children who assured the continued existence of the Minoan civilization. Because of this elevated status, Minoan women appear to have enjoyed many freedoms that were denied women in other ancient cultures. They participated in sports, hunted, and attended sports and other cultural events, such as theater.

Around 1450 BCE, the Minoan civilization began to decline. On Thera, an island north of Crete, a huge volcanic explosion killed all inhabitants of Thera and created a massive cloud of volcanic ash that engulfed Crete. Most of the island was covered in thick layers of ash that destroyed the land and made it useless for farming. Then part of the island of Thera collapsed, creating earthquakes and spawning tidal waves over 500 feet high. The waves devastated the Minoan ships, and clouds of ash suffocated animals and people.

Thus weakened, the Minoans were now easy prey for invaders from the north, mainly the Mycenaean Greeks, who eventually overthrew the Minoan government. Still, the Minoan culture influenced the new Mycenaean civilization and helped Greece again achieve great power in the Mediterranean region.

Answer the following questions in complete sentences.

1. What were some of the achievements of the Minoans?

   _____

   _____

2. How did the treatment of Minoan women differ from other ancient civilizations?

   _____

   _____

3. What eventually destroyed the Minoan civilization?

   _____

   _____

Ancient Greece: The Mycenaeans

On the mainland of Greece lived a group of people called the Mycenaeans. These people were developing culture and expanding at the very time that the Minoans were becoming weaker. The Mycenaeans invaded and conquered Crete in 1450 BCE and soon became the dominant civilization in the Aegean Sea region.

Unlike the Minoans, who had ample farmlands and fishing, living in this hilly region meant few natural resources, so the Mycenaeans became traders. They were also fine craftsmen of weapons, jewelry, and other artifacts made from imported raw materials. They were especially famous for their bronze work.

The Mycenaeans were much more warlike than the Minoans. Their lack of resources and need to acquire goods from other lands may have led them to a life of invasion and conquest. It is possible that their warlike nature caused fighting amongst their own colonies and perhaps even the collapse of their own civilization. By 1150 BCE the Mycenaean culture was weak and left them a prime target for the Dorians to invade from the north.

All of the Mycenaean cities fell to Dorian rule except for Athens, whose salvation is believed to have been a secret underground water supply in the Acropolis. The Dorians were uncivilized people possessing none of the skills of craftsmanship of the Minoans or the Mycenaeans. Trade during their rule came to a standstill. Soon all written language disappeared. Greece entered a period of decline called the Dark Age, which lasted from about 1100 BCE to 800 BCE.

Tales of the Mycenaean period were kept alive through songs and stories that were repeated during religious festivals or feasts. Around 800 BCE many people who migrated from Athens built cities and ports to expand trade once again. A new written language soon developed. The famous poet Homer wrote stories and epic poems based on the songs and tales about the Mycenaeans. This new development in writing and culture marked the end of the Dark Age.

Answer the following questions in complete sentences.

1. What were some contributions of the Mycenaeans to Greek culture? _____

_____

2. How were the Mycenaeans different from the Minoans? _____

_____

3. What happened to the Mycenaean civilization? _____

_____

4. What was the Dark Age? _____

_____

5. How did culture and trade return to Greece? _____

_____

Travel Log of Trade Routes

Pretend that you are a Greek merchant trading with other lands. Use the scale on the map to find the distance between the various locations. Choose the shortest route. Write in your travel log exactly how you would travel from one location to another. Make sure you include the directions of travel, the distance between one landform to the next, and whether you travel by land or water. Use a different color for each voyage described and trace your routes on the map.

1. Begin at the island of Corfu on the west coast of Greece and travel to Troy in Asia Minor.

2. Leave Troy and go to Knossos on the island of Crete.

3. Take your goods and return home to Corfu.

4. Which route was the longest?

_____

_____

5. Which route required travel over land and sea? _____

_____

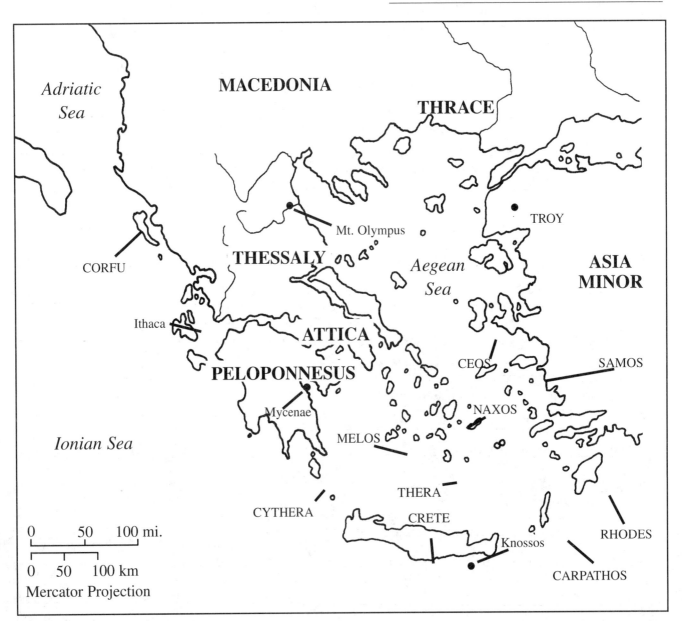

Greek Mythology

The Myth of Narcissus

Zeus, the supreme god, persuaded Echo to distract his wife, Hera, by chattering incessantly. He did this so that Hera could not keep track of Zeus, leaving him free to chase other women. However, when Hera figured out the plan, she was so enraged that she took away Echo's voice, leaving her with only the ability to repeat the final word of every message she heard. When Echo saw the extremely handsome but vain Narcissus, she fell deeply in love with him. Of course, she could not tell him of her love, but she followed him everywhere, gazing at him lovingly until he haughtily rejected her. Poor Echo hid in a cave and wasted away until only her voice remained. Then the goddess Nemesis decided to punish Narcissus by making him fall hopelessly in love with his own face as he saw it reflected in a pool. He gazed in fascination, unable to tear himself away from his image, until he gradually wasted away. In the spot where he had sat grew a beautiful yellow flower, which even to this day bears the name narcissus.

1. What did Zeus ask Echo to do? _____

   _____

2. Why did he ask her to do this? _____

   _____

3. What was Hera's reaction? _____

   _____

4. Why did Echo fall in love with Narcissus? _____

   _____

5. What was Narcissus's reaction to Echo? _____

   _____

6. What did Nemesis do to Narcissus? _____

   _____

7. What happened to Echo in the end? _____

   _____

8. What happened to Narcissus in the end? _____

   _____

The Climate of Greece and the Aegean Sea

The mainland of Greece and the Greek islands have what is called a Mediterranean climate, from the name of the sea. Most of the rain falls in the winter, so the summers are very hot and dry. Westerly winds bring much rain to the western coast of Greece. However, the systems lose much of their rain in rising above the interior mountains, so the eastern regions of Greece are drier.

Here are two maps of Greece showing the average temperatures in January (winter) and July (summer). Use the maps to answer the questions below.

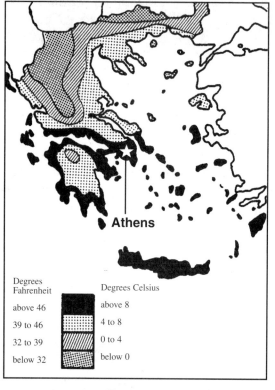

January

July

1. What is the average difference in temperature in Athens between January and July? _____

2. Where are the warmest places in Greece in July? _____

3. Where are the warmest places in January? _____

   What pattern do you see? _____

4. What portion of Greece seems to be the coldest in both months? _____

   What pattern do you see? _____

The Trojan Horse

In Homer's *The Iliad*, Greece and Troy had been battling for ten years. The Greeks thought long and hard about ways to end the war. Perhaps if they made special offerings to the gods, the gods might look favorably upon their gifts and reward them with the city of Troy. Their king, Odysseus, was struck by that idea—a gift! They would offer the Trojans a mysterious gift. They would build a huge and glorious wooden horse with a hollow belly. The horse would be left outside the gates of Troy as if it were a peace offering. Unknown to the Trojans, inside the horse's belly would be a Greek fighting force.

When the magnificent beast was completed it was pulled into place outside the massive gates of Troy. That night, under the cover of darkness, a small band of chosen warriors hid inside. When dawn broke the next day, the rest of the Greeks made a big show of leaving sadly, as if in defeat. They boarded their ships and sailed away, leaving the horse behind as tribute to their victors.

The Trojans were overjoyed. With shouts of triumph they swarmed outside the city walls. They dragged the horse through the gates of their city as a symbol of their hard-won victory. For hours the Trojans celebrated—drinking, feasting, and dancing. Later that night, when Troy was silent and still, the belly of the horse opened and the band of soldiers crept out. They quietly opened the gates to their army, which had sailed back during the night. The Greeks swept in and killed all who challenged them. The Trojan king was slain, and most of the women were taken as slaves. As they were leaving, the Mycenaeans set fire to Troy. The Greeks had finally won the war.

Read the questions and then circle the best answer.

1. **The story of the Trojan Horse is in . . .**
   a. the Bible.
   b. the dictionary.
   c. *The Iliad.*
   d. *The Odyssey.*

2. **What did the Greeks think might help end the war?**
   a. giving the Trojans more money
   b. making special offerings to the gods
   c. signing a contract with Troy to end the fighting
   d. running away

3. **What did the Greeks do to make it seem like they were defeated?**
   a. They boarded their ships and sailed away.
   b. They threw down their weapons and asked forgiveness.
   c. They asked to sign a peace treaty.
   d. They hid inside the Trojan horse.

4. **The word *slain* means . . .**
   a. captured.
   b. attacked.
   c. killed.
   d. loved.

Romulus and Remus

The history of Rome begins with the legend of Aeneas, a Trojan warrior who survived the fall of his city to the Greeks. He wandered for seven years before he settled with the Latins, a tribe on the Italian peninsula. Aeneas married Lavinia, daughter of the Latin king, became king himself, and had a son, Aeneas Silva, who founded the city of Alba Longa, 19 miles from the site of Rome.

Alba Longa became the capital of Latium and was ruled by Aeneas' descendants. One of the kings felt threatened by his brother's twin grandsons, Romulus and Remus, who were said to be sons of the god Mars. The king ordered the infant twins drowned in the Tiber River. Miraculously, they washed ashore where they were suckled by a she-wolf and later raised by a shepherd, Faustulus.

When they were grown, Romulus and Remus returned to Alba Longa, took revenge on the evil king who tried to drown them, and then set out to build their own city. They argued about where to settle; Romulus won the argument by killing his brother, after which he gave his own name to the new city, Rome.

1. What city was the capital of Latium before Rome was built?

   _____

2. Which of the twin brothers won the argument about where to settle?

   _____

3. Who was the legendary ancestor of Romulus and Remus?

   _____

4. What miracle occurred, according to the legend?

   _____

5. Into what tribe did Aeneas marry after the fall of Troy?

   _____

6. About 1184 BCE Troy fell. In 753 BCE Rome was founded. How many years passed from the fall of Troy to the founding of Rome?

   _____

Critical Thinking: Who founded your city? The United States? Was there fighting over who would be the leader? Write your answers on the back of this paper.

Emperors' Time Line

Roman emperors are known for their accomplishments or their failures. From first to last, emperors exercised real power in the government of a large land area around the Mediterranean Sea. Use the chart/time line at the right to answer the questions below.

1. How many emperors are listed on this time line?

   _____

   Did they all serve an equal number of years?

   _____

2. Who was the first emperor?

   _____

   The last?_____

3. When did the empire split into four sections?

   _____

   When was it reunited under one emperor?

   _____

4. Who served as emperor immediately before Nero?

   _____

   After Nero? _____

5. Give the years of Marcus Aurelius' reign.

   _____

6. How many emperors were named Constantine?

   _____

   Valentinian?_____

7. How many years passed from the reign of Vespasian to the reign of Gratian? _____

8. Was Tacitus emperor before or after Antoninus Pius?

   _____

   Before or after Galerius?_____

9. How many years passed from Hadrian's reign to Diocletian's reign? _____

Roman Emperors

23 BCE Augustus	282 Carus
14 BCE Tiberius	283 Carinus and Numerian
37 Gaius (Caligula)	
41 *Claudius*	*Empire split into four sections under two Augusti and two Caesars*
54 Nero	
68-69 Galba	284-285 *Diocletian*
69 Otho and Vitellius	286-305 *Maximian*
69 Vespasian	293-296 Constantius Chlorus
79 *Titus*	293-311 *Galerius*
81 Domitian	305-307 Flavius Severus
96 Nerva	
97 Trajan	308-324 Licinus
117 *Hadrian*	306-337 *Constantine I (Sole Emperor of East and West, 324)*
138 Antoninus Pius	
161-180 Marcus Aurelius	337-340 Constantine II
176-192 Commodus	337-350 Constans
193 Pertinax	337-361 *Constantius II*
193-211 *Septimius Severus*	361-363 *Julian*
	363-364 *Jovian*
198-217 Caracalla	364-375 *Valentinian I*
217 Macrinus	364-378 *Valens*
218 Elagabalus	367-383 Gratian
222 Severus Alexander	375-393 Valentinian II
235 Maximin Thrax	379-395 *Theodosius I*
238 Gordian I, II, III	385-388 Maximius
244 Philip and others	392-394 Eugenius
249 Decius and others	395-423 Honorius
253 Gallienus and others	425-455 Valentinian III
268 Claudius II	457-474 *Leo I*
269 Aurelian and others	475-476 Romulus Augustus
275 Tacitus	*(Eastern Emperors in italics)*
276 Probus	

Historical Overview of Ancient Rome

The early Romans believed a legend that claims a youth named Romulus founded the city of Rome. Historical evidence tells us that the original inhabitants of the region were simple peasant farmers called Latins who migrated to the area from Central Europe and settled along the banks of the Tiber River. In this central part of Italy the city of Rome grew to become the center of a vast empire. At its peak, the Roman Empire stretched from the Atlantic Ocean in the west to the Caspian Sea in the east. It reached northward into Britain and southward into Egypt.

While the Latins occupied the area around Rome, three other powers moved in around them. The Etruscans moved into central and northern Italy. The Greeks crossed into southern Italy. The powerful Carthaginians expanded into northern Africa. These different cultures would make lasting contributions to Roman culture and history.

Rome was ruled by kings during its first two centuries. When the Romans finally were able to defeat the last Etruscan king in 509 BCE they formed a new kind of government called a republic. In this system the elected leaders were advised by a group of men from the more powerful families.

The citizens of the Roman Republic were divided into two classes. The upper-class of noblemen and their families were called patricians. These men could hold political, military, or religious offices. The **plebeians** were the common people who comprised most of the population. For years the plebeians struggled with the patricians for equality and power.

As the Roman army marched off to expand the Republic's holdings, it waged war with many neighbors. Carthage had established many successful trading posts around the Mediterranean. Rome and Carthage became bitter rivals and fought three long and bloody battles, called the Punic Wars, in order to dominate the Mediterranean region. Rome finally defeated Carthage in 146 BCE and became the sole ruler of a mighty and gigantic empire.

How was Rome able to conquer and control so much territory and unite it under one rule? There are five main reasons.

1. Romans loved their Republic and defended it with fierce patriotic determination. They took great pride in their military successes, and they continued building and strengthening their army with the spoils of their victories.

2. Once a region became a Roman province, many of the native people were granted Roman citizenship. They then gained the benefits of Roman protection and stability. In turn, Rome taxed the people to help pay for a stronger army.

3. The Romans absorbed the achievements of the people they conquered and utilized them to help develop a lifestyle that was often more advanced and comfortable than before. Many people liked the advantages of this and willingly adopted Roman rule.

4. The Romans allowed people in conquered regions to keep their own language and religion, as long as they also worshipped Roman gods and learned Latin, the official Roman language.

5. The Romans were excellent engineers and builders. They constructed a vast network of roads throughout the Empire that allowed for more efficient travel and trade.

Historical Overview of Ancient Rome *(cont.)*

As Rome aggressively expanded its Empire, civil wars were common. Warlords fought amongst themselves, and slaves rebelled against the Roman Army. Dishonest and greedy leaders fought one another for control of the government. One such leader was Julius Caesar. He had been a successful general in the army. Back home, Caesar fought for and gained great power. He declared himself dictator. Fearing Caesar's disregard for Rome's constitution, a group of senators assassinated him. However, their hopes of saving the Republic did not materialize. Caesar's death only caused a greater struggle for power.

For several years Caesar's adopted son, Octavian, shared power with Mark Antony and Queen Cleopatra of Egypt. After defeating the Egyptians, Octavian ruled as the first emperor of Rome under the name of Augustus Caesar. Although his rule marked the end of the Republic, it also began a new era of Pax Romana, or Roman peace, and the beginning of centuries of rule by emperors.

The birth of Jesus Christ marked the change between the time eras we know as BCE and CE. The rapid growth, spread, and influence of religion in the area—mainly Christianity and Judaism—created much fear within the Roman government. Many Christians were persecuted and even put to death. Pontius Pilate ordered the crucifixion of Jesus Christ in about CE 30. The first Christian emperor did not come to power until CE 306. He was Constantine the Great, who ruled until CE 337.

After Constantine's rule ended, pagan religions were forbidden and their followers were persecuted. The mighty Roman Empire was permanently divided into East (Byzantine) and West. The Empire's weakening power allowed for more conquest by invading barbarians. Around CE 475, the Western Empire collapsed. What followed in this area was an era of unrest and turmoil known as the Dark Ages. However, the Eastern Empire continued to flourish and lasted another thousand years before it fell to the Turks. The once-great Roman Empire finally ended in CE 1453.

1. **Historical evidence suggests that the original habitants of Rome were . . .**
   a. Romulus and Remus.
   b. simple peasant farmers called Latins.
   c. Greeks who crossed into southern Italy.
   d. Etruscans.

2. *Plebeians* **were . . .**
   a. the upper-class of noblemen and their families.
   b. the emperors.
   c. the people in the conquered regions of the Roman Empire.
   d. the common people who comprised most of the population.

3. **Which of the following is NOT a reason why Rome was able to conquer and control territory?**
   a. Romans loved their Republic and defended it with fierce patriotic determination.
   b. The Romans allowed people in conquered regions to keep their own language and religion.
   c. The Romans bought land from the people at a higher price than other governments did.
   d. The Romans constructed a vast network of roads throughout the Empire that allowed for more efficient travel and trade.

4. **Which emperor's rule marked the end of the Republic?**
   a. Julius Caesar
   b. Augustus Caesar
   c. Constantine
   d. Mark Antony

Roman Monuments

Look at the list of famous monuments to Roman engineering. Then answer the questions on the following page.

Castel Sant' Angelo—built by Emperor Hadrian in CE 136 as a tomb for himself and his successors
Trajan's Column—97 foot (29.6 m) marble shaft dedicated to Emperor Trajan in CE 113
The Pantheon—Rome's only perfectly preserved ancient building; begun by Agrippa in 27 BCE became a domed, circular temple under Hadrian in CE 124, used as a church since CE 609
The Colosseum—built about CE 80, approximately a third of a mile in circumference, three tiers of arches in an oval amphitheater, seated 50,000
The Aurelian Wall—built in CE 272 to keep out the barbarians
Theater of Marcellus—finished in CE 13 and housed the great productions of Greek and Roman authors
Circus Maximus—huge chariot race track, 600 x 200 yards (549 km x 183 km), begun about 300 CE could seat 250,000
Baths of Caracalla—public baths built during the reign of Emperor Caracalla, CE 211–217
Hadrian's Arch—triumphal arch built during the reign of Emperor Hadrian, CE 117-138
Arch of Constantine—triumphal arch built during the reign of the Emperor Constantine, CE 324–337
Appian Way—ancient Roman highway begun in 312 BCE
Emperor's Palace—beginning in CE 85, emperors lived here surrounded by an army of servants and officials

The Colosseum

Roman Monuments *(cont.)*

1. Which seated more people, the Colosseum or the Circus Maximus? How many more people?

   _____

2. Which triumphal arch is older, Constantine's or Hadrian's? Approximately how many
   years older? _____

3. The Pantheon is reputed to be one of the most beautiful domed buildings in the world. How long
   was it a temple to all gods before it became a Christian church?_____

4. When was the Emperor's Palace 1,900 years old? _____

5. The Appian Way was built to let people travel to Rome. The Aurelian Wall was built to keep
   some people out. How many years passed between the construction of these two Roman projects?

   _____

6. The Emperor's Palace was a place for emperors to live; the Castel Sant' Angelo was a place for
   emperors to be buried. Which was built first? How many years passed from
   the construction of one to the construction of the other? _____

7. Chariot races were popular in Rome for a long time. Approximately how much older is
   the Circus Maximus than the Theater of Marcellus? _____

8. Approximately how tall is Trajan's Column? _____

The Roman Empire's Resources

Directions: Use the table below to complete the graph as well as the map on the following page.

Product	Country of Origin
wheat and barley	Egypt, Sicily, Tunisia, Italy
corn	Egypt, Russia, Tunisia, Sicily, Sardinia
olive oil	Spain, Tunisia, Libya, Syria, Austria, Greece, Italy
wine	Greece, Austria, Italy
silks	China, Syria
cotton	India
timber	Syria, Yugoslavia, Romania, Lebanon
marble	Northern Italy, Greece
pottery and glass	Italy, France (Gaul)
gold and silver	Africa, Egypt, Spain
lead and tin	Britain
jewels, spices, and perfumes	China, India, Syria, Turkey
wild beasts	Britain, Germany, Africa, Turkey, Algeria

Directions: Answer the following questions and complete the bar graph below.

1. Which resource is available in the most locations?
2. Which resource is found in the fewest locations?
3. List the places where food and beverages are found.
4. Which place has the most resources? List the location and the different resources.

Graph the Empire's Resources

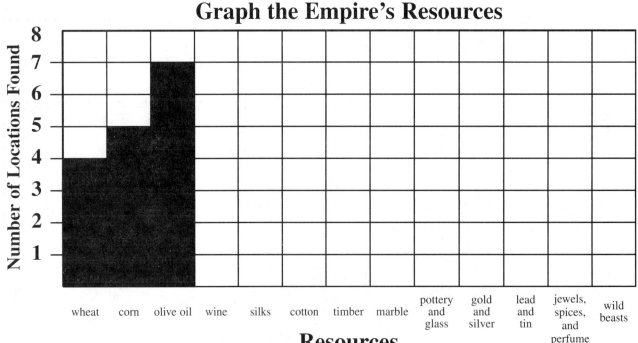

Resources

Map the Empire's Resources

Directions: Use The Roman Empire's Resources (page 186) to make a resource map of the Roman Empire. Create colored symbols to represent the resources and put them on the map key and the map.

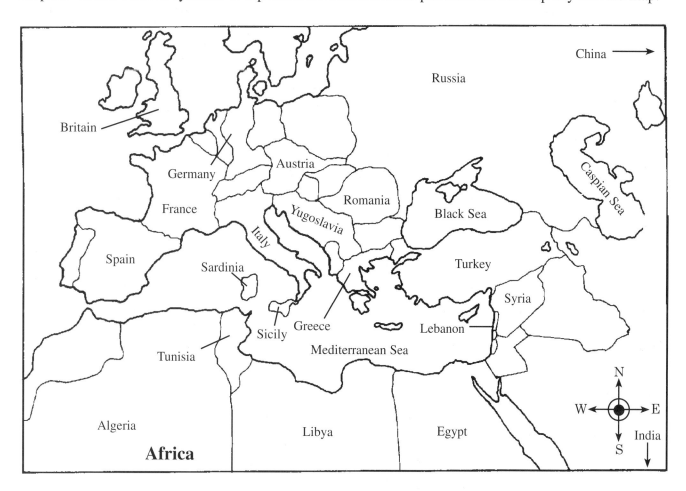

Key

wheat and barley		cotton		lead and tin	
corn		timber		jewels, spices, perfume	
olive oil		marble		wild beasts	
wine		pottery and glass			
silks		gold and silver			

Early Roman Beliefs and Worship

As Ancient Rome expanded its empire and conquered other people, Romans began to absorb and accept or modify some of the other cultures' beliefs. The Romans especially adopted and adapted the religious beliefs of the Greeks. Although early Romans thought the numina (spiritual forces) had no form, they gradually developed the belief that the gods took on human qualities and bodies.

The Romans began to identify their gods with those of the Greeks. Eventually, the two sets of gods could barely be distinguished except for their names. For example, the Greek god Zeus, ruler of the heavens and was king of all the gods, became the Roman god Jupiter. Hera, his wife, became known as Juno. Athena, the Greek goddess of wisdom, war, and handicrafts, became the Roman goddess Minerva.

Because the people of the Roman Empire came from a wide variety of cultures and heritages, they worshipped in many different ways. The Roman government tolerated this as long as they also paid homage to the official gods of Rome and participated in Roman religious rituals.

There were two basic ways to worship in Ancient Rome. The first was to worship and make offerings at your own family shrine, or lararium. Each morning the family would pay homage to the goddess of the hearth, Vesta, and to other numerous household spirits who were asked to work on behalf of the members of the family. These included Janus, who guarded the home's entrance, and Penates, who looked after the food cupboard.

The second form of religious practice was a type of public worship conducted regularly at local temples or on holy days (holidays) with special festivals. There were many temples, each dedicated to a god the Romans believed was in charge of their daily fate. However, the Romans did not go to the temples to attend religious services. Instead they went to make offerings and sacrifices. Some left coins, pieces of jewelry, small statues of the god, food, and drink. Sometimes messages would be left at the temple asking for something special or for a curse to be placed on an enemy. Animal sacrifice was common, and incense was burned at the altars where these sacrifices took place. Sacrifices ranged from a single bird to a whole herd of cattle. Different animals were sacrificed in different ways. Larger animals like boars or cows were felled with an axe.

Early Roman Beliefs and Worship *(cont.)*

Priests conducted the religious rituals, but these men were usually regular citizens who held high positions in public life. Being a priest was only one of their civic duties. The only full-time religious workers were the Vestal Virgins, young girls trained to guard the holy flame of the goddess Vesta at her temple in Rome. Of course, as in many ancient cultures, the emperor was considered the chief priest, and temples were dedicated in his honor. During one period of Ancient Roman history, emperor worship began when the emperor was declared a god after he died and was required to be worshipped as such.

Still, the attitude of the early Romans toward the gods was mixed. On the one hand they were feared, and many Romans spent a great deal of time and energy trying to win their favor. On the other hand, some Romans were doubtful about the powers of the gods. These people prayed and sacrificed in troubled times, but found the practice dull and unrewarding. Many felt the state religion lacked spiritual fulfillment, so they turned to other religions. Some of the more exotic religions of the East seemed to offer hope of eternal life and more meaning to their daily lives. A number of these cults spread across the Empire along the trade routes. The most popular included the worship of the Egyptian goddess Isis and the Persian goddess Mithras. These involved secret initiation ceremonies, holy secrets, and the promise of rebirth into an afterlife.

The Romans tolerated this diversity of religion as long as it did not interfere with or pose a threat to the Empire. This tolerance did not extend to Jews and Christians. Both of these religions refused to acknowledge and make sacrifices to the Roman gods, and for this they were brutally persecuted. Later Constantine became emperor and decreed freedom of religion. He made Christianity the official religion of the Roman Empire.

Answer the following questions in complete sentences.

   1. How were the Greek and Roman religions similar?

   _____

   _____

   2. What were the two different ways that the Romans practiced their religion?

   _____

   _____

   3. Why did participation in traditional Roman worship decrease?

   _____

   _____

   4. Why were the Jews and Christians persecuted and not people of other religions?

   _____

   _____

The Jews and the Christians

Augustus Caesar became Rome's first emperor in 27 BCE. During his reign many important events took place to help create an era of peace and prosperity. Travel throughout the Empire was made safe so that trade flourished, and many new goods made their way into Rome. People could now choose from a variety of places to settle and still be protected by the strong Roman military. Many people of all different races were now bound together under one rule. The language, customs, and religions of these various people were accepted by the Roman government as long as they didn't conflict with Roman law.

One of the most important events in the history of the world occurred around 4 BCE. Jesus Christ of Nazareth was born in the town of Bethlehem in an outlying part of the Roman Empire called Judea. The people of this region were called Jews, and their religion was Judaism. Jesus was a Jew, and the people who later became his followers were also Jews. Christianity began as a Jewish sect and has its roots in Judaism.

Although the Romans tolerated most religions of the people they conquered, Judaism clashed with Roman religion and law in too many ways. The Jews believed in one true god and refused to recognize any other. This meant they were unwilling to worship the Roman gods or the emperor as a god. The Jews also followed the teachings of their prophets and the strict laws set forth by their god in the Torah, their holy book. One of their laws forbade them to make sacrifices, which again conflicted with Roman practice. For these and other reasons, Romans fought the Jews because they believed their religion was a serious threat to the Roman Empire.

Although Judaism was a problem for Roman authorities, it was recognized as a legal religion. As Jesus grew older and began teaching, he attracted a small band of followers, or disciples. This group came to believe that Jesus Christ was the messiah (savior) and the son of God. They called themselves Christians. Even though Jews and Christians shared the same basic beliefs, the Jews did not recognize Jesus as the son of God. They believed that the messiah was still to come, and when he did, he would overthrow the Roman government and reunite the Jews. However Christians believed Jesus Christ came to give them the gift of everlasting life.

Since the number of people involved in the early Christian sect was quite small, few people throughout the Roman Empire were aware of it. This is why there are few written accounts of early Christianity. Stories of Jesus's life and teachings were collected and recorded between CE 100–200 in a part of the Christian Bible called the New Testament. Since these stories are written from the perspective of Christians to teach and inspire other Christians, the stories do not reflect the viewpoints of Jews or Romans.

As Christianity grew and spread, it became a real threat to Jewish beliefs as well as Roman authorities. The early Christians concentrated on trying to convert other Jews and were met with great resistance from Jewish leaders. Although they were charged with disobeying Jewish law, the Christians insisted that their belief in Jesus and his love were more important than the laws set forth in the Torah. Consequently, persecution of Christians came first from the Jews and later from the Romans.

Social Studies

The Jews and the Christians *(cont.)*

As Christianity spread, it became evident to the Romans, too, that something must be done. Christian settlements sprang up around Roman communities, and the Christians were unpopular because they refused to act like other Romans. The Christians kept to themselves and worshipped behind closed doors. Many Romans felt the Christians thought they were superior—like a secret elite club.

Some of the Christian ideas were shocking to the Romans. Roman order relied upon wealth and property as a status symbol, but the Christians denounced money and earthly pleasures. The Romans considered their religion and government to be linked as one, while the Christians saw them as separate. The Christians did not attend public festivals or take part in the activities of their communities because to do so would go against the laws of their religion.

Many Romans feared that the failure of the Christians to honor Roman gods would hurt the Empire. Although the Jews also refused to honor the gods, Judaism was a well-established religion and therefore excused. Soon the Christians' lack of Roman patriotism made them the scapegoat for every natural disaster that plagued the Empire.

By CE 100, to be a Christian was a crime punishable by death under Roman law. However, this policy was seldom enforced, because local officials in the provinces actually decided the fate of the Christians under their jurisdiction. Many of these officials were unsure what to do, so they let most Christians alone as long as they didn't make trouble. Still, some Christians were treated cruelly under this law. Many were forced to go into a large arena, or colosseum, to fight lions as entertainment for the Romans.

Emperor Constantine provided the turning point for the Christians. He believed the Roman government should be tolerant of all religions. He forbade the persecution of Christians and allowed them to worship openly without fear. Churches were rebuilt and congregations grew. Constantine helped Christianity spread throughout the Roman Empire. By CE 325 the Christian Church and the Roman State were one and the same. Constantine was officially baptized as a Christian shortly before his death.

The Christian church continued to grow more powerful throughout the CE 300s. Church leaders began giving orders to emperors and punishing them for going against their wishes. Just as the Romans had persecuted those unwilling to obey their religious customs, some fanatical Christians were now persecuting pagans, or those people who were not Christians or Jews. In CE 391 pagan religions were outlawed. Now it was the Christians forcing their beliefs upon others. Intolerance and persecution of those who held different beliefs had come full circle.

Directions: Answer the following questions in complete sentences.

1. **Why wouldn't the Romans tolerate Judaism?** _____

2. **How did the Jews and Christians differ in their beliefs?** _____

3. **Why were Romans suspicious of Christians?** _____

4. **When Christianity became the official religion of the Roman Empire did religious persecution stop? Explain.** _____

Compare the Religions of Ancient Rome

Read the numbered statements below that list some of the religious practices in the Ancient Roman Empire. Each statement is true for one or more of the three main religions of that era. Study each statement and relate it to each of the three religions. Then place the **number** of the statement in the appropriate section of the Venn diagram.

For example, consider this statement: * Welcomed all people into the religion. This statement is true of the Roman polytheism, which encouraged all people to worship their many gods, and of Christianity, which attempted to convert people to believe in their one god. It is not true for Judaism, which allowed only Jews. Therefore, the * has been placed on the Venn diagram in the section where the Christianity circle overlaps the Roman polytheism circle. It is not inside the Judaism circle.

Religious Statement

1. Believed in one god.
2. Believed in many gods.
3. Believed that Jesus was the messiah.
4. Did not believe that Jesus was the messiah.
5. Accepted some of the beliefs of other religions.
6. Religion played an important role in daily life.
7. Carried out sacrifices at public temples.
8. Worshipped in churches.
9. Worshipped in temples and homes.
10. Persecuted the Christians.
11. Persecuted the Jews.
12. Persecuted the pagans.

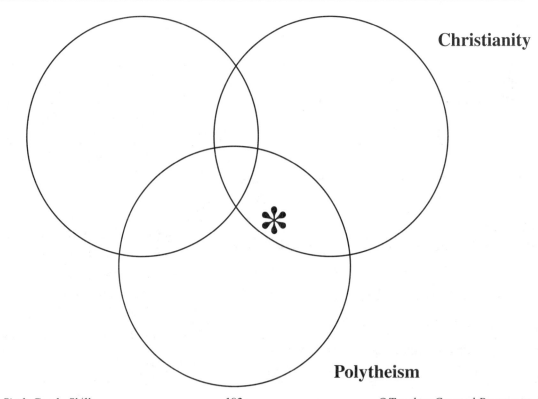

Judaism   **Christianity**

Polytheism

Cultural Time Line

To help understand the development of the ancient cultures of America, fill in the time line below showing their growth and the growth of other areas of the world.

Year	Europe	Near East and Asia	Central America and Mexico	Peru
3500–2500 BCE	3000 BCE Beginning of Minoan Age in Crete	3500 BCE First Egyptian dynasty founded		
2500–1500 BCE			2000 BCE First farm settlements in Guatemala, Chiapas, Yucatan	
1500–500 BCE				1200 BCE Chavin civilization in highlands, Coastal settlements
499–0 BCE				

Transfer the information below to the appropriate columns on the chart.

Europe

- 3000 BCE Beginning of Minoan Age in Crete
- 776 BCE First Olympic games in Greece
- 734 BCE Legendary founding of Rome
- 27 BCE Caesar Augustus crowned first Roman emperor

Central America and Mexico

- 2000 BCE First farm settlements in Guatemala, Chiapas, Yucatan
- 1500 BCE Olmec Civilization
- 300 BCE Rise of the Maya begins
- 150 BCE Teotihuacan settled by farmers

Near East And Asia

- 3500 BCE First Egyptian dynasty founded
- 2700 BCE Chinese civilization begins
- 326 BCE Alexander the Great conquers Near East
- 210 Great Wall of China built

Peru

- 1200 BCE Chavin civilization in highlands, Coastal settlements
- 100 BCE Moche kingdom on the Northern coast, Nazca ruled the south

The Land of the Maya

The remains of the great Mayan civilization are found in the Central American countries of Mexico, El Salvador, Honduras, Guatemala, and Belize. This Mayan homeland encompasses one of the most varied environments on Earth. The Northern lowlands are flat, and there is little surface water, while the Southern lowlands and the volcanic highlands are rain forests.

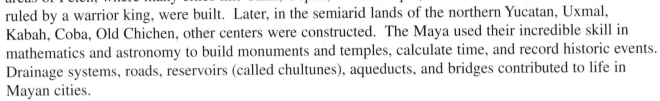

Archaeologists believe that the earliest Maya were nomads who hunted, fished, and gathered nuts, berries, and seeds for food. By the Preclassic or Formative Period (2000 BCE to CE 250), the Maya had settled in communities or villages and were farmers. Deep in the tropical rain forests, the Maya cleared the dense bush and planted corn and other crops.

In the Classic Maya Period, from CE 250 to 900, the Maya created a remarkable civilization. Civilization first flourished in the forested areas of Peten, where many cities like Tikal, Copan, and Palenque, each ruled by a warrior king, were built. Later, in the semiarid lands of the northern Yucatan, Uxmal, Kabah, Coba, Old Chichen, other centers were constructed. The Maya used their incredible skill in mathematics and astronomy to build monuments and temples, calculate time, and record historic events. Drainage systems, roads, reservoirs (called chultunes), aqueducts, and bridges contributed to life in Mayan cities.

Beginning about CE 800, the Maya abandoned their large lowland cities. Archaeologists have been unable to explain why this happened, but there are several theories, including war with Mexican (Toltec) armies, changes in climate, economic problems, famine, and overpopulation. The surviving people moved into the jungle where they lived in small villages. In the Postclassic Period (CE 900–1500), the Maya in the Yucatan blended their culture with that of Toltec invaders from Central Mexico.

The first encounter with Spanish explorers was a peaceful one with Christopher Columbus in 1502. Later Spanish explorers believed they had found El Dorado, a legendary city of great wealth. The Spanish conquered and enslaved the native people. Warfare and European diseases brought by the Spanish killed as many as 90% of the Maya. Missionaries tried to convert the Maya to Christianity.

Today, all that remains of this amazing civilization are astounding temples and magnificent cities of ruins scattered throughout Central America. Descendants of the Maya live in large cities and in rural villages. Many ancient traditions of the Maya, including planting, weaving, and the use of the calendar, coexist with modern technology.

Circle the correct answer.

1. **Which of the following is NOT a country where Mayan remains are found?**
   a. Mexico   b. El Salvador   c. Guatemala   d. Colombia

2. **The Classic Maya Period was from . . .**
   a. CE 250 to 900.   b. CE 800–1502.   c.   250–900 BCE.   d. 900–1500 BCE.

3. **Which of the following is a theory of why the Maya abandoned their lowland cities?**
   a. Fires burned down most of the cities, forcing the Maya to leave.
   b. War with the Spanish caused the Maya to move to safety in other cities.
   c. European diseases spread too easily in the lowland cities.
   d. Famine caused the Maya to leave the lowland cities.

4. **War with the Spanish and European diseases killed as many as _____ of the Maya.**
   a. 50%   b. 30%   c. 90%   d. 100%

The Inca Empire

Archaeologists have identified several groups of people who settled in ancient Peru. Along the coast the Nazca and Mochica tribes flourished from CE 200 to 600. In the highlands, near Lake Titicaca, Tiahuanaco and Huari people built roads, towns and temples. These empires collapsed about CE 1000. Then, in about CE 1200, the first Inca, Manco Capac, arrived at the Cuzco Valley.

No one is sure if Manco Capac was real or legendary. According to the traditional stories, he was the son of the Sun God, sent to earth to found a people with his sisters and brothers. They settled in the Cuzco Valley where they built a small, strong state, *Tahuantinsuyu* (The Land of the Four Quarters), ruled by the descendants of Manco Capac, who were called *Inca* (lord or king).

Then, in 1438, the neighboring Chancas threatened to invade Cuzco. The Inca, Pachacuti, lead his army to victory and expanded his control of the area. He is also credited with rebuilding the city of Cuzco. Archaeologists think this city was planned to look like a puma. Pachacuti was Inca until his death in 1471.

The rulers who followed Pachacuti were called *Sapa Inca*, and continued expanding the Inca Empire, sometimes through wars and sometimes by promising better lives. By the time the Spanish arrived in 1532, the Tahuantinsuyu people and their Inca leaders controlled the west coast of South America from Quito in the north to what is now Chile in the south, a distance of 2,170 miles (3,500 km). The empire included diverse terrain, from the Andes mountains to deserts and coastal areas. The Incas imposed their religion, laws, and Quechua language on those they conquered, and they collected taxes from the people. A vast system of roads connected all parts of the Inca lands to the capital at Cuzco, carrying armies, officials, and goods. Messengers, (called *chasquis*), used the roads to carry communications between Cuzco and its regional capitals.

At its height, the Inca Empire governed 10 million people and included parts of the present-day countries of Peru, Bolivia, Colombia, Argentina, Ecuador, and Chile.

Answer the following questions in complete sentences.

1. **What is the traditional story of Manco Capac?**

_____

_____

2. **What did the Incas impose on those they conquered?**

_____

_____

3. **What did roads connected to Cuzco help do?**

_____

_____

The Aztecs

The Aztecs were the last people to settle in the Valley of Mexico, high in the volcanic mountains of central Mexico. There, on the shores of shallow, marshy Lake Tezcoco, they built an impressive center for their empire.

The Aztecs were a semi-nomadic tribe of Chichimecs who arrived in the Valley of Mexico about CE 1200. According to oral traditions and codices (ancient manuscripts), the ancestral home of the Aztecs was Aztlan, a place northwest of Mexico City. No one has identified an exact location. Legend has it that about CE 1100 the god Huizilopochtli (Blue Hummingbird) instructed them to wander until they found an eagle on a cactus, eating a snake. Here they would build their capital.

After many stops and skirmishes, they settled on the west side of Tetzcoco, at a place called Chapultapec (Grasshopper Hill). Other tribes drove the Aztecs out, but the Colhua allowed the Aztecs to live near them in exchange for the services of Aztec soldiers. Finally tired of being under Colhuacans, Aztecs killed the daughter of the ruler, then fled into the marshy lake. On one island, they saw an eagle on a cactus. At the site of this sign, the Aztecs built their capital, Tenochtitlán.

In the 200 years from the sighting of the eagle (about CE 1325) to the arrival of the Spanish (CE 1521), the Aztecs grew to be the most powerful people in the Valley of Mexico. They adopted many elements from the cultures that had preceded them and built one of the most impressive cities of Mesoamerica.

Circle the correct answer.

1. Based on the passage, how do you think people first learned about the Aztecs?

    a. reading textbooks

    b. oral traditions and codices

    c. in the newspaper

    d. on the Internet

2. What does *Huizilopochtli* mean?

    a. Valley of Mexico

    b. Blue Hummingbird

    c. Grasshopper Hill

    d. capital city

3. The Aztec capital was named . . .

    a. Aztlan.

    b. Tetzcoco.

    c. Tenochtitlán.

    d. Mesoamerica.

4. What sign did the Aztecs look for to know where to build their capital?

    a. an eagle on a cactus

    b. a fish in the lake

    c. lightning hitting the mountain

    d. a blue hummingbird

The Water Cycle

Our Earth is a closed system. This means that all the water that ever was here is still here. How can that be? Because our Earth recycles its elements, using each one over and over again.

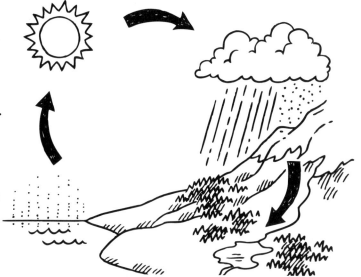

Every drop of water on the Earth has gone through the water cycle. Much of it has gone through the cycle billions of times. All of the water on Earth is always in some stage of the water cycle. The water is either in storage, evaporation, condensation, precipitation, percolation, or runoff. All of the ice frozen in glaciers and all of the water in oceans, lakes, rivers, and underground aquifers is in the storage stage. During the evaporation stage, liquid water changes to vapor. This vapor enters the atmosphere. When the vapor cools, it condenses and forms clouds. Later the clouds drop precipitation in the form of rain or snow, and the water falls back to the ground. Much of this precipitation seeps down through the ground in a process called percolation. The rest runs into streams, lakes, rivers, and oceans. Such runoff increases during storms, rainy seasons, and after snow and ice melt.

Humans have affected the water cycle for thousands of years. We dig ditches to bring water to dry land. We build dams to control flooding and provide electrical power. We drill wells to pump up groundwater. In some areas of the U.S. people have drained underground aquifers that took thousands of years to fill. As a result, the ground may begin to cave in.

The oceans hold about 97 percent of all the water on Earth. Since sea water is salty, we cannot drink it. However, if water evaporates from an ocean, it leaves its salt behind. So when it falls as precipitation, it's fresh water. The fresh water in glaciers stays frozen for hundreds of years. Thus, we cannot easily **access** this water. Most groundwater is found in the first ten miles of the Earth's crust, and we can tap this supply. Water below this depth can only return to the Earth's surface during a volcanic eruption.

The Water Cycle *(cont.)*

Comprehension Questions

1. Steam is in what stage of the water cycle?

  a. condensation   c. evaporation

  b. percolation   d. precipitation

2. Read all of the statements. Decide what happened third.

  a. An aquifer was drained.

  b. People pumped out water.

  c. Many people drilled wells.

  d. A ground depression (sinkhole) formed.

3. Water stays the longest time in which stage of the water cycle?

  a. evaporation   c. precipitation

  b. storage   d. condensation

4. Another word for *access* is. . .

  a. drink.   c. obtain.

  b. buy.   d. freeze.

5. How does an aquifer fill with water?

  a. Rainwater percolates until it reaches the aquifer.

  b. The aquifer absorbs clouds.

  c. Ocean floods fill the aquifer.

  d. People pump water into the aquifer.

6. Picture a foggy day. The fog means that water is in which two stages of the water cycle?

  a. storage and condensation

  b. percolation and runoff

  c. evaporation and precipitation

  d. precipitation and condensation

7. Should we satisfy a growing need for more fresh water by melting polar ice? Explain.

_____

_____

_____

Relative Humidity

Earth's surface is covered in water. The water is in lakes. It is in rivers. It is in oceans. The surface water is always evaporating. When it evaporates, it changes. It changes into water vapor. Humidity describes the amount of water in the air.

Air can hold only so much water. It can absorb only so much. When the air can't absorb anymore, the water vapor condenses. The water becomes more tightly packed together. It condenses into clouds. Then, the water is returned to Earth's surface. It is returned in the form of rain. It is returned in the form of snow.

People often talk about relative humidity. How is relative humidity different from humidity? Relative humidity compares something. It compares the amount of water in the air with the total of what the air could hold. Suppose the relative humidity is 50%. This means the air holds half as much water as it could hold before condensing. People talk about relative humidity because it affects the way we feel. People often say, "High relative humidity? Ugh!" Why ugh? Why don't people like high relative humidity?

We stay cool in a special way. We use evaporation. Evaporation keeps us cool. First, we sweat. Our sweat is made of water. Then, our sweat evaporates. As it evaporates, we are cooled. When the relative humidity is high, it is harder to stay cool. This is because the air has already absorbed a lot of water. It is already filled with water. It is close to the point where it can't absorb anymore. The air does not feel dry. The air feels moist.

When the air is full of moisture, it is harder for us to shed sweat. It is harder for our sweat to evaporate. Our sweat is not absorbed into the moist air. It stays on our skin. It soaks our clothes. We feel damp and hot. We feel sticky. It is hard to feel cool when one is damp and sticky.

Directions: After reading the passage, answer the questions. Circle the correct answer.

1. **When the relative humidity is high . . .**
   a. it is harder to stay warm.
   b. we stay cool in a special way.
   c. the air has absorbed a lot of water.
   d. surface water makes us feel damp and sticky.

2. **This passage is mainly about . . .**
   a. water.
   b. sweating.
   c. humidity.
   d. evaporation.

3. **There is the least chance of rain when the relative humidity is . . .**
   a. 3%   c. 53%
   b. 23%   d. 83%

4. **When our sweat evaporates . . .**
   a. we heat up .
   b. we cool down.
   c. we feel damp.
   d. we feel sticky.

5. **Think about how the word water relates to water vapor. Which words relate in the same way?**

   > water : water vapor

   a. liquid : gas
   b. gas : liquid
   c. liquid : solid
   d. solid : liquid

Cloud Formations

Meteorologists learn to read cloud formations to help them predict upcoming weather. The clouds pictured below represent some of the earth's cloud formations. See how well you can identify them. Read the definitions, noting the cloud name for each. Then write the cloud name on or near the matching cloud.

Cumulus: Dense, billowy clouds heaped upon one another. (1,600 - 20,000 ft./480 m - 6 km)

Cirrostratus: Form ice crystals that veil the sky with a milky look. (over 20,000 ft./6 km)

Stratocumulus: Large, rounded masses with light and dark areas. (ground to 6,500 ft./ground to 2 km)

Altocumulus: Have various shapes; may form bands across the sky. (6,000 - 20,000 ft./1.8 - 6 km)

Stratus: Low, smooth layer of clouds; resembles fog. (ground to 6,500 ft /ground to 2 km)

Cirrus: Wispy clouds that look like tufts of hair. (sometimes higher than 30,000 ft./9 km)

Water Words Scramble

Water makes up three-fourths of the surface of our planet. Earth has water in oceans, lakes, and rivers. It has water in the sky, under the ground, and frozen in ice. Every living thing on Earth depends on a source of water. Water is one of our most precious resources.

Directions: Each of the words in the box below has to do with water. First, unscramble the words. Then move the numbered letters to the bottom to find the answer to the bonus question.

watershed	evaporate	drinking	glacier	condensation
precipitation	chemicals	pollution	waste	sewage

1. tewas

    __ __ __ __ __
    1

2. weesag

    __ __ __ __ __ __
    2

3. gniknird

    __ __ __ __ __ __ __ __
      3

4. rsetawhde

    __ __ __ __ __ __ __ __ __
    4

5. snodacnntioe

    __ __ __ __ __ __ __ __ __ __ __ __
      5

6. linopluto

    __ __ __ __ __ __ __ __ __
    6

7. rleagci

    __ __ __ __ __ __ __
    7

8. cichleams

    __ __ __ __ __ __ __ __ __
    8

9. aceiiinopprtt

    __ __ __ __ __ __ __ __ __ __ __ __ __
    9

10. proteavea

    __ __ __ __ __ __ __ __ __
    10

Bonus: Which of the Great Lakes is the deepest?

__ __ __ __ __ __ __ __ __ __ __ __
8   1   3   4   2   6   9   4   10   7   5   10

The Rock Cycle

You have probably heard of the water cycle, but do you know that rocks are recycled too? What does the Earth look like inside?

How do we know what is inside the Earth? Can we drill into the center of the Earth?

All the rocks which are on Earth have been here since Earth first began about 4.5 billion years ago. The only new rocks are occasional meteors which are pulled toward Earth by gravity as they come near our planet. (Of course, we also have a few rocks that were brought back by astronauts who first landed on the moon.) Rocks are constantly being formed as magma from beneath the Earth's crust, which then forces its way to the surface in volcanoes. Rock is recycled through erosion forces of water, wind, and ice. Rock is also melted when it goes deep enough to make contact with the mantle of the Earth.

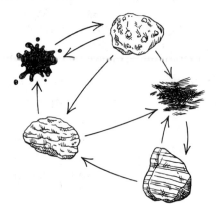

The **crust** is the hard layer of rock which covers the outside of the Earth. This layer is about 5–20 miles (8–32 km) thick and lies just above the mantle. The **mantle** is the layer just below the crust is about 1,800 miles (2,880 km) thick and consists of semisolid rock which is approximately 1,600° F (871° C). This extremely hot taffy-like layer moves slowly in convection currents between the crust and outer core. **Magma** is the semisolid material in the mantle which sometimes pours through cracks in the crust and is then called lava. When it cools and hardens into rock, it is referred to as igneous rock. Just below the mantle, the 1,400–mile (2,240–km) layer called the outer core is made of liquid iron and nickel which is 4,000° F (2,204° C). The **inner core** of the Earth consists of the heaviest elements of iron and nickel which came to rest here during the early stages of Earth's development. These metals are solid despite their temperature of 9,000° F (4,982° C).

The Earth is 4,000 miles (6,400 km) in radius; it is impossible to drill into the center because the distance and temperature are too great. Scientists know the structure of the interior of Earth through Earthquakes. The energy waves given off by Earthquakes are like sound waves, traveling faster through solid material than through liquid or gas. There are some Earthquake waves which cannot pass through a liquid. Knowing this, geologists (people who study the Earth) use the speed and direction of Earthquake waves which are picked up by instruments around the world to make a picture of the inside of the Earth.

Circle the best answer for each question.

1. **According to the passage, the earth first began about . . .**
   a. one million years ago.
   b. 4.5 million years ago.
   c. 4.5 billion years ago.
   d. 5.4 billion years ago.

2. **Which of the following is located just below the crust?**
   a. mantle
   b. magma
   c. inner core
   d. outer core

3. **According to the passage, why can't we drill into the center of the earth?**
   a. We don't have long enough drills.
   b. It would take too long.
   c. It would damage the center, causing volcanoes to erupt.
   d. The distance and temperature are too great.

4. **Scientists know the structure of the interior of the earth through . . .**
   a. volcanoes.
   b. earthquakes.
   c. tsunamis.
   d. hail storms.

Where Do Rocks Come From?

Rocks cover the entire surface of the earth, even beneath every body of water and the polar ice caps. This rock covering is referred to as the crust of the earth. Dirt or soil, which consist of crushed rock and pieces of organic material, covers some areas of the crust.

The earth's crust consists of three types of rock—igneous, sedimentary, and metamorphic. The crust is slowly and continuously recycled from one type of rock to another.

Igneous: Melted rock beneath the crust, called magma, is under tremendous pressure and sometimes rises through cracks in the crust. When magma solidifies, it is called igneous rock. Magma may cool underground within the crust or break through creating volcanoes which pour forth lava (magma above ground), which cools into igneous rock. The crust is cracked into large sections called plates. The edges of some crystal plates are forced beneath others, melting and recycling the leading edge of rock as it comes in contact with the hot magma.

Sedimentary: Sedimentary rocks consist of rocks which were once igneous, metamorphic, sedimentary or organic material. These materials are deposited in layers by wind, water, or ice. As the layers build up, the pressure packs the material together and squeezes out most of the water, forming solid rock layers. These sediments may consist of rock fragments ranging in size from large boulders to fine grains of sand and silt. These rocks may also be deposits of minerals in the form of crystals or organic sediments such as shells, skeletons, and plants. Fossils are found in sedimentary rocks.

Metamorphic: Metamorphic rock is igneous, sedimentary, or metamorphic rock which is subjected to tremendous pressure and heat by movement of the earth's crust or contact with magma. The original rock changes in appearance and often in mineral composition. For example, granite (an igneous rock), becomes gneiss, and calcite in limestone (a sedimentary rock), changes to marble.

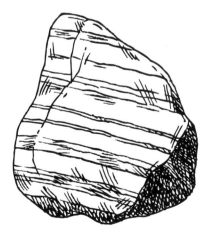

Igneous   **Sedimentary**   **Metamorphic**

Where Do Rocks Come From? *(cont.)*

Comprehension Questions

Directions: Read the passage on the previous page and then circle the correct answers.

1. **The rock covering the surface of the Earth is called the . . .**

    a. dirt.

    b. soil.

    c. sand.

    d. crust.

2. **Magma solidifies into what type of rock?**

    a. igneous

    b. sedimentary

    c. metamorphic

    d. granite

3. **True or False: Rocks are consistently recycled from one type to another.**

    a. true

    b. false

4. **Fossils are found in . . .**

    a. igneous rocks.

    b. sedimentary rocks.

    c. metamorphic rocks.

    d. volcanic rocks.

5. **Metamorphic rocks are subjected to tremendous . . .**

    a. pressure and noise.

    b. earthquakes and volcanoes.

    c. pressure and heat.

    d. heat and magma.

6. **In complete sentences, describe the rock cycle in each stage of forming the different types of rocks.**

    _____

    _____

    _____

    _____

History of the Earth

Why are there earthquakes? What could crack the Earth's crust? What makes mountains and volcanoes? How do the continents drift?

The history of the Earth is literally written in stone: fossils and rock formations. These can be interpreted by scientists to confirm what once was thought impossible— that huge sections of the Earth's crust drift on a sea of molten magma, carrying continents and the ocean floor with them. Large land animal fossils and rock layers found along the eastern coast of South America and western coast of Africa were found to be the same. Fossil specimens found in Australia and Antarctica also indicate that the same type of land animals once lived in
these widely separated areas. Plant fossils show that climates in many parts of the world have gradually changed.

Drilling samples of rock, mapping contours of the ocean floor, and plotting earthquake and volcano locations have revealed outlines of large divisions in the Earth's crust. This evidence, along with observations of volcanic activity deep under the ocean, has proven the early theories of continental drift and sea floor spreading. The theory is now referred to as *plate tectonics* and explains how continents gradually relocate over the Earth's long history. It also predicts what will happen to the crust as the energy from within the Earth's mantle continues to push the plates around, creating earthquakes, building and destroying mountains and volcanoes, and gradually changing the crust.

Answer the following questions in complete sentences.

1. What do scientists interpret to help discover the history of the earth?

   _____

   _____

2. Describe the theory of plate tectonics.

   _____

   _____

3. How did scientists find evidence that supported the plate tectonics theory?

   _____

   _____

Cracked Earth

Scientific Proof that Earth's Continents Drift

To the Students: You are a scientist who is examining the evidence which has been collected to prove that the Earth's crust is divided into plates that have gradually moved the continents around. Carefully record this information on the Cracked Earth Map on the next page.

Scientific Evidence	Code
The same fossils of large land animals are found on the eastern edge of South America and the western edge of Africa.	Green line along the east coast of South America and west coast of Africa.
The same type and age of rock formations are found on the eastern edge of South America and the western edge of Africa.	Brown line along the east coast of South America and west coast of Africa.
Fossil remains of animals like those found in Australia have been discovered in Antarctica.	Green X's on both of these continents.
A long, high ridge runs north-south along the middle of the floor of the Atlantic Ocean. Rock samples taken along the top of this ridge show the rocks are younger than those taken further away from the ridge.	Red line outlining the mid-Atlantic ridge. Brown line on the side of the ridges.
Deep-sea diving vessels investigating areas along the ridges discovered molten magma pushing up. This magma cools and becomes new rock.	Red line along the west and south edge of the Nazca Plate.
The mountains that run along the western coast of North and South America are gradually rising higher. There are frequent earthquakes in this area also. The mountains on these coasts also contain active volcanoes, like Mount St. Helens, and many dormant volcanoes.	Red line along the western coasts of North and South America.
Earthquakes happen frequently along and near the San Andreas Fault in California. This fault outlines the division between the Pacific and North American Plates.	Red line along the edge of the Pacific Plate that divides California and Baja from the North American Plate.
The Himalaya Mountains in northern India rise higher each year. There are also many earthquakes here.	Red line along the division between India and Asia.

Cracked Earth *(cont.)*

Map of Major Plates

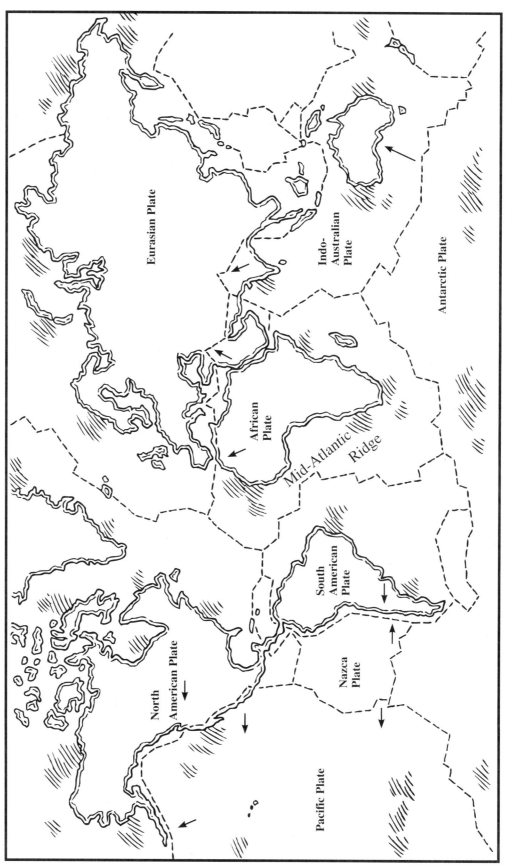

Building Mountains

Fundamental Facts

There are four different types of mountain ranges: fold mountains, block mountains, dome mountains, and volcanic mountains. All mountains are formed as a result of movement in Earth's crust.

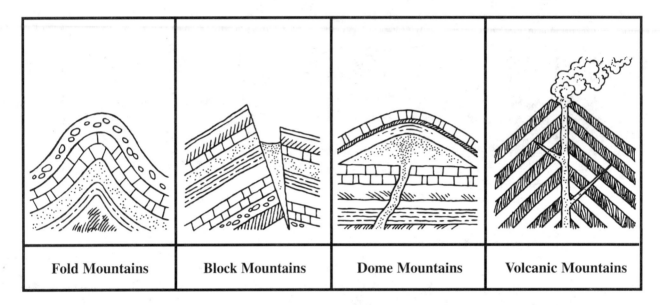

| Fold Mountains | Block Mountains | Dome Mountains | Volcanic Mountains |

Fold mountains are created when two tectonic plates collide and one plate goes under the other. All the land, rocks, and water between the two plates are pushed upward and crumbled into enormous folds. The Appalachians are fold mountains.

Block mountains are smaller than fold mountains. They are formed on fault lines when magma pushes up huge slabs of rock in the mantle, lifting up the land and splitting it apart. This creates wide rifts or cracks in Earth's crust. Great pieces of land slide down into the rifts, creating valleys with huge cliffs on both sides. The Sierra Nevada Mountains in California are block mountains.

Dome or intrusion mountains are created when swirling hot currents of magma push upward but cannot break through Earth's crust. The magma continues to press against the soil and rocks and finally spreads out in layers under the surface, forming a large rounded hump or dome-shaped mountain. The Black Hills of Dakota are examples of dome mountains.

Volcanic mountains are formed rapidly when gases in hot magma are forced upward through an opening or crack in Earth's crust. Lava slowly pours out the opening or erupts out violently forming a cone-shape mountain. The Cascade Mountains in the northwestern United States are volcanic mountains.

Use this information to help you answer the questions on the following page.

Building Mountains *(cont.)*

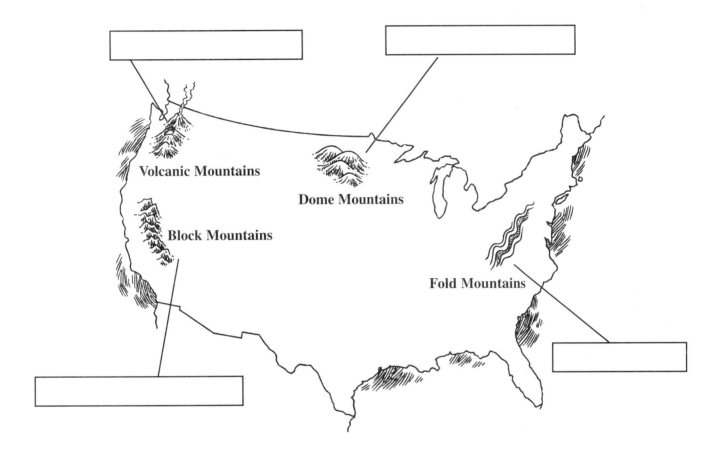

1. Write the names of the four different mountain ranges in the boxes on the map.

2. What type of mountains are the Cascades?_____

3. What type of mountains are the Appalachian Mountains? _____

4. What type of mountains are the Black Hills of South Dakota? _____

5. What type of mountains are the Sierra Nevada Mountains?_____

6. On a separate sheet of paper describe the four ways mountains are built.

Geology Facts

Directions: Discover some interesting facts about geology. Solve each problem below. Then write the answer in the blank.

1. 52 x 25	2. $4\overline{)680}$	3. $10 \times 10 =$

4.   1345
   + 438
	5. $81 \div 9 =$	6. 756
		   − 159

7.   2.5
   x 6
	8. 49
	  + 46
		9. 33
		  − 28

1. Worldwide, more than _____ volcanoes have erupted at least once during the past 10,000 years.

2. A tsunami *(tsoo-na-me)* is an extremely destructive sea wave, usually triggered by large earthquakes or eruptions, and can reach heights of _____ feet.

3. Yakima, located about _____ miles downwind of a volcano, received more than an inch of ash.

4. After observing the weird weather patterns that followed the eruption at Laki Volcano in Iceland in _____ , Benjamin Franklin became the first person to figure out that volcanic eruptions could affect climate.

5. The strength of earthquakes is measured on the Richter scale, which is numbered from 1 to _____. Most earthquakes are caused by rocks moving along faults.

6. Faults are fractures, or cracks, in rock layers along which the rocks have moved. The San Andreas fault in California, is about _____ miles long.

7. A sudden movement along the San Andreas fault in 1906 caused the destructive San Francisco earthquake. Near the city, the fault moved _____ feet.

8. In the top 10 miles of the earth's crust, _____ % of the rocks are either igneous (formed from molten magma) or metamorphic (changed by heat, pressure, or chemical action).

9. Geologists think that the age of the earth is about _____ billion years.

Rocks and Minerals Facts

Directions: Learn some facts about rocks and minerals as you find the missing words in the sentences. Use the number pairs listed in each sentence to determine the missing letters on the grid. Then, write the correct letter on the proper line in the sentence. **Reminder:** Use the numbers at the bottom of the grid to find the first number of the pair.

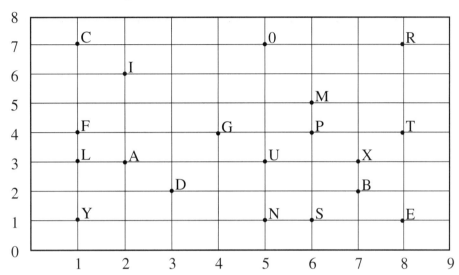

1. Sulfides are ___ ___ ___ ___ ___ ___ ___ ___ ___ that have atoms of sulfur and
              1,7 5,7 6,5 6,4 5,7 5,3 5,1 3,2 6,1
   atoms of a metal.

2. The sulfides are important because they provide important metals. Minerals that are mined for their metals are called ___ ___ ___ ___ .
              5,7 8,7 8,1 6,1

3. Pyrite is the most common sulfide mineral on earth and is found just about everywhere. Sometimes it looks like gold. Pieces in streams have fooled miners, so it was nicknamed
   ___ ___ ___ ___ , ___   ___ ___ ___ ___ .
   1,4 5,7 5,7 1,3 6,1   4,4 5,7 1,3 3,2

4. Sulfosalts are minerals that have sulfur, a metal (either silver, copper, or lead), and a semimetal. The semimetals are bismuth, antimony, and ___ ___ ___ ___ ___ ___ ___ .
              2,3 8,7 6,1 8,1 5,1 2,6 1,7

5. The ___ ___ ___ ___ ___ ___ are very important minerals. Oxygen is a part of the air
        5,7 7,3 2,6 3,2 8,1 6,1
   we breathe. It is also in water and magmas.

6. The ___ ___ ___ ___ ___ ___ ___ ___ ___ ___ are a group of beautiful and very
        1,7 2,3 8,7 7,2 5,7 5,1 2,3 8,4 8,1 6,1
   common minerals.

7. ___ ___ ___ ___ ___ ___ ___ ___ have a nitrogen atom surrounded by three oxygen
   5,1 2,6 8,4 8,7 2,3 8,4 8,1 6,1
   atoms. Sodium is a nitrate found in dry, desert areas.

8. ___ ___ ___ ___ ___ ___ is probably the most common sulfate. It has a Mohs
   4,4 1,1 6,4 6,1 5,3 6,5
   hardness of two, and can be scratched with your fingernail.

Meteors and Comets

During Columbus' first voyage to the Indies he reported seeing "...a marvelous bolt of fire fall from the heavens into the sea..." This phenomenon was actually a meteor. Learn about meteors. Read the paragraph below and then answer the questions below it.

> Meteors are sometimes called "shooting stars," but they are not stars at all. They are chunks of iron and stone that have broken off from asteroids. Meteors fall to Earth very quickly and, unlike comets, they only appear to last for a few seconds. As meteors make their descent, they become hot and begin to glow brightly. Meteors can burn up before they reach the Earth, but occasionally a meteor will hit the ground hard enough to form a crater. When a meteor makes it all the way to Earth, it is then called a meteorite. One famous meteorite crater is in Arizona. The Barringer Meteor Crater is almost 600 feet deep and was made by a giant meteorite weighing more than 500 tons (or one million pounds)!
>
> Other bright objects which can be seen traveling through space are comets. A comet is a ball of dust, ice, and gases that travels in an orbit around the sun. As it speeds along in space, the sun's light and heat cause the comet to lose some of its dust and gas. This dust and gas streams out from behind the comet forming a tail millions of miles long. Probably the most famous comet is Halley's Comet, named after English astronomer Edmund Halley. He observed and studied the comet in 1682; he predicted that it would reappear in 1759. Halley's comet has been seen every 76 years since the year 240 BCE. It was last seen in 1986. In what year will the next sighting take place?

Read each statement below. Write a **T** if the sentence is true; write an **F** if the sentence is false.

1. _____ All meteors burn up before they reach the earth.

2. _____ A comet orbits the earth.

3. _____ Meteors are composed of iron and stone.

4. _____ As meteors fall to the ground they cool off.

5. _____ The Barringer Meteor Crater can be found in Arizona.

6. _____ Comets are the same as meteors.

7. _____ Meteors are stars.

8. _____ Another name for meteor is "shooting star."

9. _____ Halley's Comet will be seen in 1999.

10. _____ Some meteorites hit the ground hard enough to form craters.

11. _____ A comet has a tail millions of miles long.

12. _____ Meteors glow brightly as they make their descent.

13. Complete the Venn diagram on the next page comparing meteors and comets.

Meteors and Comets *(cont.)*

Complete the comet and meteor Venn diagram by writing each statement below in the correct section of the intersecting circles.

- are members of the solar system
- tails are millions of miles long
- appear in the night sky for many days
- are made of iron, stone, and other metals
- have a tail

- fall quickly to Earth
- are called "shooting stars"
- orbit around the sun
- hardly made of anything
- some are visible without telescopes

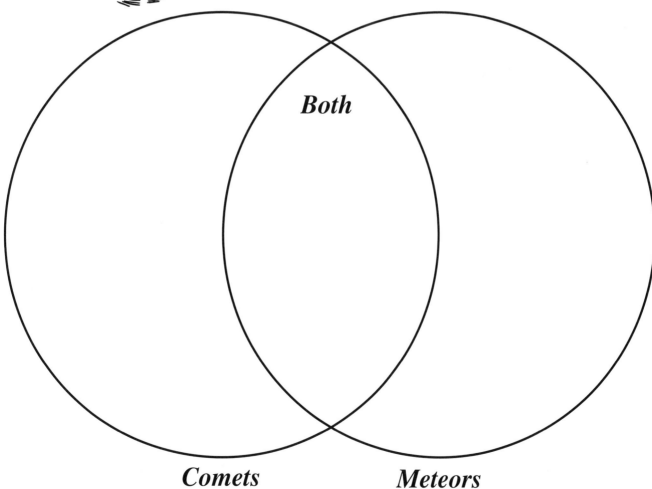

Both

Comets   *Meteors*

Asteroids

Asteroids, or minor planets, have been described as "mountains in space." They are large rocks typically ranging from a few feet to several hundred miles across. Most asteroids move between the orbits of Mars and Jupiter in what is often called the "asteroid belt." They appear star-like in telescopes. Against the background of stars, their motion is usually so slow that several hours may pass before any movement is noticed. Most asteroids within the asteroid belt never come closer than 100 million miles from Earth, but there are some which come closer to—and even cross—Earth's orbit. These objects can occasionally pass within a few million miles of us, or even within the orbit of the moon. They move so fast in this location that the change is apparent after only a few minutes. Asteroids within the asteroid belt can be observed every year, while ones passing especially close to Earth may be visible for only a few weeks or months.

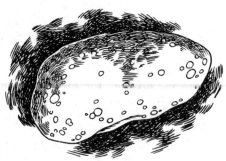

Astronomers distinguish asteroids and comets on the basis of their telescopic appearance. If the object is star-like in appearance, it is called an *asteroid*. If it has a visible atmosphere or tail, it is a comet. Scientists do not distinguish between asteroids and comets in methods to warn of impacting Earth. Both can collide with our planet.

Earth is located in a swarm of comets and asteroids that can, and do, collide with it periodically. The solar system has a huge population of asteroids and comets, remnants of its origin. From time to time some are bumped into orbits that cross the orbits of Earth and other planets. Spacecraft exploration of **terrestrial** (solid) planets and most of the moons of planets shows cratered surfaces made by continuous impacts from projectiles.

Additional evidence about asteroids near Earth has been collected since the first asteroid was discovered nearly 60 years ago. Improvements in telescopic search techniques have resulted in the discovery of dozens of near-Earth asteroids and short-period comets each year. The role of impacts in Earth's geological history, its ecosphere, and the evolution of life itself, has become a major topic of discussion among scientists.

The possible dangers of such impacts focused when, in 1989, father-and-son geologists team, Luis and Walter Alvarez, found evidence indicating that an asteroid estimated at 6–10 miles (10–16 km) long impacted Earth 65 million years ago, resulting in extinction of many life forms and ending the age of dinosaurs. The greatest risk is from the impact of the largest objects—those with diameters greater than 1/2 mile (1 km). Such impacts may occur once to several times per million years and would affect the entire planet.

Asteroids *(cont.)*

Comprehension Questions

1. **Asteroids have been described as . . .**

   a. asteroid belts.   c. comets.

   b. mountains in space.   d. meteors.

2. **Astronomers distinguish asteroids and comets on the basis of . . .**

   a. their telescopic appearance.   c. how many times they orbit Mars and Jupiter.

   b. their weight in relation to Earth.   d. how close they come to Earth.

3. **If an object has a visible "tail," it is a(n) . . .**

   a. asteroid   b. meteor   c. comet   d. star.

4. **The word *terrestrial* means . . .**

   a. outer space   b. alien   c. star   d. solid.

5. **When was the first asteroid discovered?**

   a. 60 years ago   c. 20 years ago

   b. 50 years ago   d. 75 years ago

6. **Describe the evidence and possible results found by the Alvarez team.**

   _____

   _____

   _____

   _____

   _____

Celestial Visions

In 1986, a young woman working at Palomar Observatory near San Diego, California, discovered a comet. But it did not bring her the fame and glory that befell Maria Mitchell some 139 years earlier. After all, Maria's discovery had been made without the use of the sophisticated techniques and equipment available today.

Maria's life began in 1818 on Nantucket Island in Massachusetts. Her father was a dedicated astronomer and teacher. He was also a Quaker and believed that girls deserved the same education as boys. This was at a time when it was generally considered unimportant for girls to get any education. By the time Maria was four years old she could read. At night she learned to read the stars. When she was 12 years old, she helped her father record the timing of a solar eclipse.

As a young woman, Maria worked as a librarian and continued her rooftop observations. Fortunately, the bank where her father worked had built a new observatory complete with a four-inch (10 cm) telescope. Then, on October 3, 1847, she discovered a comet and asked her father to confirm her findings. Over the course of a few days, she continued to observe the comet. Mr. Mitchell wrote to Professor Boyd, an astronomer at Vassar College in Poughkeepsie, New York. The professor, in turn, wrote of the discovery and sent a letter to the King of Denmark. A gold medal had been offered by the King to the first person finding a comet by using a telescope. After some dispute, Maria Mitchell was declared the winner.

This sudden fame opened up various opportunities for Maria. She was asked to work on a nautical almanac, which included information about tides, phases of the moon, and eclipses. In 1875, she was appointed President of the Women's Congress' third annual meeting. Maria also traveled extensively and even saw—but could not use—the Vatican's telescope in Rome. America's first woman astronomer died in 1889, in Lynn, Massachusetts.

Science

Celestial Visions *(cont.)*

Maria Mitchell became an astronomy teacher in 1865, at Vassar College in Poughkeepsie, New York. She taught her female students by sharing her work with them and by allowing students to assist her in the observatory.

Directions: Read the paragraphs below to discover some of the celestial sights they observed. Then draw the missing parts in each picture.

1. To view the total eclipse from Denver in 1877, Maria and her students had to wear protective dark glasses. The moon almost covered the sun, leaving a bright halo surrounding the moon's black disk. Color the disk black. Color the halo yellow.

2. The students watched Maria take photographs of sunspots which are huge, dark, "cooler" areas on the sun. Draw and color two sunspots on the sun.

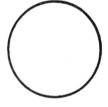

3. Maria's students discussed with her ideas about the composition of Saturn's rings. Saturn has many rings. Draw three rings around Saturn.

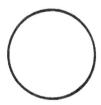

4. The students listened attentively as Maria told them her theories about Jupiter. They watched the moons travel across the face of the planet. Jupiter has dozens of known moons. Draw some moons around Jupiter.

5. Maria would call to her students to watch an unexpected meteor shower, even if it was late at night. A meteor is a chunk of rock or dust plunging to the earth. As it heats up, it leaves behind a glowing streak of light. Draw a meteor in the space provided.

The Moon

Many of the planets in our solar systems have satellites. Satellites are objects that orbit around a planet. These can be manmade or they can be natural satellites. Did you know the moon is a natural satellite of the Earth? There are moons in this solar system that are larger, but it is still very big. On the other hand, the moon is smaller than the Earth. That is why objects weigh less on the moon than they do on Earth. When the astronauts traveled to the moon, they could float and bounce around because they weighed less on the moon.

The moon does not have any liquid water on it. However, it does have craters, mountain ranges, and lava plains as well as other special features. The inside of the moon is made up of layers. Some of these layers are rock solid while others are molten like lava.

One thing that scientists have learned is that there is no wind on the moon. That is because there is no atmosphere on the moon. Because there is no atmosphere, there is no protection from the sun. The moon can get very hot during the day and very cold at night.

Humans have been able to see the moon since the beginning, but Galileo was the first person to look at the moon close up. He used a telescope to let him see things more closely. Galileo learned a lot of amazing things about the moon.

Directions: Circle the correct answer.

1. **Which paragraph explains the physical features of the moon?**
   a. first paragraph
   b. second paragraph
   c. third paragraph
   d. fourth paragraph

2. **What inferences can you make about the moon after reading this passage?**
   a. Unaided, humans cannot live on the moon.
   b. The moon used to be considered one of the planets.
   c. The moon has living organisms on it.
   d. The moon rotates around the sun more quickly than the Earth.

3. **Which statement shows the author's opinion about the moon?**
   a. Galileo learned a lot of amazing things about the moon.
   b. Scientists have been studying the moon and its surface for years.
   c. On the other hand, the moon is smaller than the Earth.
   d. He used a telescope to let him see things more closely.

Sun Storms

You know that the sun **sustains** life here on Earth. You know that you should never look directly at the sun because it could blind you. But did you know that the sun has weather? Of course it's nothing like the weather on Earth. In comparison, our most powerful storm seems like a mild breeze. And believe it or not, what it's doing up there on the sun affects us down here!

Our sun is a huge ball of burning plasma—a state of matter where gas is superheated. Most of this plasma is hydrogen gas. The sun has an 11-year cycle. Throughout the cycle, the sun has periods of major storm activity and minor storm activity. During the major storm part of the cycle, the sun has lots of solar flares. Solar flares are plasma eruptions that shoot off the sun's surface, causing solar wind. Just one average-sized solar flare releases enough energy to meet all the current power needs of the U.S. for 10,000 years! The biggest solar flares extend out into space like gigantic clouds. These clouds move a million miles per hour (1,609,344 kph) toward Earth as solar wind. When strong solar winds hit Earth's atmosphere, the night sky glows with colored lights reflecting off the ice at the Earth's North Pole. People call them the Northern Lights.

Unfortunately, solar winds don't just provide interesting sky effects. They can cause harmful magnetic storms. These storms can disrupt phone, TV, and radio signals, the Internet, and e-mail. They can make radar systems crash. They can destroy satellites and kill astronauts working outside the space shuttle. The biggest threat comes from the magnetic storm's ability to knock out electrical power. This happened in 1989 when Quebec, a large region in Canada, lost its entire electrical power grid in less than 90 seconds. The problem took so long to fix that many people had to go without heat or electricity for a month.

Sun Storms *(cont.)*

Comprehension Questions

1. **The Northern Lights are caused by . . .**

   a. magnetic storms.

   b. solar wind.

   c. plasma.

   d. hydrogen gas.

2. **What happened second in 1989?**

   a. The sun had one or more major plasma eruptions.

   b. People went without electricity for a month.

   c. Solar wind created a magnetic storm.

   d. Quebec's power grid was heavily damaged.

3. **Even small solar flares cause some . . .**

   a. solar wind.

   b. plasma.

   c. Northern Lights.

   d. hydrogen gas.

4. **An antonym for *sustains* is . . .**

   a. burns.

   b. chills.

   c. maintains.

   d. destroys.

5. **What usually protects us from the harmful effects of solar wind?**

   a. the Northern Lights

   b. power grids

   c. Earth's atmosphere

   d. plasma eruptions

6. **Picture a team of scientists discovering a way to collect and use solar flare energy. What is the expression on their faces?**

   a. excited

   b. upset

   c. annoyed

   d. bored

7. **Do you think it's important for scientists to continue studying solar weather? Explain.**

   _____

   _____

   _____

Genetics

It is hard to imagine that an Augustinian monk of the 19th century would provide the basis for modern genetics. However, that is precisely what happened.

Born in 1822 in Heinzendorf near Austria, Gregor Mendel learned his love of gardening from his father who was a farmer. Gregor attended high school in a nearby town.

Since his family was so poor and could not afford to pay the full tuition, Gregor received only half the amount of food as the other boys. He nearly starved, and the experience remained in his memory forever.

On the advice of a professor he greatly admired, Gregor entered the monastery where he could continue his studies. There he became the caretaker of the gardens and a substitute teacher for an elementary school.

From 1856 until 1864, Mendel worked with 10,000 specimen pea plants. He cross-fertilized 22 kinds of peas and studied seven characteristics of the plants. After eight years of accurate record-keeping, he formulated three laws that became the basis of the science of heredity. He proudly wrote a paper to describe his findings. No one seemed to recognize the genius of his work, though, and Gregor was crushed. In 1883, he died of a heart attack, embittered that no one recognized or appreciated his scientific revelations.

Then, in 1990, three botanists from three different countries completed papers on the heredity of plants. Each of them had come across Mendel's paper when they made a routine check of the scientific literature before they published their own findings.

In each case, Mendel's forgotten paper reached the same conclusions that they had reached. Gregor Mendel's time had finally come.

Genetics *(cont.)*

You inherit many character traits from your parents, such as eye color, hair color, and blood type. One gene comes from each parent. Many times, the gene from one parent is stronger than the other. This is called the dominant gene. The weaker gene is called recessive. Two features whose traits are controlled by gene inheritance are the fingers and the ear lobes. Discover which traits you and your family share by determining the recessive and dominant genes you inherited.

Directions: Categorize the ear lobes and fingers of members of your family by checking with grandparents, parents, uncles/aunts, brothers/sisters, or even cousins. Record your findings in the charts. Then, answer the questions at the bottom of the page.

Lobes

Joined   **Free**

Relation to you

(Check the appropriate box.)
	Free	Joined
_____	☐	☐
_____	☐	☐
_____	☐	☐
_____	☐	☐
_____	☐	☐
_____	☐	☐

Fingers

Straight   **Bent**

Relation to you

(Check the appropriate box.)
	Straight	Bent
_____	☐	☐
_____	☐	☐
_____	☐	☐
_____	☐	☐
_____	☐	☐
_____	☐	☐

Which seems to be dominant, free or joined lobes? _____

Which seems to be dominant, bent or straight fingers? _____

Cells

The cell is the smallest unit of living matter. Many living things are made up of millions and millions of cells. Cells come in all different sizes, shapes, and forms. They each have different jobs to perform as well. There are three main parts to a cell. Each cell has a cell membrane, a nucleus, and cytoplasm.

The cell membrane is found along the outer edge of the cell. It works like a filter or a sieve. It lets the good things like nutrients in, and it gets rid of all the bad stuff. It serves as a protection to the cell.

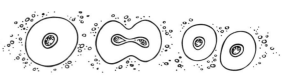

The nucleus of a cell is like the brain of the cell. It is dark and is usually located in the center of the cell. It controls all the actions of the cell. The nucleus also contains the DNA. The DNA is like a blueprint or a plan that the cell will use to reproduce.

The cytoplasm is located inside the cell membrane and around the nucleus. It is a jelly-like substance. This is where all the action takes place. The cytoplasm responds to the nucleus. This is where the cell uses the nutrients. It is made of water and other chemicals. Cells can live for different amounts of time. Cells are constantly reproducing.

Directions: Circle the correct answer.

1. **What are the three parts of a cell?**
   a. cell membrane, shell, cytoplasm
   b. cell membrane, brain, cytoplasm
   c. cell membrane, nutrients, cytoplasm
   d. cell membrane, nucleus, cytoplasm

2. **What does the word** *sieve* **mean as used in the passage?**
   a. strainer
   b. proof
   c. instruction
   d. plan

3. **What role does DNA play in the cell?**
   a. It depends on the amount of cytoplasm in the cell.
   b. It carries the information to the brain.
   c. It carries the overall plan or blueprint of the cell's reproduction.
   d. It depends on how many years it has been a cell.

4. **Which paragraph helps answer the previous question?**
   a. first paragraph
   b. fifth paragraph
   c. third paragraph
   d. fourth paragraph

Atomic Numbers

All matter is composed of molecules. These molecules, in turn, are made up of atoms. Atoms are the smallest particles of matter. Within each atom is a nucleus or center. Electrons revolve around the nucleus, and are arranged in orbits. For example, an atom of lithium can be illustrated like this:

Since there are three electrons, its atomic number is 3. Use the chart below to identify the elements pictured. Write the name of the element on the space provided.

Element	Symbol	Atomic #
Helium	He	2
Nitrogen	N	7
Oxygen	O	8
Sodium	Na	11
Aluminum	Al	
Sulfur	S	
Argon	Ar	
Calcium	Ca	

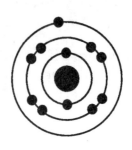

_____

2. _____

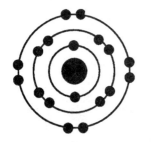

3. _____

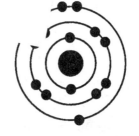

4. _____

5. _____

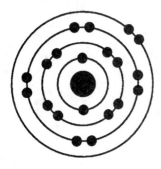

6. _____

7. _____

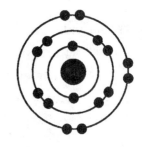

8. _____

Matter

What is matter? Everything is made up of matter. Matter is made up of tiny particles called atoms, molecules, or ions. Matter is ordinarily found in three states. These states are liquid, gas, or solid. There are two forces at work regardless of the state of matter. These two forces are energy and attraction. Energy makes the matter move. Attraction pulls and keeps the particles together.

Solids are packed together. Examples of solids are wood, plastic, stone, and iron. You can hold solids in your hand. Liquids are a state between gases and solids. Liquids flow and change shape. The best example of a liquid is water. Gases are floating around you and inside bubbles. Gases don't have any particular shape, but they are fluid. They can also be compressed. "Vapor" and "gas" mean the same thing.

Matter can change from one state to another. For example, a liquid can change to a solid or gas. Solids can change to a liquid. Temperature influences the changes in matter from one state to another. For example, heating a liquid can turn it into a gas. Cooling or freezing a liquid can turn it into a solid. Scientists continue to study matter, molecules, and ions to better understand our world.

Directions: Circle the correct answer.

1. **After reading the passage, what do you think would happen if a liquid was boiled?**
   a. It would immediately double in size.
   b. It would turn into a gas.
   c. It would turn into a solid.
   d. Scientists have not yet determined what happens in this case.

2. **The main idea of this passage is . . .**
   a. to inform the reader about what happens when it is raining.
   b. to inform the reader about the definition of matter.
   c. to inform the reader about how important it is to see ice, rain, and condensation.
   d. to share general information about the universe and how it is organized.

3. **Where can you find information about the three types of matter?**
   a. second paragraph
   b. all three paragraphs
   c. third paragraph
   d. first paragraph

Fixed by Bacteria

We need nitrogen. Nitrogen is a chemical element. Nitrogen is essential for all forms of life. When something is essential, it is needed. It is necessary. All proteins contain nitrogen. Proteins perform essential tasks, or jobs, in living things. They provide structure. They control the rates of chemical reactions. Nucleic acids contain nitrogen, too. DNA is a nucleic acid. So is RNA. DNA contains genetic information. RNA translates the genetic information. It translates the information into protein production.

Nitrogen is a gas that has no color. It has no taste. It has no odor. The air we breathe is made up mostly of nitrogen. In fact, around four-fifths of the air we breathe is nitrogen. But we cannot use the nitrogen in the air. We cannot use the nitrogen when it is in the form of a gas. Most living things can't. So how do we get our necessary nitrogen?

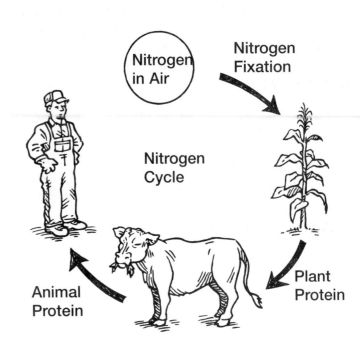

The answer lies with bacteria. Some bacteria can use nitrogen in the air. They convert it. They change it. They convert it to a compound we can use. A compound is a substance. It is formed from two or more chemical elements. The bacteria "fix" the nitrogen. They "fix" it into a compound we can use. This process is called nitrogen fixation.

The bacteria live on plants. They live off of the plants, too. They get their food from the plants. But the plants get something from the bacteria. They get fixed nitrogen. They get essential nitrogen in a form they can use. They get nitrogen compounds. What does the plant do with the nitrogen? The plant uses it to make proteins.

The bacteria help the plants. Plants help the bacteria. The bacteria and plants have a symbiotic relationship. A symbiotic relationship is a relationship that benefits both organisms. Both the bacteria and plants are helped. They both benefit. So how do people get their nitrogen? People eat plants. They eat plant seeds like corn, rice, and beans. They eat animals that eat plants and seeds. They get essential nitrogen and proteins from what they eat.

Fixed by Bacteria *(cont.)*

After reading the passage, answer the questions.
Circle the correct answer.

1. **This story is mainly about . . .**
   a. nitrogen in the air.
   b. how we get and use nitrogen.
   c. bacteria that make nitrogen.
   d. nitrogen and chemical elements.

2. **About how much of the air we breathe is made up of nitrogen?**
   a. one-fifth
   b. one-fourth
   c. four-fifths
   d. five-fourths

3. **Think about how the word convert relates to change. Which words relate in the same way?**

   convert : change

   a. bacteria : fix
   b. benefit : help
   c. use : nitrogen
   d. symbiotic : relationship

4. **What translates genetic information?**
   a. RNA
   b. DNA
   c. proteins
   d. nucleic acids

5. **Which answer lists how useable nitrogen gets to people in the right order?**
   a. bacteria, plants, animals, air, people
   b. plants, animals, air, bacteria, people
   c. air, plants, bacteria, animals, people
   d. air, bacteria, plants, animals, people

Fire Fuels the Cycle of Life

True or false: forest fires can be good for an ecosystem. Think it's false? No, it's true! Forests actually need fires to release the minerals stored within dead and living plants and trees. Fires keep the forest from taking over the meadows that border it. After a large fire, these fields grow rapidly because of the nutrients set free by the blaze. Forest fires make new habitats, encouraging greater plant and animal variety. The greatest number of different species is found about 25 years after a major blaze.

In 1972 when scientists found out that fires were helpful, national parks adopted a new policy: No one would fight any fire started by a lightning strike. Most fires caused by lightning would go out by themselves in a few hours. This would result in **minimal** damage while allowing natural and necessary blazes.

However, during the summer of 1988, Yellowstone National Park had a serious drought. No rain fell. Old, dead pine trees lay stacked on the forest floor like logs in a fireplace. On June 14 lightning started a fire. Due to the policy, it was left to burn. When it still hadn't gone out on its own after five weeks, things looked grim. Finally, people started fighting the fire. By then the situation was completely out of control. The fire raged all summer, stopping only when snow fell in September. The gigantic blaze had destroyed almost half of the Park, burning about a million acres (405,000 hectacres). It seemed like a big disaster.

Yet in a forest the cycle of life is based on fire. Just one year after Yellowstone's huge fire, its forest showed new growth. Its most plentiful trees, lodgepole pines, have cones that actually need the high temperatures of a fire to open and drop their seeds. Their tiny saplings poked up through the charred soil. A flowering plant called fireweed blanketed the area. Scientists figured that Yellowstone's cycle of life includes a major fire every 200 years.

After another 200 years, Yellowstone will burn again, and the cycle will start over.

228

Fire Fuels the Cycle of Life *(cont.)*

Comprehension Questions

1. **How is a forest fire beneficial?**
   a. It gives firefighters jobs.
   b. It releases trapped nutrients from plants and trees.
   c. It gives scientists a chance to study forest fires.
   d. It attracts lightning strikes away from people's homes.

2. **What happened second during the summer of 1988?**
   a. People did not respond immediately.
   b. Lightning caused a forest fire in Yellowstone National Park.
   c. The fire was stopped by snowfall.
   d. New habitats formed.

3. **The 1988 drought caused Yellowstone National Park to. . .**
   a. be cooler than normal.
   b. support greater plant and animal variety.
   c. have very dry conditions.
   d. attract more lightning strikes than usual.

4. **An antonym for minimal is. . .**
   a. costly.　　b. much.　　c. little.　　d. limited.

5. **Based on Yellowstone's forest fire cycle, prior to 1988, when had its last major blaze occurred?**
   a. around 1588　　　　c. around 1788
   b. around 1688　　　　d. around 1888

6. **Picture Yellowstone in October of 1988. What do you see?**
   a. Firefighters are spraying water on a huge forest fire.
   b. Most of the trees have colored leaves, and colored leaves blanket the ground.
   c. Tiny pine trees and flowering fireweed are everywhere you look.
   d. There's snow on the ground, and few standing trees are black and bare.

7. **Do you agree with the policy of allowing fires started by lightning to burn themselves out? Explain.**

   _____

   _____

   _____

Answer Key

Page 8

1. B   9. B
2. A   10. B
3. B   11. A
4. A   12. B
5. B   13. A
6. A   14. B
7. B   15. A
8. A

Page 9

1. The sun set on the horizon. Wasn't the sight astonishing?
2. When the snowflakes stop falling, we will go to the store.
3. Where did you get that beautiful, blue ribbon?
4. Hurrah! We can finally go swimming in the ocean since the storm has abated.
5. When will the sound of cracking thunder stop frightening me?
6. The daffodils are blooming all over the hillside, creating a waving carpet of yellow.
7. The gazelles ran smoothly and silently in the distance.
8. When will the moon escape from behind the clouds?
9. Wow! I am impressed with the colorful vibrancy of fall.
10. How often will you be able to come over to my house this summer?
11. Although I like the refreshing coolness of snow cones, I usually don't like ice cream.
12. Why is the wind picking up speed? Will there be a hurricane?
13. The puppy quickly scurried under the bushes, hoping that nobody had noticed him.

14. I will be glad when this project is over and I feel a sense of accomplishment.

Page 10

1. Michael shouted, "Let's get busy with the paint!"
2. "Those who deny freedom to others deserve it not for themselves," stated Abraham Lincoln.
3. "Has anyone in this group ever climbed Mount Everest?" asked the mountain guide.
4. Mr. Cummings said, "Please watch your step through the pond."
5. Donna and Chandra complained, "We don't want to do the dishes."
6. "Help!" cried the frightened girl as she gasped the end of the rope.
7. "What is the time difference between New York and Los Angeles?" he asked the flight attendant.

Page 11

Tuesday, March 16, 1999
Dear Aunt Judy,
I want to thank you for the lovely new dress you sent me for my birthday. I'm sorry you were unable to attend my party on Saturday, March 13. We had lots of fun. I plan to come visit you in Lynchburg, Virginia, this summer. Mother wants you to check your calendar for July. She has booked me on a flight to arrive Wednesday, July 27, in the evening. Please write or call to let us know if that is all right. I can't wait to see you!
Yours truly,
Kara

Kara James
7008 Milton Road
Los Angeles, CA 90049
Mrs. Judy Kimball
1454 Dresser Road
Lynchburg, Virginia 20546

Page 12

2. women's careers
3. my friend's comments
4. my baby's toys
5. its horn
6. the passengers' tickets
7. the children's clothes
8. Chris' store or Chris's store
9. an artist's paintbrush
10. the hostess's invitations

Page 13

Exercise 1

1. teachers'
2. country's
3. children's
4. Ross' or Ross's
5. men's
6. cities'
7. dogs'
8. Argus' or Argus's
9. Karla's
10. girls'

Exercise 2

1. A   6. A
2. B   7. A
3. B   8. B
4. A   9. A
5. B   10. A

Page 14

Answers will vary

Page 15

1. On our first trip to California, I wanted to visit the San Diego Zoo; my little sister wanted to go to Disneyland.
2. Our parents settled the dispute for us: they decided we could go to both places.
3. At the zoo we saw a zebra, elephant, and lion; the tigers were not in their display area.
4. Three days later we went to Disneyland; it has imaginative rides.

5. We can't wait to vacation in California again; there are so many sights to see.

Page 16

Answers will vary

Page 17

Part I

Answers will vary.

Part II

1. family
2. sister-in-law
3. trolley car
4. herd
5. class
6. editor-in-chief
7. pile
8. passers-by
9. flock
10. group

Page 18

1. a. churches
   b. trees
   c. bushes
   d. boxes
   e. peaches
   f. buses/busses
2. a. geese
   b. men
   c. feet
   d. lice
   e. teeth
   f. women
   g. children
   h. mice
3. a. potatoes
   b. photos
   c. volcanoes
   d. hippos
   e. heroes
   f. tomatoes

Page 19

1. big truck, little car
2. good book
3. cute kitty, sweet face
4. nice (Ms. Bronowski)
5. delicious cake
6. silly thing
7. chocolate ice cream
8. red car, blue one
9. old (book)
10. shiny, new penny

Answer Key (cont.)

Page 20
Exercise 1: Accept appropriate responses.
Exercise 2: Accept appropriate responses.

Page 21
Exercise 1
1. talks
2. is
3. ran
4. read
5. enjoyed
6. think
7. hope, get
8. like
9. had
10. was

Exercise 2
1. plays (A)
2. watches (A)
3. likes (A)
4. looks (L)
5. spit (A)
6. is (L)
7. seems (L)
8. looked (A)
9. saw (A)
10. is (L)
11. asked (A)
12. heard (A)
13. sounded (L)
14. is (L)
15. like (A)

Page 22
1. known, frozen
2. chosen, began
3. worn, stolen
4. chosen, torn
5. rung, have
6. stolen, known
7. have, sung
8. driven, begun
9. began, chosen
10. fell, frozen
11. worn, rung
12. fallen, broken
13. sang, chosen
14. brought, stolen
15. rang, began

Page 23
Exercise 1
1. I
2. me
3. We
4. she
5. heI
6. them
7. they
8. her, us
9. us
10. me

Exercise 2
1. We
2. us
3. I
4. him, her
5. we
6. me
7. him, me
8. us
9. me
10. him, her
11. her
12. He, I
13. her, him
14. He
15. They
16. I
17. we, they
18. him, her
19. her
20. them, us

Page 24
Accept appropriate responses

Page 25
Exercise 1
1. at the South Pole
2. during the speech
3. with the bathwater
4. in the pan
5. on TV
6. under the table
7. to the movies
8. across the road
9. on the table
10. to the top

Exercise 2: Accept appropriate responses.

Page 26
Exercise 1
1. but
2. or
3. so
4. if
5. until
6. after
7. and
8. since
9. although

Exercise 2: Accept appropriate responses.

Page 35
1. familiar
2. accommodate, appropriate
3. vacuum
4. license
5. separate
6. irrelevant
7. guarantee
8. calendar
9. foreign
10. embarrass
11. privilege
12. weird
13. rhythm
14. a lot

Page 36
1. license
2. guarantee
3. appropriate
4. calendar
5. vacuum
6. weird
7. irrelevant
8. rhythm
9. embarrass
10. a lot
11. accommodate
12. privilege
13. familiar
14. foreign
15. separate

Page 37 and 38
1. c
2. b
3. c
4. c
5. a
6. b
7. b
8. a
9. c
10. b
11. c
12. c
13. a
14. b
15. c
16. c
17. a

Page 39 and 40
1. b
2. a
3. c
4. a
5. b
6. b
7. c
8. b
9. c
10. b
11. b
12. a
13. c
14. a

Page 41
1. assent, ascent
2. course, strait
3. coarse
4. compliment
5. cite
6. taut
7. there, their
8. lesson, lessen
9. presence, presents
10. passed, past

Page 42 and 43
1. c
2. a
3. b
4. a
5. b
6. c
7. c
8. a
9. b
10. c

11. b
12. c
13. a
14 b
15. b
16. b
17. a

Page 44
A.
1. G
2. F
3. E
4. H
5. B
6. D
7. A
8. I
9. C

B.
1. ophthalmologist
2. neonatologist
3. criminologist
4. ornithologist
5. mineralogist
6. psychologist
7. etymologist
8. histologist
9. radiologist

Page 49
1. Wayne did not go to school.
2. He missed so much school.
3. He decided to start working on his attendance.
4. He did not think that his brother and mom cared about his decision.
5. He felt better.

Page 51
1. b
2. a
3. b
4. c
5. d
6. c

Page 53
1. b
2. a
3. c
4. c
5. a
6. d

Page 55
1. a
2. b
3. c
4. c
5. d
6. b
7. Accept well-supported answers.

Page 57
1. c
2. b
3. b
4. c
5. d
6. c

©Teacher Created Resources, Inc.   231   #3945 Mastering Sixth Grade Skills

Answer Key *(cont.)*

Page 59
1. d   4. c
2. d   5. a
3. b   6. c

Page 61
1. a   4. b
2. d   5. b
3. d   6. d

Page 63
1. c   4. b
2. d   5. b
3. a   6. b

Page 65
1. b   4. a
2. d   5. d
3. b   6. c

Page 82
1. -10   11. -6
2. -8   12. -2
3. +7   13. +7
4. -16   14. -24
5. -21   15. -4
6. -24   16. -23
7. -13   17. +25
8. +10   18. -3
9. +2   19. -25
10. -13   20. -15
　　　　21. -21

Page 83
1. +6   12. -34
2. -4   13. -110
3. +16   14. -32
4. -59   15. -56
5. +11   16. -40
6. -13   17. +450
7. -22   18. -579
8. +31   19. +176
9. -23   20. -1
10. -22   21. -198
11. -21

Page 84
H. 2   K. -6
Q. 4   Q. -4
D. -2   X. -21
B. -18   S. -1
F. 0   A. -9
G. -11   Y. 6
O. -3   U. 11
W. -15   E. -16
Y. 5   P. 22
J. -21   T. 3
Z. 8   R. -20
N. 1   L. -41
M. 12   C. 13

I. -15
Riddle: He thought he would be a good drill sergeant.

Page 85
1. 36   15. 8
2. 9   16. 81
3. 25   17. 16
4. 4   18. 729
5. 100   19. 125
6. 121   20. 32
7. 125   21. 196
8. 216   22. 1
9. 81   23. 225
10. 512   24. 400
11. 49   25. 900
12. 1,000   26. 1,600
13. 343   27. 2,500
14. 169

Page 86
1. $3 \times 3 = 9$
2. $7 \times 7 = 49$
3. $4 \times 4 = 16$
4. $9 \times 9 = 81$
5. $2 \times 2 = 4$
6. $8 \times 8 = 64$
7. $10 \times 10 = 100$
8. $6 \times 6 = 36$
9. $11 \times 11 = 121$
10. $12 \times 12 = 144$
11. $2 \times 2 = 4$
　　$4 \times 2 = 8$
　　$2^3 = 8$
12. $3 \times 3 = 9$
　　$9 \times 3 = 27$
　　$3^3 = 27$
13. $5 \times 5 = 25$
　　$25 \times 5 = 125$
　　$5^3 = 125$
14. $7 \times 7 = 49$
　　$49 \times 7 = 343$
　　$7^3 = 343$
15. $4 \times 4 = 16$
　　$16 \times 4 = 64$
　　$4^3 = 64$
16. $6 \times 6 = 36$
　　$36 \times 6 = 216$
　　$6^3 = 216$
17. $10 \times 10 = 100$
　　$100 \times 10 = 1,000$
　　$10^3 = 1,000$
18. $9 \times 9 = 81$
　　$81 \times 9 = 729$
　　$9^3 = 729$
19. $11 \times 11 = 121$

$121 \times 11 = 1,331$
$11^3 = 1,331$
20. $12 \times 12 = 144$
　　$144 \times 12 = 1,728$
　　$12^3 = 1,728$

Page 87
1. $12   7. $270
2. $20   8. 156
3. +42   9. -64
4. $7   10. 15
5. -9   11. $5
6. +10   12. +20

Page 88
1. 72   16. 4,800
2. 72   17. 2,800
3. 42   18. 2,800
4. 42   19. 2,700
5. 80   20. 2,700
6. 80   21. 4,200
7. 170   22. 4,200
8. 170   23. 4,125
9. 190   24. 4,125
10. 190   25. 1,125
11. 600   26. 1,125
12. 600   27. 1,541
13. 2,000   28. 1,541
14. 2,000   29. 714
15. 4,800   30. 714

Page 89
1. 504
2. 504
3. 300
4. 300
5. 600
6. 600
7. 6,000
8. 6,000
9. 80,000
10. 80,000
11. 180,000
12. 180,000
13. 3,750
14. 3,750
15. 12,300
16. 12,300
17. 379,500
18. 379,500
19. 264,264
20. 264,264

Page 90
1. 18,759
2. 35,322
3. 53,656
4. 2,700

5. 27,315
6. 11,856
7. 10,486
8. 38,684
9. 53,504
10. 69,894
11. 22,275
12. 26,862
13. 18,018
14. 18,785
15. 53,754
16. 25,806

Page 91
1. $93.96
2. $4.47
3. $105.30
4. $69.93
5. $53.38
6. $420.52
7. $585.39
8. $256.50
9. 2.646
10. 1.872
11. 2.6628
12. 0.00228
13. $6.30
14. 4.78
15. 137.74
16. $1.38
17. $8.37
18. .1218

Page 92
1. 11r1   14. 18r2
2. 16r4   15. 11r2
3. 13   16. 16r3
4. 11r1   17. 23
5. 28r2   18. 6r4
6. 24r3   19. 8r4
7. 9   20. 9r2
8. 34   21. 10
9. 13   22. 5
10. 10r6   23. 12r2
11. 11r1   24. 21r3
12. 14r1   25. 23r1
13. 16r1

Page 93
1. 21r17
2. 31r14
3. 32r12
4. 31r10
5. 15r2
6. 11r2
7. 42r5
8. 21r22

Answer Key (cont.)

9. 23r13
10. 13r25
11. 22r6
12. 32r17

Page 94
1. 8,400 ÷ 40 = 210
Check: 210 x 40 = 8,400
2. 41,916 ÷ 28 = 1,497
Check: 1,497 x 28 = 41,916
3. 33,320 ÷ 136 = 245
Check: 245 x 136 = 33,320
4. 3,600 ÷ 90 = 40
Check: 40 x 90 = 3,600
5. 8,928 ÷ 9 = 992
Check: 992 x 9 = 8,928
6. 28,917 ÷ 81 = 357
Check: 357 x 81 = 28,917
7. 35,620 ÷ 260 = 137
Check: 137 x 260 = 35,620
8. 180,930 ÷ 37 = 4,890
Check: 4,890 x 37 = 180,930
9. 8,840 ÷ 65 = 136
Check: 136 x 65 = 8,840

Page 95
1. 0.21 lb.
2. 100.2 ounces
3. 1.09 ounces
4. 10.2 candies
5. 45.1 lb.
6. 80.5 ants
7. 969.624 ounces
8. $0.23
9. $0.38
10. 157.68 lb.

Page 96
1. 5
2. 0.14
3. 10.80
4. 625
5. 0.01
6. 0.04
7. 0.03
8. 750
9. 175
10. $81.25
11. 5.7
12. 0.04
13. 4.9
14. 80
15. 50
16. 7/20
17. 8/125
18. 3 2/5
19. 3 1/8

20. 3 1/8
21. 4 5/8
22. 21/2500
23. 66 ¾
24. 159/500
25. 1/16
26. 4 ¼
27. 1 1/10
28. .8
29. .38
30. .67
31. .78
32. .83
33. .63
34. .33
35. .7

Page 97
1. 2   16. 40
2. 4   17. 700
3. 7   18. 800
4. 9   19. 400
5. 10   20. 900
6. 8   21. 500
7. 11   22. 300
8. 12   23. 600
9. 13   24. 100
10. 15   25. 3,000
11. 14   26. 9,000
12. 20   27. 5,000
13. 30   28. 6,000
14. 70   29. 7,000
15. 80   30. 8,000

Page 98
1. 4
2. 6
3. 12
4. 5
5. 8
6. 9
7. 11
8. 1
9. 3
10. 10
11. 7
12. 2
13. 50
14. 60
15. 20
16. 10
17. 80
18. 70
19. 30
20. 130
21. 90
22. 40

23. 120
24. 110
25. Answers may vary.

Page 99
1. 10   9. 0
2. 30   10. 20
3. 25   11. 86
4. 1   12. 36
5. 63   13. 8
6. 53   14. 5
7. 6   15. 18
8. 18

Page 100
1. 53   9. 95
2. 15   10. 22
3. 41   11. 46
4. 10   12. 6
5. 11   13. 138
6. 61   14. 44
7. 38   15. 2
8. 34   16. 21

Page 101
1. 0   9. 9
2. 18   10. 45
3. 20   11. 29
4. 24   12. 58
5. 27   13. 107
6. 70   14. 117
7. 13   15. 72
8. 2   16. 58

Page 102
1. 1/3
2. 6/7
3. ¼
4. ½
5. 17/20
6. 1 11/35
7. 5/18
8. 1/20
9. 1/5
10. 19/24
11. 11/20
12. 11/16
13. 10 7/12/06
14. 3 3/8
15. 3 2/9

Page 103
1. 13/20
2. ¾
3. 7/8
4. 1/6
5. 4/9
6. 11/12
7. 7/8

8. 9/10
9. 8/9
10. 11/15
11. 3/20
12. 7/24
13. 26/21 = 1 5/21
14. 35/24 = 1 11/24
15. 22/18 = 1 2/9
16. 5/24
17. 13/36
18. 14/72 = 7/36
19. 59/42 = 1 17/42
20. 29/24 = 1 5/24
21. 3/20
22. 23/18 = 1 5/18
23. 55/60 = 11/12
24. 25/30 = 5/6

Page 104
1. 1/12   12. 3/5
2. 5/12   13. 2/5
3. 2/9   14. 4/15
4. 1/9   15. 4/15
5. 1/6   16. 1/6
6. 11/24   17. 5/42
7. 1/9   18. 3 3/10
8. 3/7   19. 3/10
9. 1/3   20. 3/64
10. 1/6   21. ½
11. 9/16

Page 105
1. 3/8
2. 2/21
3. 9/40
4. 6/35
5. 1/6
6. 1/6
7. 2/7
8. 2/9
9. ¼
10. ¾
11. ¼
12. 1/6
13. 3/20
14. 35/72
15. 1/8
16. 1/10
17. 1/5
18. 2/9
19. 3/5
20. ½
21. 1/5
22. 2/27
23. 3/7
24. 15/154
25. 11/16

©*Teacher Created Resources, Inc.*   233   *#3945 Mastering Sixth Grade Skills*

Answer Key (cont.)

26. 1/8
27. 4/39
28. 2/7
29. 11/30
30. 4/47
31. 17/611
32. 7/4,000

Page 106
1. 2
2. 2
3. 2
4. 4
5. 3
6. 4
7. 1 3/4
8. 5/6
9. 7/6 = 1 1/6
10. 9/5 = 1 4/5
11. 7/2 = 3 ½
12. 1
13. 3
14. 8
15. 1/3

Page 107
1. 11/14
2. 1 13/18
3. 14/19
4. 82/87
5. 18/29
6. 1 ¼
7. 2/3
8. 5
9. ¾
10. ¾
11. 2 1/6
12. 3/7
13. 5/12
14. 8/9
15. 1 5/27
16. 3/10
17. 3 1/9
18. 6 ¼
19. 9 ¾
20. ¼
21. 24/133
22. 5/64
23. 2 31/32
24. 33 ¾
25. 18/175
26. 1/32
27. 150
28. 7 ½
29. 4 2/27
30. 10

Page 108
1. 4 1/6
2. 3 ¼
3. 8
4. 5 3/7
5. 3
6. 23/7
7. 28/5
8. 65/9
9. 35/8
10. 29/10
11. 2 1/5
12. 4 ¾
13. 9 3/5
14. 9 ¼
15. 0.25
16. 0.75
17. 6.20
18. 0.5
19. 0.38
20. 0.6
21. 3.6

Page 109
1. 12
2. 24
3. 40
4. 21
5. 31.5
6. 50.4
7. 43.5
8. 122.4
9. 18.8
10. 9.9
11. 18.2
12. 33.6
13. 40
14. 77
15. 1.75

Page 110
1. 0.7
2. 0.4
3. 0.75
4. 0.15
5. 1.75
6. 26/100
7. 3/100
8. 2/10
9. 78/100
10. 825/1000
11. 1/20
12. 1/50
13. 1/8
14. 1/25
15. 6 9/10
16. .06, 6%

17. .70, 70%
18. .63, 63%
19. .03, 3%
20. .31, 31%
21. 25/100, 0.25
22. 2/100, 0.02
23. 0.5/100 or 5/1000, 0.005
24. 33/100, 0.333
25. 40/100, .04

Page 111
1. $42.29
2. $196
3. $16.20
4. $0.25
5. $1,372.70

Chart
1. 1/10, .10, 10%
2. ¼, .25, 25%
3. 9/20, .45, 45%
4. 3/20, .15, 15%
5. 4/5, .80, 80%
6. 5/6, .833, 83.3%
7. 77/100, .77, 77%
8. 1/20, .20, 20%
9. 11/50, .222, 22%
10. 2/5, .40, 40%

Page 112
1. a. 12, 25, 25, 35, 73
   b. 73 – 12 = 61
   c. 34
   d. 25
   e. 25
2. a. 23, 23, 30, 49, 51, 88, 100
   b. 100 – 23 = 77
   c. 52
   d. 49
   e. 23

Page 113
3. a. 18, 18, 24, 36
   b. 36 – 18 = 18
   c. 24
   d. 21
   e. 18
4. a. 22, 22, 36, 42, 70, 84
   b. 84 – 22 = 62
   c. 46
   d. 39
   e. 22
5. a. 170, 200, 305
   b. 135
   c. 225
   d. 200

e. none
6. a. 22, 45, 66, 66, 69, 77, 89
   b. 67
   c. 62
   d. 66
   e. 66

Page 114
1. **Mode:** 13 **Median:** 13 **Mean:** 9.6 (10)
Most representative: mode and median
Reason: They reflect the values best and are midway between high and low values.
2. **Mode:** 23 **Median:** 23 **Mean:** 23.3 (23)
Most representative: 23
Reason: They are all the same.
3. **Mode:** 8 **Median:** 8 **Mean:** 8.3 (8)
Most representative: all
Reason: They all are the same value.
4. **Mode:** 46 **Median:** 49 **Mean:** 51.9 (52)
Most representative: mean and median
Reason: They are closer to the center of the numbers in terms of value.
5. **Mode:** 23 **Median:** 29.5 **Mean:** 32.3 (32)
Most representative: median and mean
Reason: The mode is too near the first values; the others are representatives of the numbers.

Page 115
1. 65
2. 65
3. 64
4. 31
5. 73
6. 74
7. 74
8. 48

Page 116
1. 37
2. 38.5
3. 60%
4. 20

Answer Key *(cont.)*

5. 300
6. 80
7. 100 and 80

Page 117
Check students' stem-and-leaf plots
1. 19
2. 20
3. 4
4. 848
5. 870
6. Answers will vary.
7. 23
8. 32
9. 134.5
10. 141

Page 118
1. 6   **Frequency**
2. 1   Cat 8
3. 4   Dog 12
4. 5   Snake 2
5. 2   Bird 3
6. 11   Mouse 3
7. 18   Hamster 4
8. 2   Fish 6
9. 4   Other 3
10. dog
11. snake
12. 5
13. 41
14. 27

Page 119
1. 54
2. 32
3. 4
4. 15
5. 2
6. New York
7. 257
8. 281
9. There are more votes in California
10. 13
11. Illinois and Texas; New York and Ohio
12. All states have at least 12 votes.

13. The graph can make the total of California's votes look many times greater than that of the smaller states. There is a distortion due to the scale.

Page 120
1. 30%
2. 5th/8th
3. 60%
4. no
5. 45%
6. 40%

Page 121
Riddle: Outback
Stems 4, 5, 6, 7, 8, 9, 10
Leaves
7,
7, 8
2, 3, 3, 7
0, 4, 5, 9, 9
0, 1, 3, 7, 8, 8
1, 1, 3, 3, 6, 6, 8
0, 0, 0
Number of leaves
1, 2, 4, 5, 6, 7, 3
Letters
O, U, T, B, A, C, K

Page 122
Answer: The girl necks-door.

Page 123
1. Check student graphs.
2. Check student graphs.
3. T-shirts ¼
    Sneakers ½
    Athletic Posters 1/8
    Other 1/8
4. Check student graphs.

Page 124
1. (11, 5)
2. (3, 0)
3. (6, 1)
4. (12, 12)
5. (4, 4)
6. (10, 8)
7. (8, 6)
8. (2, 11)
9. (6, 10)
10. (3, 7)
11. (1, 3)
12. (10, 2)

Page 125
Answer: Steal its chair.

Page 126

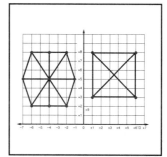

Page 127

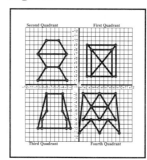

Page 129
1. library
2. town hall
3. gas station
4. (11, 1)
5. (4, 4)
6. (-5, -9)
7. park
8. (-10, -7)
9. (-9, 5)
10. general store
11. drug store
12. III
13. I
14. II

Page 131

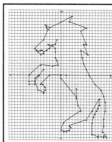

Page 132
1. 84
2. 60
3. 24
4. 120
5. 66
6. 27
7. 78
8. 68
9. 8
10. 1
11. 2
12. 4
13. 5 2/3
14. ½
15. 2 ½
16. 4 ½
17. 8
18. 2
19. 4
20. 2 1/3
21. 2
22. 1

Page 133
1. 8 fl. oz.
2. 15 fl. oz.
3. 32 fl. oz.
4. 48 fl. oz.
5. 64 fl. oz.
6. 72 fl. oz.
7. 32 fl. oz.
8. 64 fl. oz.
9. 160 fl. oz.
10. 96 fl. oz.
11. 4 qt.
12. 16 qt.
13. 128 fl. oz.
14. 60 qt.
15. 1,920 fl. oz.
16. 16 fl. oz.
17. 48 fl. oz.
18. 112 fl. oz.
19. 40 pints
20. 176 cups
21. 120 pints
22. 1,280 fl. oz.
23. 34 cups

Page 134
1. C
2. B
3. C
4. A
5. A
6. m
7. km

Answer Key *(cont.)*

8. cm
9. cm or mm
10. mm
11. cm
12. m
13. km
14. B
15. A
16. C

Page 135
1. 1
2. 500
3. 3
4. 100
5. 5
6. 900
7. 6.5
8. 330
9. 1
10. 1
11. 6
12. 5
13. 8
14. 7
15. 7.53
16. 8.35
17. 400
18. 3,000
19. 700
20. 6,000
21. 900
22. 10,000
23. 680
24. 15,500
25. 0.004
26. 0.007
27. 65
28. 0.07
29. 0.65
30. 0.004
31. 6.5
32. 4,00
33. 0.004
34. 7,500
35. 4,00
36. 6.5
37. 0.225
38. 3,500
39. 225,000
40. 0.057

Page 136
1. 130 yds.
2. 260 cm
3. 330 ft.
4. 630 m
5. 250 cm
6. 722 mm
7. 221 mm
8. 85.8 cm

Page 137
1. 80 m
2. 150 cm
3. 124 yds.
4. 105 mm
5. 100 in.
6. 75 mm
7. 92 ft.
8. 114 cm
9. 194 m
10. 323 mm

Page 138
1. 31.4 in.
2. 37.68 m
3. 28.26 in.
4. 25.12 ft.
5. 47.1 cm
6. 62.8 m
7. 78.5 ft.
8. 94.2 in.

Page 139
1. $2,400 \text{ m}^2$
2. $3,000 \text{ ft.}^2$
3. $1,600 \text{ yds.}^2$
4. $2,800 \text{ cm}^2$
5. $1,800 \text{ mm}^2$
6. $6,300 \text{ mm}^2$
7. 42 m^2
8. $4,900 \text{ ft.}^2$
9. $5,980 \text{ ft.}^2$
10. $1,504 \text{ in.}^2$

Page 140
1. 750 m^2
2. $1,000 \text{ mm}^2$
3. $1,386 \text{ ft.}^2$
4. $4,920 \text{ in.}^2$
5. $2,324 \text{ cm}^2$
6. 31.5 m^2
7. $2,296 \text{ mm}^2$
8. 24.8 ft.^2
9. $14,400 \text{ in.}^2$
10. 38 m^2
11. $4,840 \text{ mm}^2$
12. 23.25 in.^2
13. 19.84 m^2
14. $61,200 \text{ cm}^2$

Page 141
1. $180 \text{ mm}2$
2. $680 \text{ ft.}2$
3. $440 \text{ in.}2$
4. 792 m^2
5. $1,680 \text{ cm}^2$
6. 475 ft.^2
7. 638 yards^2
8. 14.08 cm^2

Page 142
1. 78.5 in.^2
2. 28.26 m^2
3. 254.34 yards^2
4. 152.16 cm^2
5. 113.04 ft.^2
6. 379.94 m^2
7. 314 in.^2
8. $5,024 \text{ cm}^2$

Page 143
1. $1,320 \text{ mm}^3$
2. $2,520 \text{ ft.}^3$
3. $6,250 \text{ m}^3$
4. $30,000 \text{ cm}^3$
5. $36,960 \text{ in.}^3$
6. $5,400 \text{ mm}^3$
7. 47.25 m^3
8. 32.55 cm^3

Page 144
1. 549.5 cm^3
2. 502.4 inc.^3
3. $2,009. \text{ ft.}^3$
4. $10,173.6 \text{ cm}^3$
5. $1,205.76 \text{ in.}^3$
6. $1,130.4 \text{ m}^3$
7. $1,692.46 \text{ mm}^3$
8. 602.88 cm^3

Page 145
1. 24 in.^3
2. 48 ft.^3
3. 80 mm^3
4. 40 in.^3
5. 200 in.^3
6. 150 cm^3
7. 210 m^3
8. 346.7 ft.^3

Page 146
1.
   face 1: 32 m
   face 2: 32 m
   face 3: 40 m
   face 4: 40 m
   face 5: 80 m
   face 6: 80 m
   total 304 m
2.
   face 1: 35 ft.
   face 2: 35 ft.
   face 3: 20 ft.
   face 4: 20 ft.
   face 5: 28 ft.
   face 6: 28 ft.
Total 166 ft.
3. face 1: 110 cm
   face 2: 110 cm
   face 3: 55cm
   face 4: 55 cm
   face 5: 50 cm
   face 6: 50 cm
Total 430 cm
4. face 1: 63 mm
   face 2: 63 mm
   face 3: 70 mm
   face 4: 70 mm
   face 5: 90 mm
   face 6: 90 mm
Total 446 mm
5.
   face 1: 200 in.
   face 2: 200 in.
   face 3: 220 in.
   face 4: 220 in.
   face 5: 110 in.
   face 6: 110 in.
Total 1,060 in.
6.
   face 1: 120 m
   face 2: 120 m
   face 3: 108 m
   face 4: 108 m
   face 5: 90 m
   face 6: 90 m
Total 636 m

Page 147
1. H – T; ½
2. 1 – 2 – 3 – 4 – 5 – 6; 1/6
3. 1 – 2 – 3 – 4 – 5 – 6; 1/6
4. 1 – 2 – 3 – 4 – 5 – 6; 2/6
   = 1/3
5. Red – Green – Blue
   – Black; ¼
6. Red – Green – Blue
   – Black; 2/4 = 12/
7. Red – Green – Blue
   – Black; 0
8. Red – Green – Blue
   – Black; ¾
9. HH – TT – HT – TH; 2/4
   = ½

Page 148
1. 1/8 or 12.5%
2. ½ or 50%
3. 2/8 or ¼ or 25%
4. 2/8 or ¼ or r25%

Answer Key *(cont.)*

5. 100%
6. 100%
7. ¼ or 25%
8. ¼ or 25%
9. 2/4 or ½ or 50%
10. 2/4 or ½ of 50%
11. ¾ or 75%
12. ½ or 25%
13. ¼ or 25%
14. 2/4 or ½ or 50%
15. 2/8 or ¼ or 25%
16. ½ or 50%

Page 149
1. 2/5
2. 2/5
3. 1/5
4. 0/5
5. 3/10
6. 2/10 or 1/5
7. 1/10
8. 5/10 or ½
9. 5/10 or ½
10. John's
11. No. She only has a 1/10 chance.
12. 5/26
13. 21/26
14. 1/26
15. 0/26
16. 9/26
17. 3/26

Page 150
1. .1 or .10; 10%
2. .1 or .10; 10%
3. .3 or .30; 30%
4. .3 or .30; 30%
5. .1 or .10; 10%
6. .5 or .50; 50%
7. .4 or .40; 40%
8. .0 or .00; 0%
9. .2 or .20; 20%
10. .5 or .50; 50%

Page 151
1. n = 11
2. n = 3
3. a = 4
4. n = 25
5. a = 15
6. n = 26
7. x = 27
8. n = 10
9. a = 20
10. n = 31
11. x = 25
12. a = 14
13. y = 24
14. a = 91
15. n = 27
16. a = 65
17. x = 38
18. n = 66

Page 152
1. n = 5
2. n = 11
3. n = 3
4. a = 4
5. n = 7
6. n = 10
7. n = 5
8. a = 6
9. a = 15
10. n = 20
11. n = 60
12. a = 60
13. n = 16
14. n = 60
15. a = 64
16. n = 160
17. a = 70
18. n = 40

Page 153
1. 1
2. 4
3. 6
4. 10
5. 3
6. 5
7. 8
8. 12
9. 7
10. 9
11. 15
12. 13
13. XXI
14. XXII
15. XXIII
16. XXIV
17. XXV
18. XXVI
19. XXVII
20. XXVIII
21. XXIX
22. 30
23. 26
24. 33
25. 35
26. 29
27. 38
28. 39
29. 34
30. 37
31. XLV
32. XLIX
33. XLVIII
34. XLVII
35. XVI
36. XLVI
37. XXVII
38. XXXVII
39. XXIX
40. Answers will vary.
41. Answers will vary.
42. Answers will vary.

Page 154
1. 2000
2. 2001
3. 2005
4. 1900
5. 1800
6. 1803
7. 1912
8. 1950
9. 1983
10. 1600
11. 1718
12. 1998
13. MM
14. MMI
15. MMX
16. MCM
17. MCMLX
18. MDCCC
19. MCMX
20. MCMXL
21. MDCCCLXXXI
22. MDCLIV
23. MCDXCII
24. MDLXXXVIII
25. 5
26. 10
27. 50
28. 100
29. 500
30. 1000
31. 2000
32. 300
33. 1500
34. 1700
35. 3650
36. 1666
37. LXIII
38. XCVII
39. CC
40. L

Page 155
1. 1 two
2. 10 two
3. 11 two
4. 100 two
5. 101 two
6. 110 two
7. 111 two
8. 1000 two
9. 1001 two
10. 11 two
11. 101 two
12. 10 two
13. 1001 two
14. 100 two
15. 110 two
16. 111 two
17. 1 two
18. 1000 two

Page 156
1. 0011
2. 0101
3. 0110
4. 0111
5. 0010
6. 0100
7. 0001
8. 1000
9. 1001
10. 1011
11. //// /, 0101
12. // /, 0011
13. ///, 0100
14. //// // /, 0111
15. ////////, 1000
16. //, 0010
17. //// //, 0110
18. //////// /, 1001
19. //////// // /, 1011
20. //////// //, 1010
21. //////// ////, 1100
22. //////// //// // /, 1111
23. //////// //// //, 1110
24. //////// //// /, 1101

Page 157
1. Someone born in 1760 BCE is older.
2. The difference is 500 years.
3. The difference is 2,960 years.
4. Answers will vary. One possibility is 1450–1550.
5. It is the 21st century.

Page 159
1. c
2. d
3. b
4. d
5. a
6. c

Answer Key *(cont.)*

Page 161
1. artifacts and relics found through archaeological digs
2. a. a bank tank at Mohanjo-Daro: ritual bathing important to Hindus
   b. terra-cotta figurines: some of them represent fertility, strength, rebirth, and continuity, central to Hindu faith
   c. bulls: represent virility, sacred to the Hindus
3. agricultural people, dependent on water, water still sacred to Hindus

Page 163
One of the seven wonders of the world is the pyramid of Khufu at Giza.

Page 164
1. d
2. b
3. a
4. c

Page 165

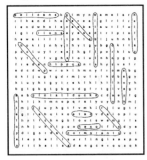

Page 167
1. b   4. d
2. a   5. d
3. c   6. c

Page 169
1. a   4. c
2. c   5. d
3. b   6. b
7. Accept reasonable answers.

Page 170
1. Any three – Nubia, Punt, Lebanon, Kush
2. cinnamon and myrrh
3. north
4. Accept any reasonable answer.
5. Any four – Mycenae, Crete, Cyprus, Lebanon, Nubia, Kush

Page 171
1. Polytheism is the worship of many gods.
2. By praying, the Egyptians believed they could protect themselves from their enemies, sickness, evil spirits, and forces of nature.
3. It was the pharaoh's duty to feed and protect the gods, as well as keep everything in proper order for them.

Page 173
1. Both believe in reincarnation, karma, and leading an honorable life without harming others. Hindus worship many gods, yet Buddhism presents no gods.
2. Siddhartha felt that starving himself didn't bring him any closer to the truth. The hermits felt this showed his weakness.
3. Reincarnation is the idea that the soul lives on after the body dies and is reborn in the body of another human or living form. Karma, the good or bad deeds performed, travel with the soul into the next life. Good Karma brings the soul closer to enlightenment, bad Karma inflicts more suffering. The cycle is finally broken when one reaches enlightenment, and enters nirvana, and never returns to Earth again.

Page 174
1. The Minoans constructed a large naval and merchant fleet of ships. They crafted delicate jewelry, clothing, and ornaments. Minoan potters were regarded as the best in the world.
2. Minoan women were held in high status and participated in sports, hunted, and attended sports and other cultural events.
3. Though many factors contributed to the decline of the civilization, the Minoans were eventually overthrown by the Mycenaean Greeks.

Page 175
1. The Myceneans contributed weapons, jewelry and other artifacts to Greek culture, especially their bronze work.
2. The Myceneans were different from the Minoans in that they did not have many natural resources, and therefore became traders.
3. All of the Mycenaean cities fell to Dorian rule except for Athens.
4. The Dark Age was a time between 1100 BCE and 800 BCE that was a period of decline for Greek culture. Trade and written language came to a standstill.
5. Culture and trade returned to Greece through stories and poems written by Homer, who based his writing on the songs and tales of the Myceneans.

Page 176
Answers will vary.

Page 177
1. Zeus asked Echo to distract his wife Hera by talking to her.
2. Zeus asked Echo to do this so that Hera wouldn't notice that he was flirting with other women.
3. Hera figured out what Zeus and Echo were up to and became furious. She took away Echo's ability to speak normally, leaving her only able to repeat the last word spoken to her.
4. Echo fell in love with Narcissus because he was so handsome.
5. Narcissus rejected Echo.
6. Nemesis punished Narcissus by making him fall in love with his own reflection.
7. Echo hid in a cave and wasted away until all that remained of her was her ability to repeat the last word spoken to her.
8. Unable to move away from his beautiful reflection, Narcissus wasted away at the edge of the pool until he vanished. A yellow flower grew in the place where he had sat.

Page 178
1. 18 C (64.4 F)
2. Along the coasts.
3. Southern coast & along Gulf of Corinth. Near the water.
4. The interiors. Places closer to water are generally warmer.

Page 179
1. c
2. b
3. a
4. c

Answer Key *(cont.)*

Page 180
1. Alba Longa
2. Romulus
3. Aeneas
4. Romulus and Remus survived an attempt to drown them as infants, and were suckled by a she-wolf.
5. Latins
6. 1184–753 = 431 years

Page 181
1. 62 (plus others); no
2. Augustus; Romulus Augustus
3. CE 284; CE 324
4. Claudius; Galba
5. CE 161–180
6. 2; 3
7. 367–69 = 298
8. after; before
9. 284–117 = 167

Page 183
1. b
2. d
3. c
4. b

Page 185
1. Circus Maximus: 200,000
2. Hadrian's arch: 199 years
3. 485 years
4. 1985
5. 584 years
6. Emperor's Palace: 51 years
7. 313 years
8. 97' (29.6 m)

Page 186
1. olive oil
2. cotton, lead, and tin
3. Egypt, Sicily, Tunisia, Italy, Russia, Sardinia, Greece, Austria

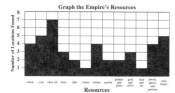

Page 187
Check student maps.

Page 189
1. Both Greek and Roman religions had many gods that were similar to each other.
2. Romans worshiped at their own family shrine, and also at temples for public worship.
3. Many Romans felt the state religion lacked spiritual fulfillment, and found the practice dull and unrewarding. They sought out other religions.
4. Jews and Christians were persecuted because they refused to acknowledge and make sacrifices to the Roman gods.

Page 191
1. The Romans wouldn't tolerate Judaism because Jews wouldn't worship Roman gods or make sacrifices to them.
2. Christians believed that Jesus Christ was the messiah and son of God, while Jews believed the messiah was still to come.
3. Christians refused to act like other Romans, kept to themselves, and worshiped behind closed doors.
4. Religious persecution did not stop when Christianity became the official religion because Christians began persecuting pagans.

Page 192

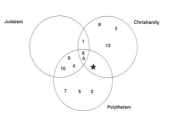

Page 193

Year	Europe	Near East and Asia	Central America and Mexico	Peru
3500–2500 BCE	3000 BCE Beginning of Minoan Age in Crete	3500 BCE First Egyptian dynasty founded		
2500–1500 BCE			2000 BCE First farm settlements in Guatemala, Chiapas, Yucatan	
1500–500 BCE	776 BCE First Olympic games in Greece; 734 BCE Legendary founding of Rome		1500 BCE Olmec Civilization	1200 BCE Chavin civilization in highlands, Coastal settlements
499–0 BCE	27 BCE Caesar Augustus crowned first Roman emperor	326 BCE Alexander the Great conquers Near East; 210 Great Wall of China built	300 BCE Rise of the Maya begins; 150 BCE Teotihuacan settled by farmers	100 BCE Moche kingdom on the Northern coast, Nazca ruled the south

Page 194
1. d
2. a
3. d
4. c

Page 195
1. b   3. c
2. b   4. a

Page 196
1. the traditional story of Manco Capac is that the was the son of the Sun God, sent to Earth to found a people with his brothers an sisters.
2. The Incas imposed their religion, laws, and language on those conquered.
3. Roads connected to Cuzco helped carry armies, officials, goods, and messengers.

Page 198
1. c   4. c
2. a   5. a
3. b   6. d
7. Accept well-supported answers.

Page 199
1. c   4. b
2. c   5. a
3. a

Page 200
1. cirrus
2. cirrostratus
3. altocumulus
4. stratocumulus
5. cumulus
6. stratus

Page 201
1. waste
2. sewage
3. drinking
4. watershed
5. condensation
6. pollution
7. glacier
8. chemicals
9. precipitation.
10. evaporate

Bonus: Lake Superior

Page 202
1. c   3. d
2. a   4. b

Page 204
1. d   4. b
2. a   5. c
3. a
6. Accept well-supported answers.

Page 205
1. Scientists interpret fossils and rock formations to help discover the history of the earth.
2. Plate techtonics is the theory that the Earth's continents drift and eventually relocate.
3. Scientists find evidence supporting plate techtonics by drilling samples of rock, mapping contours of the ocean floor, and plotting earthquake and volcano locations.

Answer Key *(cont.)*

Page 207
Check student maps.

Page 209
1. Cascades—Northwestern U.S.
   Sierra Nevada—Western U.S.
   Black Hills—North Central U.S.
   Appalachians—East Central U.S.
2. Cascades—volcanic mountains
3. Appalachians—fold mountains
4. Black Hills—dome mountains
5. Sierra Nevada—block mountains
6. Accept responses that reflect information presented on Page 208.

Page 210
1. 1300
2. 170
3. 100
4. 1783
5. 9
6. 597
7. 15
8. 95
9. 5

Page 211
1. compounds
2. ores
3. fool's gold
4. arsenic
5. oxides
6. carbonates
7. Nitrates
8. Gypsum

Page 212
1. F
2. F
3. T
4. F
5. T
6. F
7. F
8. T
9. F
10. T
11. T
12. T

Page 213
Comets
- tales are millions of miles long
- appear in the night sky for many days
- have a tail
- orbit around the sun
- hardly made of anything

Both
- are members of the solar system
- some are visible without telescope

Meteors
- are made of iron and atoms
- fall quickly to earth
- are called "shooting stars"

Page 215
1. b
2. a
3. c
4. d
5. a
6. Luis and Walter Alvarez found evidence that a huge asteroid hit Earth 65 million years ago, resulting in many life forms becoming extinct, including the dinosaurs.

Page 217
Check student pictures.

Page 218
1. b
2. a
3. a

Page 220
1. b
2. c
3. a
4. d
5. c
6. a
7. Accept well-supported answers.

Page 223
1. d
2. a
3. c
4. c

Page 224
1. sodium
2. nitrogen
3. argon
3. aluminum
5. oxygen
6. calcium
7. helium
8. sulfur

Page 225
1. b
2. b
3. b

Page 227
1. b
2. c
4. b
4. a
5. d

Page 229
1. b
2. a
3. c
4. b
5. c
6. d
7. Accept well-supported answers.